Successful
Consulting
Anna Hipkiss

For UK order enquiries: please contact Bookpoint Ltd,
130 Milton Park, Abingdon, Oxon OX14 4SB.
Telephone: +44 (0) 1235 827720. Fax: +44 (0) 1235 400454.
Lines are open 09.00–17.00, Monday to Saturday, with a 24-hour
message answering service. Details about our titles and how to order
are available at www.teachyourself.com

Long renowned as the authoritative source for self-guided
learning – with more than 50 million copies sold worldwide – the
Teach Yourself series includes over 500 titles in the fields of
languages, crafts, hobbies, business, computing and education.

British Library Cataloguing in Publication Data: a catalogue
record for this title is available from the British Library.

This edition published 2010.

Previously published as Teach Yourself Consulting

The **Teach Yourself** name is a registered trade mark of
Hodder Headline.

Typeset by MPS Limited, A Macmillan Company.

Printed in Great Britain for Hodder Education, an Hachette UK
Company, 338 Euston Road, London NW1 3BH, by Clays Ltd,
Elcograf S.p.A.

The publisher has used its best endeavours to ensure that the URLs
for external websites referred to in this book are correct and active
at the time of going to press. However, the publisher and the author
have no responsibility for the websites and can make no guarantee
that a site will remain live or that the content will remain relevant,
decent or appropriate.

Hachette UK's policy is to use papers that are natural, renewable
and recyclable products and made from wood grown in sustainable
forests. The logging and manufacturing processes are expected to
conform to the environmental regulations of the country of origin.

Impression number   11

Year   2020

Front cover: © Steve Wisbauer/Stockbyte/Getty Images

Back cover: © Jakub Semeniuk/iStockphoto.com, © Royalty-Free/
Corbis, © agencyby/iStockphoto.com, © Andy Cook/
iStockphoto.com, © Christopher Ewing/iStockphoto.com,
© zebicho – Fotolia.com, © Geoffrey Holman/iStockphoto.com,
© Photodisc/Getty Images, © James C. Pruitt/iStockphoto.com,
© Mohamed Saber – Fotolia.com

Contents

Meet the author

I am a successful independent business consultant, but that alone does not qualify me to be the author of this title. What inspired me to write this book was not just my experience of consulting, both internal and external, but the fact that I've managed teams of consultants, sold consulting and been a client of many consultants over the years. All these different perspectives enable me to give you the best routes to success in consulting.

Unusually, my career spans several disciplines – HR, Marketing and IT Services Management, which eventually led me to become the General Manager of an IT company in the finance sector. Before that, I worked in the engineering, consumer products and IT industries. I have employed numerous consultants in all these fields as external suppliers, and have worked with many internal consultants. I have also been an external HR consultant, and an internal Marketing consultant. In my role as IT Services Director, I ran a division which included 150 software consultants (all permanent employees), so I really have approached the subject from every angle!

Apart from my breadth and depth of experience, I also aim to bring to the subject a fresh approach, firmly anchored in the real world, which offers practical material that you can put to immediate use to help you along the road to success.

About this book

If you are a consultant in any field, working independently, or for any size of organization, from the multinational to the man plus dog, then this book is for you!

You may not call yourself a consultant. For example, you might be an engineer – civil or software – the key point is that you offer your technical expertise to a client – that is our definition of a consultant.

The aim of this book is to help you to become the very best consultant in your field by building up your client facing and commercial skills, and by showing you how vital these are. In some ways they are more important than your technical expertise. If you find that surprising, read on – this is definitely the book for you!

This book started from my e-learning program: 'The Consultant's Guide to Consulting' (see 'Taking it further', page 303), and it has been interesting to discover how differently the two media are composed. In a book you have the luxury of words, which are used sparingly on screen. In a program you have more scope for interaction. I believe that I have now produced two pieces of learning, which are quite different but complementary, and they can be used in tandem, or in sequence.

It has been a delight to meet so many consultants, and to have room in the book to quote them extensively. Irene Nathan made the comment: 'I often consult other consultants on different subjects, as part of my learning process. I believe you need to keep yourself fresh and alive and learned and knowledgeable – that is the most important thing you can offer, whatever your subject.'

This illustrates a major theme of the book – the consultant's love of self-development. I have really enjoyed having this personal opportunity to consult so many people, which I can share with you now.

DISCLAIMER

As I have gone to great lengths to use real case study material in this book, I have gone to similar lengths to disguise the companies and the people involved, to protect everyone's confidentiality. If, in creating these disguises, I have used names which you recognize, then this is unfortunate, because, as they say at the beginning of all the best books, all the names I have used for disguise are fictional. Any resemblance to real people or companies is purely coincidental.

Only got a minute?

Imagine you are facing an angry client. You thought all was going well, and the report was due on Friday. It's Wednesday morning, and your client tells you the deadline is today, not Friday.

Encapsulated in this scene are many of the challenges you will face as a consultant, and there are solutions provided to all these issues in this book.

One of the worst sins you can commit as a consultant is to set unrealistic client expectations. Did you promise Wednesday and forget? Worse, did you promise Wednesday thinking it would not matter if you were a bit late?

If you agreed Friday, do you have written evidence, or was it just part of a discussion? You won't win any points from the client by telling them they are wrong, unless you can point to objective evidence. Even then, does it help? The client wants the report today, whatever the agreement was. Did you understand that at the time, or have they just moved the goal posts?

Client communication is another critical area, and client understanding too. Spending time discovering that your client has a temper, or a conveniently short memory, can pay dividends. How best to do that is an art we will explore.

So can you produce a Wednesday rabbit out of a Friday hat? This is where flexible thinking and really understanding the client's needs will help. Why exactly do they want the report today? Do they need all of it? What will they do with it between now and Friday?

It is easy to be mesmerized by client demands, particularly if they are angry, and you appear to be in the wrong. Tell yourself that 'there is a solution to every problem' and if you can believe that, just for a while, you may find you can provide something on Wednesday that will bridge the gap until Friday.

The book contains many case studies and real-life examples like these to help you in the most practical way on route to success as a consultant.

5 Only got five minutes?

Are you cut out to be a consultant? By reading this book you will learn how to be a good one, and how to develop the skills and commitment to do what it takes to succeed. Here you have the opportunity to evaluate how well you fit the consultant role. We will deal first with factors that are common to all consultants: employed or self-employed, internal or external.

Expertise

It goes without saying that you will have some expertise to offer – be it in tax planning or designing websites. You may be the best web designer in Britain, but unless you have the awards to prove it, that fact may not get you very far, because beyond a certain competence level, all unknown consultants look alike to the person who wants to hire one.

Unless your expertise means that you can offer some tangible benefit – a complete site in two hours, or guaranteed high response rates, then your USPs (unique selling points) as a consultant need to be focused in other areas.

Personal qualities

What clients want most of all from you are three things:

1 Integrity – can they trust you?
2 Reliability – will you keep your promises?

3 Credibility – do you convince them and others that you know your stuff?

Trust is fundamental – your relationship will not work without it.

Reliability means doing what you say you will do, every time. If your style is a bit erratic, and deadlines to you are a guide, not an unmissable target, then seriously consider how you will manage this critical element of consulting.

In relation to credibility, it is one thing to be an expert, it's quite another to appear to be one, and you need to do both.

Apart from these fundamental personal qualities, let us now look at the interpersonal skills that will make you a starring consultant.

Ask good questions. Listen to the replies.

First, you will be a good listener. Did you expect me to say a fluent speaker? Well, some level of articulacy is vital, but much more important is the ability to listen to what the client wants. Lots of consultants fail to do so, and end up delivering their 'standard package', or worse, something that is not quite what the client asked for. Linked to this is the ability to ask the right questions, in order to have all the material you need to draw conclusions. No point in listening if the client is not giving you the information you need.

Stay off the pedestal

What goes with the above is a lack of arrogance, which is not quite humility, but does mean that you never assume you know what the client's problem is before they've told you, and you never assume you know what the client wants until you have asked all the right questions and listened carefully. Certainly you would never imply that you are the expert, and are therefore superior in any way. Most clients think they know something about what you do, and there is always a risk that this arrogant stance may be misplaced, as well as a complete turnoff for the client.

Client first

You will always put the client first, and never ever be seen to be doing anything which puts your interests before those of the client. As with all things a consultant does, you need to be seen to do them, as well as doing them. A skill which is really useful here is the ability to step into the client's shoes and see things from their point of view. When you have that perspective it is much easier to see what to avoid, or to anticipate needs. You can also demonstrate how your solution is tailored for them, even if it is hardly tailored at all.

Applied realism

You will have a firm grasp on reality, and the ability to assess situations objectively. This means that when it comes to setting client expectations, you will do so without a trace of optimism. Under-promise and over-deliver will always be your motto. The thought of over-committing fills you with horror, and although you probably have a strong desire to please the client, you are able to think consequences, and go beyond the moment to what will happen if you say yes now, and then disappoint the client in two weeks' time, when you have not quite managed to meet that deadline.

Cool and considered

Linked to your very realistic outlook is a total lack of impulsiveness. You stay cool under pressure, you do not give knee-jerk reactions, and when the client asks for something, you give a considered reply that sets the right expectations.

You are also calm when the client is not. If you come under fire, whether justifiably or not, you do not rise to the attack, but can judge whether to push back, or whether to leave the client to cool down before you deal with the issue calmly and objectively, always maintaining the client relationship.

Respect

Just as you are always respectful of the client, it is important to ensure that they respect you too. This can be a difficult balancing act, when your aim is to please the client and respond well to their requests, no matter how unreasonable, but there will come a time when you know the client is abusing the relationship, and that is the time to push back and show that there is a limit to how much they can push you around. Normally, doing this results in a better, healthier relationship, and the book contains some good examples of when and how to do this.

Keep learning

You are the expert, of course you are, but that does not make your expertise invulnerable. The best consultants keep learning, not because they have to, but because they want to. If you are not interested in developing your expertise, perhaps it is time to find a new one, which holds your interest. It is certainly time to ask yourself whether your specialism excites you and enables you to be inspiring to others.

Having looked at common factors to all consultants, let us now look at whether you are best suited to working in an organization, or going it alone.

Employee or self-employed?

You have a report to write. How do you feel about the prospect of working from home for a day? If you want to run a mile, and need interruptions after the first half hour, this does not augur well for self-employment. If you welcome a day's peace and quiet, to get on with things uninterrupted, this is a better sign.

Does a day's peace and quiet mean just that, or does it mean doing a few domestic chores, maybe a few personal emails, and other bits and pieces that swallow up your time? We are testing here for self-discipline: can you sit down and get on with things, or are you always looking for displacement activities?

You may think it would be different if you work for yourself, and it might be, but will you be happy in this environment, on your own, with no structure to your day, and no one to talk to? Being self-employed can be very lonely, and you won't have the support structure of an organization around you. Buying stamps or filing will suddenly appear on your task list.

Of course, you have lots of freedom, and you can choose whether you want that project in Belfast or not, but you will have to generate your own business, and many consultants find that hard. There are ways round it, though, and you can become an associate consultant to other, larger organizations. Your fees are less, but they generate your business for you.

Can you live with an irregular income flow? Unless you are unusually lucky, you will find that your work flows erratically: sometimes too much, sometimes not enough. If you start on your own, the ideal way is to win some business before you leave employment, so you have some immediate income. Otherwise, you need to allow from three to six months to develop a pipeline and you will not have any income during that time.

The organization type

From the above, you will gather that someone who is best fitted to be a consultant within an organization has the following characteristics:

▶ likes/needs the security of a regular income/benefits
▶ prefers to be given a structure to work within

- is happy to be 'sent' to distant or unappealing places on projects
- enjoys the contact and stimulation of being part of a consulting team
- does not want the responsibility of selling to generate own income
- needs organization rules and requirements to help with self-discipline
- likes the prestige of belonging to a bigger organization

If you are now clearer on where your future as a consultant lies, it will give you focus as you explore all these areas and many more in what follows. In particular, there are profiles of successful consultants, both employed and self-employed, which will give you a very practical view of what makes them successful.

Acknowledgements

I have consulted many consultants and employers of consultants in writing this book, and I would like to thank them all for their very rich contribution, in particular:

The late Sir John Harvey Jones

Mary Ahmad – Corporate HR Partners

Mark Brown – Innovation Centre Europe

Sue Goble – Siebel Systems UK Ltd (now part of Oracle Corporation)

Vic Hartley – Vertex Consultants

Mary Hill – Pecaso UK Ltd (now part of Accenture)

Peter Honey – Peter Honey Learning

Gill Hunt – Skillfair

Steven Hunt – MWH

Frank Milton – IBM

David Mitchell – Oracle UK Ltd

Irene Nathan – Interpersonal Relations Group

Leon Sadler – SAP UK Ltd

Penny Stocks – Ernst & Young LLP

Finally, I would like to thank my husband Richard, for his unfailing support, and Lesley Gosling, for her inspiring vision!

1

What do you want from this book?

This chapter covers:
- *what this book has to offer you*
- *how to use this book as a self-employed consultant*
- *how to use this book as a corporate consultant*

What if ...

... every consulting project I did counted as a stunning success?

... all my clients were perfectly reasonable and a pleasure to deal with?

... business just flowed in my direction, with no effort at all?

This book is about helping you to make those dreams come true. You may be a seasoned professional, or new to this field. You may work alone from an office in your spare room, or you may be employed by one of the major consultants. The aim of this book is to help you on your way to achieving greater success as a consultant.

Why this book is different

This book is different from other books you may read on the subject, because apart from offering you plenty of 'real meat' or serious content, in the way that most books offer you things on a plate, it also provides you with a knife and a fork, and an appetite, which is what you will find in the early chapters. You may feel that you already have these, but it is worth checking. They will make the difference between just reading a useful book, and actually doing something with what you have learned from it.

THINKING INSIDE AND OUTSIDE THE BOX

What you will get on your plate is plenty of sensible, 'inside the box' thinking, spiced with lots of practical experience. The way we help you to develop your appetite, and the tools we give you to consume what is on that plate, are generally 'outside the box' ideas. As an example, we cover classic ways of handling conflict, with gritty case studies from real life. We also give you a new tool to help you get inside the head of your opponent, to better understand how to meet their needs and reach a successful outcome. As with any aspect of a book, you can take it or leave it, but consider it before you decide!

GETTING INSPIRED

When you embark on a road that is new to you, but well trodden by others, it is very helpful to have a role model to inspire you. Someone you can relate to, whose footsteps you feel capable of following. We have therefore included a number of potential role models for you to choose from, and details of the road they followed to success. We ask you to work on the principle that if they can do it, so can you! You may not believe this one hundred per cent, but if you take on the belief temporarily, and act as if it were true, this opens up your mind and your options for achieving success.

SOURCES OF LEARNING

The learning in this book will come from three sources. First of all from you, as we help you to unpick your own magic and apply it in different ways to different situations. It is easy to underrate your own skills. Have you noticed that people admire a skill in you that you simply take for granted? We will examine how to transfer that skill and broaden its use.

> ## Insight
>
> We often take our strengths for granted, or may not even be aware of them. Other people may recognize what you are good at, and don't say – not deliberately, but because they think you know that you have a special knack with customers when things go wrong, or can conjure up a spreadsheet in no time.

The second source of learning will be from studying the experts, the special group of consultants we have chosen as models for success. These are prominent figures in their different fields, who have a track record we want to emulate, and skills we want to analyse and use.

The third source of learning will be from all the real life case studies, which are woven into the book. Not just from our experts, but from many different sources. They are, of necessity, anonymous, in order to honour that key commitment of any consultant to protect client confidentiality, but they are no less real for that, and provide solid experience that we can learn from. Often these examples cover what went wrong, as well as what went right, so that we can learn from others' mistakes as well as their expertise.

When you have absorbed all three sources of learning, we will challenge you to be creative in applying ideas in new ways, to enable you to capture and develop the difference that makes the difference – that will deliver greater success to you as a consultant in whatever way you choose to define it.

Using this book if you are a self-employed consultant

This book covers all the skills you need to be a successful consultant: these do not change with your employment status.

However, you also need skills in running a business, such as finance and marketing. In Chapter 20 you will find information on marketing your services. In Chapter 21 we cover the elements of setting up and running an independent business.

Some of the material in this book refers to the consultant as part of a project team, and suggests that you refer to your manager for advice. You may often work alone with the client, and certainly will not have a manager to refer to. However, you will often be part of a client team, even if that is not specifically your brief, and it is important to take team considerations into account. Similarly you may be working as part of a provider project team, in which case, although you are not an employee, you will certainly be acting as part of that provider's organization, and will have a project manager to refer to.

When you are working alone and you hit a real problem, instead of taking advice from your non-existent manager, think of a mentor or a friend who could be a sounding board for you, and perform much the same function as a manager. Many lone consultants have very useful reciprocal relationships, where they offer each other advice and support. It is a kind of 'buddy' system, which is very useful to cultivate. So when you see the words 'Consult your manager', think in terms of a helpful colleague.

Using this book if you are a corporate consultant

You will find this book a source of rich material. It often takes the viewpoint of a consultant who is part of a project team, frequently based on a client site. It deals with the problems that a consultant faces internally within his or her own organization, as well as externally with the client. The manager who is never there when you need them; the colleagues who let you down; the training that you miss; the left hand who never tells you, the right hand, what they are doing; the conflict between loyalty to your distant company, and to your good friend the client; the recognition and career progression that you do not get when you are hidden away on some remote site. If these issues sound familiar to you, then read on because the book contains much experience and potential learning on these subjects.

Because many consultants, unlike you, are self-employed, with concerns about things like VAT and being lonely, we have also included a chapter on setting up your own business. It contains several case studies, including people who have moved from being an employed consultant to setting up on their own. You may find it useful to understand this perspective, if only to confirm to yourself that this is not a career route for you!

The thinking behind this book

Much of the content of this book is built on years of practical consulting experience, and the perspectives of many different people. This will take you a long way along the road to success.

A new way of thinking will take you further and faster along that road. Adopting it will open your mind to new perspectives and enable you to see how you might find the difference that makes the difference for you.

Insight

Learning more facts about consulting will be very useful, and will take you a long way, but it may not enable you to make a step change in performance. To do that you need to examine your beliefs, and find any that are holding you back or leading you astray. Start by taking on some new ones...

To think in this new way, you simply adopt some new beliefs, such as, 'There is a solution to every problem.' You may believe this already, so that will be easy! You may be saying no, you simply do not accept that a nice solution is sitting round every corner. That is a very normal response, so could you just try the belief on for size, and see how it feels, knowing you can take it off again? Doing this is the equivalent of adopting a presupposition – something which you do not have to permanently accept, but which you hold for the time it is useful to you.

So can you now adopt the presupposition that there is a solution to every problem, whilst you are reading this book, and seeking to find ways of becoming more successful as a consultant? Can you see how enabling it will be, if you can hold that belief for this period?

If you can, you are ready for the whole list. These are the presuppositions that you will find useful to hold whilst you are becoming a more successful consultant.

- ▶ **There is a solution to every problem.**
- ▶ **The map is not the territory.** *This means that the way I see things – my map – is not the same as anyone else's, nor is it ever going to be a completely accurate view of the piece of the earth it claims to represent. Everybody sees life in different ways, even though they think they are seeing the same thing! This is a vital presupposition when managing a client relationship.*
- ▶ **The meaning of communication is in the response you get.** *In other words, what you intended to say is irrelevant; it is what the person hears that matters.*
  A man might say to his wife 'Is it time for lunch?'
  She might hear, 'Lunch is late, you are failing in your domestic duties, and are therefore less lovable.'
  The husband might be amazed by that, when all he was really doing was checking the timing of a meal!
- ▶ **There is no failure, only feedback.** *This is a very constructive way of looking at life. Learning usually involves making mistakes of some kind. Those mistakes are usually a vital part of the learning process. When you do something incorrectly, you learn how to adjust so that you do not repeat the same mistake again. Sometimes it takes many attempts before you get it right. In a learning environment, such as a training course, this is considered normal; in the 'real world', it is often*

viewed as unacceptable. Obviously you make every effort to avoid failure, but when it happens, treat it as a source of learning, and you will progress farther and faster towards success.

▶ **If someone else can do something, so can you.** *This is linked to another presupposition:*

▶ **Everyone already has everything they need to achieve what they want.** *If you can believe both of these things on a temporary basis, it will enable you to do so much more. You are almost certainly going to want to say that an unfit 40-year-old could never become an Olympic athlete, and of course there are going to be some physical limitations, but they do not generally apply to becoming a consultant, do they?*

▶ **The person with the most flexibility in thinking and behaviour has the most influence on any interaction.** *This is a vital presupposition, which underlies most of the teaching on negotiation and influencing skills. Overt exercise of power, unless taken to extremes, will not necessarily win the battle against the flexible thinker.*

▶ **If you always do what you always did, you will always get what you always got.** *The fact that you are reading this book suggests that you want to do things differently, so adopting all these presuppositions is a great place to start.*

Here is an example of taking on a presupposition:

Kay hates giving presentations. Her boss, Nigel, is a brilliant public speaker, witty and fluent; just being with him makes her feel more inadequate. When she thinks about the presupposition 'If someone else can do something, so can you', she thinks of Nigel and dismisses it. Just the thought of him stops her taking it on.

Now she forces herself to imagine that she does believe she can do public speaking – she can't quite make the stretch to Nigel, who seems at Olympic standard to her, but she can imagine being competent, perhaps very competent. As she imagines that, she starts to think about what she needs to do to get her to that comfortable level of competence. The presupposition is enabling her to move forward on a path towards success.

Closing thoughts

What the mind can conceive and believe, the mind can achieve.

Napoleon Hill

Seize opportunity by the beard, for it is bald behind.

Bulgarian Proverb

STEPS TO SUCCESS

▶ Go through each of the presuppositions, and test to be sure that you can take it on while you are learning. If you find a particular presupposition difficult, ask what is stopping you taking it on temporarily? Then imagine what it would be like if you could ... What would you be able to do differently?

▶ Take each one in turn and test it out. If it is difficult, do what Kay did, focus on what stops you, and then go beyond it.

▶ In this same context, think of people you know who, in your view, are good consultants. Imagine what specific advice they might give you to enable you to hold these presuppositions, and to take you forward on the road to success.

2

Consulting excellence at work

This chapter covers:
Insights from three successful consultants on:
- *their route to success*
- *key learning points along the way*
- *common success factors*

Throughout this book there are contributions from consultants in many different fields, at different stages of their career, all very successful, all potential role models.

The corporate consultant

In this chapter we will examine some career success stories, so that you can take a look at what they have achieved, and how they have achieved it. These are all consultants working for large organizations, so we will see how they have risen up the organizational ladder. Apart from describing their career, they also have valuable insights into many aspects of the role of a consultant, which reinforce many of the messages in this book.

THE INDEPENDENT CONSULTANT

Similarly, in the chapter on starting your own business, we profile consultants who have been successful independently, and again include valuable insights into the consulting role. Not surprisingly, there are some common themes which emerge.

Case study: Penny Stocks, Partner, Ernst & Young

CAREER PATH

Despite her very senior position, Penny gave a very down to earth view of business consulting. 'It is very hard work, and not nearly as glamorous as people think. Projects happen in Crewe, Glasgow and Liverpool, not always in Paris and Rome, as people like to imagine. And when you do go to Paris, you only see an office and the airport! At 4 o'clock in the morning when the photocopier has stopped working and you have a presentation to deliver at 8 am is when you discover what real hard work means.'

Despite these comments, Penny clearly loves consulting, and she described how she came to be a Partner of a very large consulting organization in her late thirties.

'I studied management sciences at Manchester University in the early eighties. This was the time when Margaret Thatcher was embarking on her union reforms, and I was inspired by that, so I joined Rover cars as a graduate trainee in HR. I started in the field of Industrial Relations, but I found it to be all talk and no action, so I moved into HR more broadly and worked in three very different departments, gaining experience particularly in managing change. Then I was approached by Price Waterhouse, and I became a consultant, learning the basics of the profession, which I would describe as really understanding the client's problems, scoping the work accurately, and then delivering a high quality product. In those days a sale worth £20,000 merited a bottle of champagne. Today, a sale would need to exceed a million before we celebrate.

'The core of my work was around helping people make the journey into change, and that was very difficult to sell, because it is so intangible. I therefore set about translating jargon into tangible and practical things that clients will buy.

'After seven successful years I started to run out of space and so I joined Ernst & Young, who were just struggling with the concept of framing their people offering, and so this was the perfect opportunity for me. I joined as a Managing Consultant with a staff of five, which I grew to thirty, eventually becoming Vice President. Through the merger with Cap Gemini the team grew to sixty. Our role to date has been to help clients manage the people part of organizational change. A new software system, or the outsourcing of – say – the finance function, all of these changes have major people implications. I then had the opportunity to join Ernst & Young as a Partner.'

Penny speaks with passion and enthusiasm for what she does. It is easy to see how she would succeed in convincing a cynical client to spend real money on 'intangibles'!

SECRETS OF SUCCESS

When asked to what she attributed her success, she was very clear:

- ▶ *'You need to have a belief in what you want to do.'*
- ▶ *'You take risks. You are prepared to put your head above the parapet and stand out amongst your peers.'*
- ▶ *'You focus on doing an excellent delivery job, and building a good track record.'*
- ▶ *'You find good mentors. Some you just take to, others you seek out and develop the relationship.'*
- ▶ *'You become a leader amongst your peers. You develop your own brand, and then just deliver. For example, my brand is being able to put forward successful and practicable ways to help people change as part of major transformation projects.'*

KEY LEARNING POINTS AS A CONSULTANT

Penny listed three major learning points:

1 *'Agree with a client exactly what they are expecting. Both the deliverable and the way you will work with them. It is in this*

area that most litigation takes place, so it cannot be agreed at too granular a level – almost down to storyboards of the project.'

2 'Be very clear on who the client is – who is paying the bill. It can often happen that the project sponsor is not your most frequent contact. Sometimes consultants are hired over the head of the person you deal with day to day. Sometimes that person may feel threatened or alienated and may not wish to co-operate with you. It is vital to maintain your link with the sponsor in this situation.'

3 'Take time to listen to the client and to really understand what the issue is. Do not produce your standard solution and then try cutting and pasting to make it fit.'

CAREER ADVICE TO CONSULTANTS

When hiring a young consultant, Penny considers that previous line experience can be a real asset.

'It really helps if people have done a proper job. Consulting isn't a proper job, it's too much fun! Seriously, particularly in the change management field, it makes it a lot easier to look at a client across the table and be firm by having been out there yourself. It may be different in the technical areas. [In effect, the company does hire graduates into other disciplines.] One of the changes in the market is an increasing desire for content – knowledge and experience. Clients are getting more sophisticated. They are no longer satisfied with the people who have read the books. They want consultants who have a lot of knowledge and experience and can give practical guidance and advice.

'I also look for exceptional communication skills, the ability to listen, understand and form a view very swiftly. The person must very quickly have presence when meeting clients, and not be fearful of walking into difficult situations. There will be times when things won't work with the client, and they need to have the inner strength to take the knocks and move on. Few clients tell you that you have done a good job, so you need confidence and a belief in yourself. Finally I want a really good team player, and lots of enthusiasm.'

THE WORST SINS A CONSULTANT CAN COMMIT

According to Penny, they are:

1 *'Arrogance. Not listening. Already knowing the answer.'*
2 *'Complaining and moaning about the client internally, but in a public place. Confidentiality is a fundamental commitment to the client, and you never know who's listening. If the client has weaknesses, they have asked for your help, so you should respect that.'*
3 *'Taking the Big Company approach: "We are the great ABC ... consultants, and we will do it to you, not with you."'*
4 *'Finally there's the opposite of arrogance, not being challenging enough to the client. Giving them what they want and not what they need.'*

'As an example of that, I was working with a company who were planning to restructure. The managing director gave me his ideas on this, and I went away and did my research and analysis, and it would have been very easy to give him a proposal along the lines he had suggested. In fact I proposed something different that meant making some tough decisions about the management team. It wasn't what he thought he wanted, but he did finally agree that it was what he needed.'

Unlike many consultants, Penny did not have a fund of 'clients from hell'. 'I guess I've just been lucky with my clients,' probably says more about Penny than it does about her clients.

'I remember a particularly difficult client situation where I was given a recruitment brief, and I just couldn't find anyone. All I could do was demonstrate to them how thoroughly and innovatively I had gone about the job. I had literally tried everything.

'I went back to the client to report on my huge effort with no result, and I talked it through with him and said what was blindingly obvious – that this job is very difficult to fill. In the end we agreed I would do some organizational design work, and solve the problem a different way. This did produce a solution. Shortly afterwards the client merged with another company, and I got the merger work too.'

Penny's honest and open approach to what she does clearly wins the trust of her clients, and delivers more business. This is also her approach with her own team, where a priority for her is to generate a culture 'which makes it OK for people to ask for help'.

'I give my team space to grow and develop, and offer them formal training, but everyone has responsibility for their own learning, and to create their own "brand". I have my own personal development plan, which apart from formal training and reading, also consists of a network of people, inside and outside the organization, with whom I arrange coaching sessions, and who regularly give me frank input and tell me how it really is.'

Case study: Leon Sadler, Regional Professional Services Director, SAP

CAREER PATH

Leon Sadler is a Director of Professional Services for SAP – the huge international software company which provides corporate systems to many large organizations. Still relatively young, Leon has an enviable career track record. 'I have been doing the same job for two years, which is a first for me!' he said.

'My career began with disappointing A levels. I discovered girls and fast cars at the time when I should have been working for good grades. I therefore ended up doing a course called Manufacturing Systems at Hatfield Polytechnic. It comprised work on several MRP (Manufacturing Requirements Planning) systems, with practical in-company placements. People often say they barely use 10 per cent of their degree – I have used at least 90 per cent of mine!'

Anderson Consulting came to Hatfield on the milk round, and Leon joined them, rising through the ranks over the next four years, benefiting from the pressure to achieve and develop which is broadly prevalent in large consulting groups. A move out of the manufacturing sector, and the departure and retirement of two of his key mentors told Leon it was time to move on. He joined a small software company, which took a good product to market too early. 'I learned more in one year with that company than in four and a half years with Anderson. I resigned, and two weeks later, the company went into receivership. These two events were not connected!'

He resigned to come to SAP as a Production Planning Consultant. From that position he was asked to head up the logistics consulting team of five consultants. Several promotions later, Leon now has a team of 280 staff, and complete responsibility for the consulting operation for the region.

SECRETS OF SUCCESS

In talking to Leon, a number of things became apparent which help to explain his success. He actively seeks and uses mentors in the organization. He also networks very well: building relationships is clearly a strength. He is very open about what he does not know, and an obvious consequence is that it frees him to seek help from mentors or experts or more experienced staff. 'Seeking mentors is not necessarily a hierarchical thing. I go where the expertise is, at any level.'

He is a risk taker. 'Better to make 100 decisions and be prepared to get 10 wrong, than only to make 50.' As part of his risk taking he will take things on – and then worry afterwards how he will cope.

THE WORST SINS A CONSULTANT CAN COMMIT

Leon listed the following:

1 *Not knowing when to say 'I don't know' and just winging it. It is always better to say that you'll find out.*

2 *Failing to deliver on your promises. If you say you'll do something – do it!*

3 *Not managing customers' expectations. What a customer expects from you is down to you – you can control it, so why over-commit?*

CUSTOMER RELATIONSHIPS

On dealing with clients, Leon said, 'It's a cliché, but people buy from people. In a previous company I was part of a bid team who lost a big project. Two of us were able to go back and ask them why we lost, and although we met all their technical criteria, they told us that they didn't like us! Not us individually, but the whole team, who they knew well as they had already done some work for this client. It was quite a shock, but a salutary lesson.

'My approach to new customers is that I endeavour to create opportunities and give them reasons to trust me. When I'm working with a client, the aim is to be smiling, positive, never moody, never lose a sense of humour, whatever the client throws at me. My first boss at Anderson said to me, "If the client asks you to sweep the factory floor, you ring me and tell me, and then you go and sweep the floor!" I've never been asked to sweep the floor, but a client who is under huge personal stress said to me recently, "I can be as horrible to you as I like, and you will have to take it." That's the reality of consulting, and some people find that hard to swallow.'

Leon is also very aware that consultants are often drawn to the profession because they enjoy change. Implementing a major new software system is a major change for an organization. 'Often the people at the receiving end do not enjoy change, so our presence can be a threat to them, whether real or imagined. It's as well to hold that perspective when dealing with clients.'

Leon's experience of difficult clients is summed up as a culture mismatch. 'In this company, we collaborate with clients, working with them as a team in partnership. I know that sounds corny, but that's what we do. This works very well with most clients, but a few clients have a culture where they believe that external suppliers are not to be trusted. The best way to treat these money-grabbing consultants, therefore, is to beat them up regularly, because they will cheat you otherwise. Given this mentality, it is very difficult to do a good job for this type of customer, because of the basic lack of trust. We can only do our best to be as honest and open as possible, and consistently demonstrate our trustworthiness.'

CAREER ADVICE TO CONSULTANTS

Leon's advice to consultants keen to progress their career is not to make this their sole intent. 'If you push your career in people's faces it is likely to be counter productive. If you are seen to be doing things only for self-advancement, then that is likely to make you very unpopular. Focus on doing the very best job you can right now, and that will take you a long way along the road to advancement. Being part of a team is key to most roles, and someone with a focus only on their next step up the ladder will not be seen or accepted as part of the team, because people will feel that your own aims will always take priority over the team's goals.'

KEY LEARNING POINTS AS A CONSULTANT

Leon values learning very highly, and sees failure as part of the learning process. He coaches skiing as a hobby, and has a role model in John Shedden, father of British skiing. 'Top skiers push themselves to the limit in how quickly they can learn new techniques, so they may fall down as much as one run in ten. That's quite a lot of falling down. If you are not falling over at all, maybe you are not learning, not growing, not pushing yourself as hard or fast as you could be. I expect to "fall down" or make mistakes fairly often – it's a good sign.'

Leon also places a high value on teamwork. As a rugby player for 27 years, he has a very graphic description of what teamwork means. 'I was a rugby forward, and the pack have to operate as a unit. If a forward scores a try, it's the pack's try, not an individual's forward try. In the pack we rely on each other entirely, if you cannot trust each other implicitly in the scrum, you can end up with a broken neck. So I am very ambitious for my team to win, not just me.'

SECRETS OF SUCCESS

Leon said that he did not really see himself as successful; he is dedicated to doing a really good job of whatever he is doing now, and does not have a long-term focus on a career ladder. This response matches his learning philosophy – success is an end point, whereas Leon is on a journey – like the ski slope – always pushing himself towards further growth.

Case study: David Mitchell, Head of E-Business Practice, Oracle

CAREER PATH

David has held a number of senior consulting positions in his three and a half years at Oracle, the major software company, with responsibility for teams of over 150 consultants, the latest being the strategically most critical consulting group – the E-Business team.

'There are two types of consulting,' David explained. 'Expert (or content) consulting, is where you have the know-how. Process consulting is where you understand the process of doing consulting to enable you to help your clients come up with their own answers, without being an expert. It is vital that clients are part of this process. My current organization combines the two types, and this is a very powerful proposition for the client.'

David's career began with a degree in geography, followed by a second degree in social geography and additional study of geographic information systems (GIS). As part of this degree he studied riot control, working with the police in Brixton – not something he has applied directly in his subsequent career, he was careful to point out.

After becoming a university lecturer for a while, he decided to move into industry, and joined Bartholomew's, best known for their maps, to work on GIS systems. From there to Unisys, and then on to Coopers and Lybrand before joining Oracle. 'It was at Coopers that I received my "real" consulting training. They had a simple model:

> *Listen*
> *Think*
> *Consult (with your colleagues, not the client)*
> *Act (note this is only 25 per cent)*

In my book, consulting firms are called this because they consult each other, not their clients. This is the leverage that big firms have.'

If you do not follow the sequence you may fall into what David eloquently expressed as 'Premature elaboration'! The obvious example of this is the young consultant, not long out of university, who feels a great pressure to deliver value for his very expensive daily fee, and rushes in with answers without even knowing the questions!

CAREER ADVICE TO CONSULTANTS

'You need to learn consulting as a profession. It's not just being an expert. You tend not to be taught those skills in supplier consulting organizations. Do a proper apprenticeship in one of the big consulting groups – learn the process consulting skills.

'On the other hand, don't join one of the big consulting groups unless you've got something to contribute. If you join straight from university, you will be given fairly basic things to do because you are not proven. If you have industry expertise, it's much better.

Having some experience in industry in a non-consulting role is good. If you are a technical guru, you can go straight in, but you are unlikely to go anywhere senior without full consulting skills. It's quite a fine art to decide what to do when.

'If you go into one of the big groups, go with your eyes open and see organizations as they are, and not as you want them to be. Lots of their business is very basic work, delivering systems – it's not all Board-level strategic stuff. If your expectations are too high, you will get frustrated when you find yourself writing sets of user procedures for the maintenance department of an electricity company!

'Work out how long you want to be there. Is it two years for the experience and a badge for the CV, or five years for that plus some seniority, or is it your end profession? Be clear on what you want to get out of it, otherwise you may drift and not get what you need. Proactively manage your career.

'Expect hard work and social disruption – it is not a nine-to-five profession. You must be clear on that before you go into it. Note that many of the best insights into a consulting project happen in the bar after work. It's easy to find yourself doing nothing but work. You need to learn how not to kill yourself with overwork, and to balance your lifestyle. Note also that the further you go up the ladder, the more the job becomes a combination of sales and delivery, which may or may not be what you enjoy doing.

'Finally, a key point about being in your comfort zone. As a rule of thumb, if you are not petrified twice a week, you are not stretching yourself enough as an individual, and in what you can do for clients. If it's too easy, you are not trying hard enough!'

We will hear more from Penny, Leon and David in other parts of the book, just as we will introduce other successful role models in other chapters. In advance of that, let us look at common factors in their success.

Common success factors

Learning
Common to all the consultants is a commitment to learning.
As Frank Milton, formerly a partner at Price Waterhouse Coopers,
and now a leading management consultant with IBM, put it,
'You need fluency in business, and you need currency – what's
happening now, and what are the future trends.' David Mitchell
ascribed part of his success to 'being a polymath', having great
breadth of knowledge across many subjects.

Personal development
Beyond learning is a burning enthusiasm for self-development,
whether expressed as falling down on the ski slope, or being
petrified twice a week!

Interpersonal skills
Excellent interpersonal skills are common to all, resulting in
the comment from some of them that they are lucky with their
clients. For luck read: 'I have the ability to get on with and bring
out the best in even the most difficult people.' The claim of
luck was not false modesty, just a taking for granted of a
natural skill.

Professionalism
This whole book is about being a professional consultant, so it
would take too long to list all the virtues displayed here. Many of
their comments are quoted in the next chapter.

Drive
A high level of drive and enthusiasm means that they make the
most of opportunities, and are recognized and promoted for it.
Steven Hunt, Client Services Manager for MWH, said: 'You need
to be able to see opportunities, and make the most of them. I took
on a high-risk project after several people had turned it down, but
to me it was a great opportunity – I saw the upside.'

Risk taking

This also illustrates another common characteristic: they are all prepared to take risks, and 'put their head above the parapet'.

Self-belief

This is very evident in all they say, and as Penny puts it 'you develop your own brand' which means you can easily sell yourself to a client or an employer. As David commented, 'Consultants are selling themselves all the time, whatever they are doing.'

Networking

Networking is something they all do, although, as Penny said: 'I do it intuitively, and it works well. If it were obvious that I was networking just for personal gain, such as career advancement, then people would see through that very quickly.'

Building a track record

This is linked to Leon's comment about not thrusting your career aims into people's faces. The message is again consistent: do a really good job now, build a track record, and that achievement will take you towards the next career step.

Mentors

Mentors are also important, and the key is to go and find them, if they do not naturally appear. Mentors are obviously most influential if they are senior, but you can find mentors at any level, and benefit from their expertise.

It is easy to derive some key beliefs that they hold about being a consultant, and link that to our list of presuppositions. From the information they have given us, it is not difficult to see that they would be comfortable with most of those listed in Chapter 1, not least:

▶ *There is no failure, only feedback. (Ski slopes come to mind!)*
▶ *If someone else can do something, so can you.*

- *Everyone already has everything they need to achieve what they want.*
- *If you always do what you always did, you will always get what you always got. (You certainly won't be petrified twice a week!)*

Closing thoughts

The way to do is to be.

Anon

Our greatest glory is not in never falling, but in rising every time we fall.

Confucius

STEPS TO SUCCESS

▶ As you read about all the different consultants described in this book, identify the one who most closely matches your role model.

▶ Analyse what they have achieved and how they did it.

▶ Identify the gap between their skills, knowledge and experience and yours, and incorporate that into your career plan.

▶ Analyse their beliefs, and try them on for size. Act as if they were true, and see what that does for you.

3

....

What makes a successful consultant?

This chapter covers:
- *putting yourself in the client's place*
- *client concerns when hiring*
- *the worst sins a consultant can commit*
- *definitions of success*

What makes a successful consultant? There are many different answers to this question, and the important point is that you will have your own. You may have it now – a clear image or a strong feeling that signals success. You may not yet be sure, so test out your thinking here.

Sir John Harvey Jones gave this advice to business consultants:

'Consulting is all about interpersonal skills, in particular knowing how to tailor your advice to the optimum of what the organization will take on board and implement. It is the art of being super-blunt but telling the truth in as acceptable a way as one can, and humour helps a great deal in this process. There is nothing easier than giving advice, and nothing more difficult than implementing it in the real world. I think it is important to hold that perspective as a consultant, particularly if you are not yourself the deliverer.'

Frank Milton added to Sir John's list: 'To be really good you need:

▶ *Fluency – in all aspects of business, as well as your special expertise.*
▶ *Currency – knowing what's happening now, and what the future trends are.*
▶ *Personability – the ability to connect with people.*
▶ *Punch – the ability to make a difference. Can you say and get away with what others would not say? (Like telling the client that they haven't got a cat's chance in hell of doing whatever!)*

'When I recruit a young consultant, I look firstly at the academic attainment, then for evidence of success and advancement early in the career with a good employer. Finally I look for something extraordinary on the CV, something in any field which is an indicator of their spark and drive – the personability and the punch.'

Just as they say that beauty is in the eye of the beholder, so the worth of a consultant is measured by the client. You may believe that you have expertise beyond question, but if your client is not happy with what you have provided, then there is no success – only a dissatisfied client, who may well relay their feelings about you to others. Sometimes a client wants the expert to confirm that what they are doing is right. You may think there is a better way, but that may not be what the client wants to hear.

Insight

It can be a very difficult decision whether to tell the client what they want to hear, or to give them some home truths. If you decide on the latter, will you still be around to influence them is one of the key questions to ask yourself. If you do the former, does it compromise your professionalism?

I did some work recently for a services company who are installing a new system. The Board had questioned the plan, and my client simply wanted external confirmation that the plan was sound.

I could have told them about better systems, about different implementation plans, but that was not the brief. Had their system been flawed, then I would have been compromising my professional integrity by endorsing it, which is something I would not have been prepared to do. The reality was that their plan was solid – not the best, but certainly much better than the average. I had no difficulty in endorsing the plan. The client is happy, the Board satisfied by an external assessment, and the plan can be implemented quickly. This constitutes success all round, although not by the rules of the perfectionist.

Putting yourself in the client's place

A critical skill of any consultant is to see things from the client's point of view. If you can work out exactly where your customer is coming from, and what they really want from you, you are already close to succeeding. Just as in the example above, many clients do not hire you on the strength of your technical expertise alone. In some cases other factors are far more important. It may be that they want you to do a sales job on the Board for them – that your authority and gravitas will impress, despite the fact that there are more qualified people available to them internally.

It may be that your fit with their culture is vital. If, say, they have a very aggressive style, then a delicate flower of a consultant with refined skills and no backbone will not be able to operate effectively in their organization. Becoming a cultural chameleon is a prime skill in a consultant.

Insight
Who is your client? This may sound obvious, but sometimes the needs of the person who commissioned the work from you and the needs of their organization may conflict. Recognizing this is critical, and needless to say, needs the most careful handling.

An insecure client may be buying your expertise to cover his back. The saying goes that 'nobody ever got fired for buying IBM'. Some people need official reassurance and endorsement. It is very important to recognize this at the outset, because you will need to make sure that your client is never exposed; that he (or she) is always wrapped safely in the protective covering of your authority and expertise. To do really well, you will shine as much of the glory on them as you can – make the right remarks to the right people to enhance their image. This may win you more work in the long run, as the client will see you as a safe supporter, which is just what insecure people need.

Case study: Siebel Systems (now part of Oracle Corporation)

Sue Goble, Head of Consulting at Siebel Systems, stands out when it comes to identifying with the client. She has such a clear and systematic way of doing this that it merits a special look.

Sue joined Siebel in 1996 as a Technical Account Manager, when there were only eight people in Europe employed by Siebel. Now there are about 2500. The aim of the role is to work alongside the client and the partner to ensure effective project implementation. She managed the first major projects in the UK, and then gradually rose within the rapidly expanding organization (an average of 30 per cent revenue growth quarter on quarter!) to her current position where she has a team of 100 consultants working for her.

The major focus of the company, however, is on customer satisfaction. You may think this is not surprising for a company that sells Customer Relationship Management systems, but in the software world in particular, it is not unusual for the cobbler's children never to have had shoes. Not so with Siebel. They use their own software, and beta test it in house on their own live system before it goes anywhere near a customer. Core to the company's commitment to the client is the quarterly customer satisfaction survey, on which everyone in the company is targeted, to varying degrees. This survey consists of a series of paired questions, such as: 'How did you rate the technical expertise of the Siebel consultant?' and 'How important is this to you?'

So if a customer gives the consultant a rating of 7 out of 10, on a subject he rates as 10 out of 10, then there is a difference of 3 points, and that difference will give Siebel staff a lot of pain. This happened some time ago, and a certification programme was introduced as a result. Now the difference is less than one point on technical expertise. The Siebel standard is a maximum of two points.

She says, 'This company-wide focus on customer satisfaction also means that consultants are not left to pick up the pieces after sales have done their bit. In other organizations, once the sale is made, then it's over to post sales, and they can sort any problems out. Because of the way we are measured, if there is a problem, everybody cares about it.'

Siebel also have an implementation effectiveness survey, and even when the account has reached a level of maturity, there is still a six-monthly satisfaction survey. Surveys may be overkill for your business, or you may do them anyway. The key point is that you are really trying to step into your client's shoes, and find out how they feel at every stage. Then, having discovered the answers, it is what you do with the results that matters. Sue spoke of this whole process with overwhelming enthusiasm, and it is clear that Siebel really want this feedback, and that they are really motivated to act on it immediately and truly serve the customer.

Client concerns when hiring

Suppose you are going to hire a consultant today?

Let us imagine that you are running a department in a large company, and you have just been asked to lead a project in your area. It involves doing something you have never done before, but nobody knows that. You feel a bit uncomfortable about this, but decide that the best thing to do is to bring in an expert in that area. What will you be looking for from that expert? Can you describe the person you are looking for?

As you think about the answers to these questions, think about the priorities for you in this situation. Jot down a list before you read on, because this list will almost certainly be one that you will be measured by, when you are being considered by a client.

Insight

It's always instructive to put yourself in your client's shoes. In this case, you are thinking, 'What would I want from a consultant?' as opposed to, 'What do my clients want from a consultant?' You may find you answer these questions differently – spend time understanding why.

A Finance Director, who had commissioned many projects in his time, produced the following list:

▶ *'Integrity is top of my list. If you can't trust them, they're no good to you. Same with reliability. It's no good having the world expert if you can't be sure they'll deliver.'*
▶ *'Next it's credibility. No good being an expert if you can't convey it and impress the right people with the authority of your views.'*
▶ *'After that it's technical expertise – but it needs to be intelligible – if not to me then to my staff. That's different from credibility – you can blind people with science so they believe you're the expert, but then if they can't understand a word ...'*

So his priorities are:

1 *Integrity*
2 *Reliability*
3 *Credibility*
4 *Technical expertise.*

It is interesting to see that expertise does not feature in his top three needs. How did your list compare?

Next he was asked what concerns he has when hiring a consultant.

'I often have to check if the organ grinder who comes to sell to me will be despatching one of his monkeys to do the work. That can be a problem with the larger firms. I also worry about being taken in by some sort of façade. If I don't know their field of expertise, and that's often why I'm hiring them, then I worry that they might pull the wool over my eyes. That's when I make an assessment about integrity. The more glib they are, the more uncomfortable I get. It's such a surprise when someone tells me they don't know something. If it's not central, then that can be just the indicator I need that they are more trustworthy than most.'

This is a very interesting comment. He is asking for your expertise, but is reassured when you say that you do not know about some peripheral area. This is a tightrope to be walked, as other clients may well be worried that there is a gap in your knowledge, and in a different situation, this could count against you. What it demonstrates is that unless you are talking expert to expert, then the client feels at a great disadvantage in his ability to judge you, and since he cannot judge the facts of your know-how, he is looking for other things to tell him how trustworthy you are, and that your expertise is not a clever sham.

Insight

How can I demonstrate trustworthiness without just saying the words? Clients make judgements on tiny things such as your punctuality. Did you do exactly what you said you would do in setting up this meeting? Are you able to say 'I don't know' on some minor issue that demonstrates honesty?

Hold this perspective in mind when you are presenting to a prospective client. If they know their stuff, you can talk technically as equals. If they do not know your area of expertise, think how you can appear to them to be reassuringly well qualified, and absolutely trustworthy. Imagine a conversation like this:

'And I just know all there is to know about landscape gardening, believe me. I can tell you at once that your Robinia pseudo-acacia frisia needs moving.'

'My what?'

'Look, just trust me on this, okay? Leave it all to me and I'll have it sorted in no time.'

How do you think the owner of the garden is feeling? Delighted by a show of expertise? Reassured by the words 'trust me'? Almost certainly not!

Just as 'with respect' usually means the opposite, so 'trust me' is a very dangerous phrase to use. The reasons that the client finds to trust you need to be implicit in what you say, not explicit. We will explore this subject further in Chapter 15 on Building Client Relationships. The bottom line is that trust ranks way above technical expertise, so bear that in mind as you overwhelm the client with the breadth and depth of your specialism.

On the other hand it may be that your client knows a great deal about the project content, in which case you must avoid the other pitfall, described here by Sir John Harvey Jones:

'I believe that consultants will be able to do their job better if they have had some real management experience. Without this, consultants are likely to take the theoretical view, and generally things are not done according to the textbook, even in the best of companies.

'Lots of consultants have a catch-all solution, which they apply to everything, irrespective of what the client's real needs are. They also will often vocalize what the organization already knows – the classic of borrowing your watch to tell you the time.'

Mark Brown, Visiting Professor of Innovation at Henley Management College, was equally concerned about the calibre of consultants in the market today:

'I have a prejudice about business consultants. There are lots of people out there who call themselves consultants, but who have very little in the way of skills and experience. There are lots of second-hand car salesmen in this field, and there is a huge variation between the deeply dodgy and the quite spectacular. If the medical profession operated this way, I think we'd be seriously worried about falling ill!'

Given this kind of view, it makes the need for integrity and credibility even more essential. If you are thinking that this does not apply to me, that I just turn up and deliver technical input, well, think again! You may be a small cog in a big project team, with no significant client contact, but there will be some, somewhere, even if it is only at the coffee machine. You are always representing your company, and just the wrong word thrown in as a casual remark can create waves of concern in the client. Whatever your role, you need to be very clear what it is you and your team are delivering to the client, and what part you play in that.

The principles therefore apply whether you are a project manager or a junior consultant in a large firm, or if it is just you alone. You are selling at least one thing in all your dealings with a client, and that is yourself. You represent your company, and so you are 'selling' your company all the time.

The worst sins a consultant can commit

On sins the Finance Director did not hesitate.

▶ *'The first is promising the earth, and then barely managing a single continent! I do wish people wouldn't over-commit – it is so unnecessary!'*
▶ *'The second is failing to keep me informed when things go off track. This deprives me of the opportunity to do something about it. It makes me very angry when this happens.'*
▶ *'The third sin is incompetence, and I put it third because consultants can control the first two – incompetence tends to be harder for them to manage!'*

Note again that the priority for the client lies in his ability to trust and rely on you as a person, more than on your expertise.

This question was asked of many consultants, and they replied at different levels.

Not listening to the client was top of the list: 'The single biggest skill that a consultant can learn is to listen ...' to quote Janet Simmons at Pecaso, and almost everyone else made the same point.

Insight

Listening is not enough, though. You have to do something with what you hear. When a client tells you they don't want something that you then include in your proposal, it looks like you have not listened or worse, that you have, and you know better!

Joint top of the list was this one, best expressed by Frank Milton: 'Loss of integrity. Everything you say has to be visibly traced back to the benefit of the client and not the consultant.'

Frank extended this in a different direction: 'Being intellectually honest is very hard to do. Sometimes you know something for sure; sometimes you just have an instinct for something. Consultants can get seduced into saying things at the wrong weight, because they get used to being the experts, and so they say something categoric, when really they are not sure at all.'

Janet at Pecaso put this same point in a different way: 'Misleading the customer by pretending knowledge you don't have. So you say no to the client because it's the safest option, when it could be that yes is true, and you are depriving them of something that they could have, if you bothered to find out.'

She also talked about the importance of involving the client, which again has been a critical point many consultants have made, although more in the sense of getting them to buy into the solution, and understand any bad news that may be coming from the project findings. Janet came from a different angle: 'It's a sin not to keep the customer fully involved, so that they know all the good things that are going on, and feel part of the success.'

Mark Brown took this further: 'I see a big difference between content and process consultants. A company may get an excellent content report from one of the top consulting groups, and put it in a drawer. I deliver some content, but I also work on process with the client in a highly collaborative way, so that they feel they own the result. We develop the plot together, so that they feel they invented the plot. I say to them what goes wrong is down to me, what goes right is down to you. In business I do two things which are equally important. I help them to innovate, and then I help them to learn how to persevere to make their innovation happen. This has to be about process consulting and about full client involvement.

Insight

Mark raises the vital distinction between content and process consulting. If you give the client content, you are not necessarily helping them to help themselves. Give the client process, and then they can.

'Another cardinal sin is arrogance. Someone once said that if a company is young and growing they need consultants. On the other hand, if the company is large and fixed in its ways they need insultants, but they are quite likely to throw them out, because they won't want to hear what they have to say, by their very nature!'

Closing thoughts

Diamonds are nothing more than chunks of coal that stuck to their jobs.

Malcolm Stevenson Forbes

We are what we repeatedly do. Excellence, then, is not an act, but a habit.

Aristotle

STEPS TO SUCCESS

Your success with any individual client relies as much, if not more, on your skills in managing the client relationship, than on delivering technically. If we take it as read that you would not get in front of the client without a good level of expertise in whatever field they need, then the qualities or skills that will make the difference can be itemized as:

▶ *Your ability to see things from the client's perspective, and truly understand what they want from you, which may not always be what they say they want.*

▶ *Your ability to state clearly how you will deliver what they want, matching any of their implicit needs with implicit content from you.*

▶ *Your ability to convince the client that you have the qualities of integrity and reliability they are looking for, in ways that are more implicit than explicit.*

▶ *Your ability to demonstrate your expertise clearly to the non-expert client, without making them feel disadvantaged, or overwhelmed, or patronized.*

If you can do all these things, and then deliver on them, you will be able to win business, and then win repeat business and get referred business, which is the most effective route to success.

4

Setting a clear vision

This chapter covers:
- *how to create a clear vision*
- *how to set a compelling goal*
- *how to define and measure success*
- *do you have an absolutely clear idea of what you are aiming for?*
- *can you describe how you will be different when you have reached your goals?*
- *do you know what measures you will use for your success?*

An American university has published a study on a group of people who participated in a very interesting research experiment. They had a daily exercise routine to develop their muscles, but this routine was entirely in their heads. They imagined the exercises, and then they visualized the growing strength in their muscles. This was tightly monitored, as was their physical activity, and the results were similar to a control group who did actually do the physical work. Their muscle strength improved to a similar level, yet they had only imagined the exercises and imagined the result.

It is rare to be able to show such a concrete result of our mental power. The most quoted examples tend to be those of Olympic gold medallists, whose training consists as much of the visualization of winning, as it does of the physical exercise.

The power of belief

Whichever example you choose, the message is the same: If you can believe you can do it, and see yourself doing it, then you will do it. We started work on beliefs in Chapter 1, and we shall return to that. We shall also be giving you lots of practical input to enhance your skills – that is the bulk of the book. However, in this chapter we want to help you to focus on 'winning the race', on that 'increased muscle power'. Whatever your goal is, we want you to be absolutely clear about it, and to be able to experience the outcome right now.

In sporting terms your goal could be to win the Olympic gold medal for javelin throwing. That is a clearly defined outcome, with at least one measure of success – the medal. Other measures could be how you will feel when you win, or how proud your parents will be. The next stage in this process is to create the vision of how you will win: run the whole event in your head, which ends with the medal. In doing this you will see, feel and hear the whole thing. You will experience every aspect of what you will do to succeed. Then you will run through all this several times, so that the vision becomes familiar, so that when you do it for real, it will not be for the first time, you will have been there before, and the outcome is assured!

It is easy to do that for something as clear and focused and measurable as winning an individual sporting competition, you may say. Being a consultant is far more complex; there are unpredictable people interactions that may affect my performance, which would mean lots and lots of permutations and a very blurred vision!

Insight

Don't dismiss the sports analogy as too far removed from your reality. It should be your gold standard. For example, for you and for your clients' sake, you want the finishing line to be as clear to them as it is to an athlete on the running track.

What is your outcome?

This is where defining your outcome is so important. What exactly does consulting excellence mean to you? In Kay's case (discussed in Chapter 2), it is all about giving presentations. She feels comfortable in the consultant's role, except in this one area. For her, imagining the result is the challenge. She would like to see herself 'doing a Nigel': being relaxed, fluent and witty, holding the audience in the palm of her hand. She feels this is too big a stretch for her in one go. She will save that for stage two. Her stage one vision is of herself as a confident and fluent presenter, well received by her audience.

Neil, on the other hand, is new to the consulting role, and feels he could improve in all areas. He works on two scenarios: the first one is building a good relationship with his client. He imagines them in a meeting together, relaxed and smiling as they hold a project review. Neil is feeling completely comfortable, despite the fact that he has just covered a tricky point, and has another one to deal with.

The second scenario is around report writing. He imagines a delighted client holding Neil's report and saying, 'This is excellent, Neil, just what we needed, very clear and to the point, but comprehensive too!'

Neil knows that there are other things that he would like to achieve, and some of these may be things he does not know about yet. That is one of the reasons for reading this book! He can return to this section and review his outcomes as he progresses in his learning, and so can you.

ACTIONS

Take some time now to work out what it is that you really want to achieve. If you feel uncomfortable about doing this, it is an excellent sign that you really do need to do it! If you have a long list, prioritize, and take the top two for now. You can come back and deal with others as you progress.

When you have an absolutely clear view of your outcome, try
going there. If you were Neil, you would step into that meeting and
feel that feeling of comfort and confidence. As he does this, Neil
will discover that he quite likes the client, knows quite a bit about
him, and can enjoy his company – he is quite surprised to learn all
this, but it just flows from the outcome that he imagines. How else
would he be feeling so relaxed and comfortable?

He then worries that this outcome will be totally client dependent –
fine for the ones he likes, but what about the ones he does not like?
He has another go at imagining the meeting with a more difficult
client. He finds it a little harder, but he can still see someone with
shared goals, that he has taken time to get to know, and whose
respect he has won through his technical skills. Perhaps he is not
quite as relaxed as in the first meeting, but he is still comfortable
and confident in dealing with difficult issues.

Step into your outcome

Stepping into your successful outcome is an excellent test, and it
will give you more information than you expect. You may want
to make some notes so that you can make the outcome more vivid
when you return to it. Create a really clear picture in your mind,
then step inside it and see what happens. If you have difficulty
creating mental pictures, and some people do, then perhaps an
impression with feelings and sounds would work for you. The
point is that you are sure of the outcome, and can move into that
world and experience the feelings, hear the sounds, see what is
around you, and know that this is where you want to be, and that
this is where you can be.

Does stepping into your outcome feel strange? Are you wondering whether to bother? Try it, and see. Remember that you don't want to be always doing what you always did, so try something different and see what you get! Do it wholeheartedly though, not just a little skip in and out!

Kay does not expect applause after a client presentation, but she does hear those positive murmurings that you get when someone has just impressed you. She also sees approbation in the eyes of her colleagues. She hears the interest in the clients' voices as they ask her questions. She feels confident as she gives quick and easy answers. She sees the nods as her replies are accepted. She sits down with a wonderful feeling of accomplishment, reinforced by the sense of approval she gets from the people in the room, both her clients and her colleagues. She delights for a few moments in her glory, and freezes her image right there.

Measures for success

This is a very clear outcome, and it also contains measures for success. Kay can now describe how she will feel when she succeeds, and how her audience will react. She might want to add other measures. She might ask a colleague to give her feedback after the meeting. She might want an unprompted compliment from one of her colleagues whose opinion she values, provided that she knows they are capable of giving unprompted compliments. Some people never do, no matter how well deserved the compliment would be, so if she sets that as a measure, she will never reach it!

Getting the measures clear is a key part of the process. If you set measures which are outside your control, such as the one above, you may be setting goals which are unrealistic, and a permanent barrier to success. If we look at Neil again, who has writing a good client report as his outcome, he creates some very specific measures.

He decides that he will ask three people the same set of questions, after they have given him unprompted feedback. Assuming the feedback does not already cover these areas, he will ask: 'Is it clear? Does it meet your requirements? Is it easy to read? How could I improve it?'

Neil has found a colleague, Jack, who is his mentor for report writing. Jack helps Neil with reports, and Neil helps Jack with the new project management software they have just installed. It is a good arrangement. Neil prepares his report and shows it to Jack, modifies it and shows it to his manager, modifies it and gives it to the client.

So now Neil will ask all three people the four questions, and providing he gets positive answers to the first three from them all, he will consider that to be success. He will still expect to get suggestions for improvement, but that will not affect the success rating, because you can always improve, wherever you are on the scale. He also does not need overwhelmingly positive answers from each one, just positive will do, and they can be positive from Jack and his manager after revisions too. Apart from to the client, he does not have to deliver right first time to the other two.

You may be thinking that this level of detail is unnecessary; that you will know when the client is happy with your report, and there is no need for all this. In fact, this process is doing two things. Firstly, it is reinforcing your outcome, so that it becomes part of you. Secondly, it is helping you to frame your outcome and how you will reach it. Neil might just have had a picture of a perfect report, lying on his desk, as his target. This is not an outcome to inspire him to achieve. Now he has the image of giving it to a satisfied client, and hearing the positive answers to his questions. Which would you feel more motivated to achieve?

A positive frame

You may have noticed that all of the outcomes that we have described are framed positively. We only talk about producing a good report, we do not refer to improving a bad one. Kay is not aiming to reduce her nervousness; she is aiming to be confident. This may seem obvious, but we often tend to express what we want in negative, rather than positive terms.

'I want to escape from this awful weather!' rather than, 'I'd love a holiday in the sun.' When you define your outcome(s), be sure you are moving towards the sun, not running away from bad weather. The reason for this is simple. Aiming for a positive gives you a much clearer focus, and takes you faster to success. Imagine this conversation between Sandra and Lionel:

'I just want to be a better consultant.'

'What does that mean?'

'Well, I'm not as technically capable as I should be, so I want to be better qualified, and I don't feel my image is right, so I'd like to change that somehow.'

'So what do you want?'

'Better qualifications and a better image, I suppose.'

'How could you express that positively?'

'I want to get the chartered qualification and look like a serious professional!'

There is quite a lot more work to do on what 'a serious professional' looks like, but Lionel is now on a positive road to the sun, and is no longer escaping from bad weather!

> ## Insight
> Now ask yourself, 'What do I want? What does my "sunshine holiday" look like?' You will gain so much more from this book if you take time to define a really good outcome for yourself.

At this point in the chapter we are going to assume that you have now created a positive outcome, with measures for its success. If you have not done this yet, do it now, in order to be able to test it thoroughly.

Testing an outcome

We are now going to apply some tests to this outcome, to ensure that it is really solid, and therefore really achievable. We will take Kay's presentation skills as an example throughout.

The first question to ask about it is would you like it in other contexts?

Kay certainly would! She has been invited to speak at conferences before, and has always turned down the opportunity. Also there are social occasions where she would like to have this skill available to her. The next question is:

What is important to you about achieving this outcome?

Kay is ambitious, and she knows that this will be an important career hurdle for her to overcome to make her way up the ladder.

What is the real problem or issue?

Kay is nervous and self-conscious when speaking to a group.

How is your present state useful to you?

Being nervous means that she minimizes the amount of exposure she gets, so she reduces the potential to make a fool of herself as much as possible.

Insight

This can look like a silly question, but it often uncovers reasons why change does not happen. Smoking can keep you slim, and this fact alone can stop people giving up. Their present state has real value to them.

Is the reward for the achievement of the outcome big enough to compensate you for the loss of how things are now?

Kay is scared, but she is forced into giving more client presentations, so the only option is to sacrifice her career in order to avoid any kind of public speaking. She is too ambitious to give this up, so the reward for achievement will be worth it.

A classic example of where this is not the case is the person who wants to give up smoking. Take the case of Sheila, who has just been told to give up by her doctor. She cares about her own health, but she enjoys cigarettes more. The reward for giving up smoking is not high enough for her to achieve it.

Is the outcome representative of who you are and who you want to be?

This outcome is exactly in line with Kay's career aspirations. She is very comfortable with this question. Asking Lionel about his image change might generate some interesting discussion.

Is it worth what it takes to get it?

Kay has no doubts.

What resources do you need, both physically and mentally?

External sources of information and guidance, plus time and courage.

What action steps can you commit to? Especially the first step?

Kay is going to finish reading this book, and she is going to talk to Nigel about training.

And what will help you maintain it?

She would like to find a mentor, someone she can make a fool of herself in front of, and not worry about it.

Testing your own outcome

Now work through these questions yourself, to test your own outcome. If you are happy with the answers to all these questions, then you have a well-formed outcome, which will deliver success. If you find difficulty, particularly in balancing the rewards of change against staying as you are, then work on those issues. If you ignore them and just carry on, the chances of success are clearly lower, and you risk falling into the category of yet another failed non-smoker!

Find an outcome that delivers greater rewards than those you get from staying as you are. It may be that you do not change the outcome at all; you focus on those rewards, enhance them, find more of them, or see more disadvantages in not changing. However you do it, the end result will clear your path to success, and remove any nagging doubts from the back of your mind, so that you can just go for it!

Here is a review of the questions to test your outcome:

1 *What is your outcome?*
2 *Would you like this outcome in other contexts?*
3 *What is important to you about achieving this outcome?*
4 *What is the real problem or issue?*
5 *How is your present state useful to you?*
6 *Is the reward for the achievement of the outcome big enough to compensate you for the loss of how things are now?*
7 *Is the outcome representative of who you are and who you want to be?*
8 *Is it worth what it takes to get it?*
9 *What resources do you need, both physically and mentally?*
10 *What action steps can you commit to?*
11 *What is the first step?*
12 *What will help you maintain it?*

Closing thoughts

Obstacles are those frightful things you see when you take your eyes off your goal.

Henry Ford

Good, better, best; never let it rest till your good is better and your better is best.

Anon

STEPS TO SUCCESS

▶ *Clarify your vision of what you want.*

▶ *Define your outcome in positive terms.*

▶ *Step into the outcome.*

▶ *Test your outcome using the 12 questions.*

5

Bringing power to your aim

This chapter covers:
- *turning your outcome into reality*
- *finding your commitment strategy*
- *moving from thinking to making it happen*

In the last chapter you created at least one crystal clear outcome.
You are now probably wondering why you need to read a chapter
on commitment. As we have already mentioned, most books simply
offer you knowledge and experience on a plate, which you may
devour voraciously, or hardly pick at. This chapter focuses on your
appetite. Just offering you useful information may be helpful, but
how much more helpful it will be if we offer you tools for learning,
and, more importantly, for making things happen. You still have
the choice. You can skip these chapters and grab a handful of what
Chapters 8 onwards contain. In other words, treat this like any
other business book on the shelf. That would be a pity, though,
because the skills you learn here are not just applicable to learning,
they apply to achievement too. They do not just apply to business
either; you can apply them to any aspect of your life. So if you
are feeling impatient to get to the 'real content', then go there and
come back if you wish to, the choice is always yours; but there is a
great deal to be gained by acquiring the techniques we cover here,
so why not give them a try?

Commitment strategy

You may or may not be surprised to learn that you have a commitment strategy. It can take many forms, and will be entirely individual to you. Emma, for example, needs to see something in writing before she can commit to it. It needs to be all laid out in sequenced detail, she needs time to reflect on it, and then she can commit. Ron, on the other hand, needs a clear picture in his head, which he discusses with at least two and preferably three people. If those discussions go well, he gets a comfortable, positive feeling and he is ready to commit.

Insight

Questions you may be asking now include: is it likely that people will behave that consistently? Do I do that? You may feel you commit to things in lots of different ways. If these are your thoughts, then yes, people are usually consistent over similar things. So the commitment to get a cup of coffee may vary from the commitment to buy a house, but for big decisions to change, you can expect to discover that you have a consistent strategy. Now the question is, what is it?

Think about a time when you proactively made an important personal decision that involved successful commitment to a new path. A change of job, house or partner are the most obvious ones. Now analyse how you made that commitment to change.

Here are some key variables to help you.

▶ *How long did the process of committing take?*
▶ *Did it involve talking to other people about the commitment?*
▶ *Did you talk to yourself (internally or externally!) about the commitment?*
▶ *Did you get a clear picture or form a strong impression of the new path?*
▶ *Did you get a particular feeling during and at the end of the commitment process?*

Let us take Bill as an example. He had been unhappy in his job for a while, and wanted a change. So far, he's 'escaping bad weather'. He looks in the papers and sees a job as a travel guide – he is currently working as a junior accountant. He feels excited at the thought of being a travel guide, and now he is focused on his 'holiday in the sun'. This is literally the case here, and he does some research on the Internet. He gets a book out of the library. He goes for a long walk and talks to himself about it. He can't quite see the picture, but he forms this lovely idea of being on a Greek hillside in the sunshine, surrounded by his flock of happy tourists. He can feel the heat of the sun, and hear himself talking about his passion, Greek history. It feels right for him. He is committed. He rushes home to apply for the job. He does not get it, nor the next one, but by this time he has targeted specialist historical agencies, and several months later, one of these takes him on, as a trainee guide.

Bill is unusual in that he does not see clear pictures, but the sounds and feelings are so strong that they create a different kind of imagery, which is just as effective. He also has no need to discuss things with people, but talking to himself is very important, and doing the necessary groundwork too; he is clearly not going to do things on the spur of the moment.

Contrast what you do with what Bill does, as an aid to understanding your own strategy. When you have worked it out, you may want to write it down, because you will need it to make your outcome(s) happen.

Insight

For some people, time may be an important element in their commitment strategy. Ask yourself a series of questions: How long do I need to decide? Who, if anyone, do I need to discuss the decision with? What information do I need in order to feel comfortable with the decision? How do I want to feel when I'm committed?

Are you thinking that you have already done this in order to get to your well-formed outcome? That may be true, but just test it.

If you always bounce things off a close friend, and you have not
done that yet, then take the time to do it. It may seem unnecessary,
but we are more creatures of habit than we realize, and that chat
with a friend will be a missing brick in your commitment structure
if you do not include it! Just be sure that you have identified all the
steps, and followed them for each outcome, and then you have the
firmest possible commitment to achieving your goal.

Sharing your outcome

Having done that, the next step is to share your outcome with
others. You have made the outcome real to you. Bill knows just
what it is like on that Greek hillside. Now he is going to tell people
about it, and the more he talks about getting there, the more likely
he is to succeed. Other people will reinforce the internal reality he
has created, and may even be able to help him on his way, but this
is not the main reason why he tells them; it is to make achieving
that outcome part of his life. People recognize his aim and his
commitment, and can share the image of where he is heading, so all
this becomes normal. Bill is surrounded by people who know what
he wants and why, and who therefore expect him to achieve it.

Insight
Who should you tell first? Find the person who will be the
most enthusiastic audience to start with. Then you can start
working up to those who may be more challenging.

You may think that telling some people may have the opposite
effect; that they will kill your idea and tell you that it is unrealistic
and you will never make it. Avoid this kind of person if you can,
but if they are central to your life, then view them as a challenge.
What is most important here is that they can really understand
your outcome, so that you can describe it to them as vividly and
enthusiastically as you can. Here the use of metaphor will help you
a great deal.

Worth a thousand words

Most people are able to create mental pictures of some kind, and they are much more comfortable with concrete things than abstract concepts. So if Jon tells you that he is preparing a report on industrial unrest in the automotive industry, that will not convey the message as clearly as if he were to say: 'I'm preparing a report on why car workers go on strike.' Now images can start to form of picket lines and union leaders, and his message is clear.

What helps even more in this communication process is the use of metaphor. Jon may say that his report will contain some illuminating concepts. Or he could use a metaphor and say that his report will be a searchlight, showing clearly to his readers what lurks in the shadowy corners of this subject. You are probably more interested in reading it now, and you are starting to imagine what might be in those shadowy corners, whereas the prospect of a few illuminating concepts did not do a great deal for you.

Insight

Think about how you would describe to someone your aim to be a top management consultant. How could you use metaphor to bring that to life?

Kay is talking to her partner, who is only half listening. She begins by describing herself giving a superb client presentation. 'And when I've overcome that hurdle, I'm going to volunteer to speak at the next industry conference. I've got a lot to say about the current hot topic, and I shall really let them have it! I'll prepare something really stunning, covering all the angles – a real firework display! I can hear the applause now!'

Kay's partner is surprised by the evident passion in what she says. 'Wow, I'm convinced already – and I've no idea what the content is. You really mean this, don't you!'

As time goes by, he will ask her how the plans for the firework display are going. He has latched on to this metaphor, which conveys to him so clearly what Kay is aiming for. This serves to reinforce Kay in her resolve, now that she has shared her outcome with him.

If you find the right metaphor, you will discover that you talk about your outcome with natural enthusiasm, if not passion. This will convey itself strongly to the person you are talking to, as it did with Kay's partner. If you get a neutral response, check that they are listening before you do anything else! If they are paying attention, then something is missing from your message, and it may just be the amount of feeling that you put into its delivery. When you get that response, you will find that it reflects the energy and enthusiasm you feel for your outcome. You are committed.

Closing thoughts

Wherever you go, go with all your heart.

Confucius

There's no scarcity of opportunity to make a living at what you love. There is only a scarcity of resolve to make it happen.

Wayne Dyer

STEPS TO SUCCESS

▶ Test your commitment strategy on your outcome.

▶ Create a metaphor around your outcome that really feels right for you.

▶ Tell people about your outcome, using the metaphor.

▶ Check their responses – positive or negative means you have made an impact, neutral means you have not made that impact, or they are not listening!

▶ Recognize the power and excitement that you generate when you are committed.

6

Assessing your resources

This chapter covers:
* *valuing what you already have*
* *obtaining feedback*
* *receiving feedback*

This chapter is about foundations to build on. Thinking of yourself as a house under construction, your building may be at any level from ground to roof, when it comes to consulting skills. You might need everything from sturdy walls upwards, or just an elegant chimney to finish things off. The critical point here is that you know which elements are solid, which need reinforcement, and which do not exist yet, and this may not be the simple matter that you think it is.

Jane was doing a part-time finance diploma. She sailed through the class work, did her revision, and sailed through the exam. She was devastated to learn that she had failed. Her tutor, just as surprised, made a formal enquiry, and discovered that she had simply not read the questions properly. She had been marked fairly and correctly. Jane believes she pays meticulous attention to detail, as well as being naturally talented at finance, yet the facts say something different. She therefore sees solid foundations to build on, where in reality there is only a shaky construction which will collapse under the slightest pressure.

Jane's story is alarming. 'Do I have blind spots like that?' is
the natural question that springs to mind. This applies to our
strengths as well as any weaknesses.

Valuing what you already have

Ken has never been comfortable with computers. He uses them,
of course, everybody does, but never with a feeling of ease and
comfort. He usually gets some help with even the simplest project
plan – not a problem really, as people are always happy to help
Ken. Once he gets a project plan in his head, he can really get the
hang of things. He can sniff out problems that other people simply
cannot detect. He can manipulate the data without needing to
see the screen again. Ken considers himself to be a poor project
planner. He believes that his skill with project software is deficient,
and what he does mentally with a plan is a poor substitute. He
assumes everybody can manipulate plans in their head, because he
finds it so easy.

Like Ken, we can often undervalue skills that for us, require no
effort. We think nothing of being able to run up a spreadsheet,
or to just lean on old Ted a bit to persuade him to do that little
favour. It is vital to get an objective view of these skills, which
others will value far more than you do.

It is even more important to get feedback on a skill that we
think that we are good at, but in reality, we are not. This is harder
in some ways, because we may be completely unaware of our
shortcomings. The starting point needs to be with someone you
can trust to give you some honest answers to some straight
questions.

It may be helpful to list the skills that you have identified as being essential to your role as a consultant. Here is a suggested list – yours may vary.

Specialist expertise
Project management
Client management
Working as part of a project team
Working alone
Projecting the right image
Building client relationships
Influencing skills
Negotiation skills
Managing conflict
Political awareness
Running client workshops/project meetings
Presentation skills
Report writing

Obtaining feedback

The reason for your list is to identify your areas of competence, excellence, and those that you need to work on. If you could put the appropriate ticks and crosses against each item on the list, and then give it to your boss, his boss, a few colleagues and several clients for their honest comments, then that would be a pretty comprehensive assessment programme. It is also fairly unlikely that you will be able to do all of this, but it serves as an ideal to work from.

If you are an independent consultant, then clients, colleagues and a business buddy are your best sources. When you work alone, it is much harder to get feedback from people other than clients who see you in action as a consultant. However, you need the feedback just as much, so just talking through with your buddy how you handled a particular situation will enable them to give you a view. It will only be second hand, but when first hand is not possible, second hand is still valuable.

The best sources of feedback are those people who see you operating in your consultant role, whose judgement you trust, and who are capable of being honest with you. Ideally at least one of these people should be a client. Obviously not a new client, and possibly not a current one, but you might have a long-standing client who you feel very comfortable with, and you might be able to have a conversation like this:

'John, I'm working on a personal development programme at the moment, and I'd appreciate some input from you. Are there any areas of my role where you think I could improve? Things that I could have done better for you?'

This may well lead into a conversation about your specialist expertise, which is fine. If it stops there, continue as follows:

'Thanks for that, John. Now is there anything on the non-technical side that you can think of?'

If this does not produce anything, prompt with:

'What about the personal side, wheels I might have oiled, people I might have managed better, that sort of thing?'

If nothing is forthcoming after this, then you will probably want to stop, unless you know them really well, and can cajole them further. Otherwise, play safe with a client relationship; do not risk pressing it too far.

Insight

Asking for feedback is hard, but the results are more than worth it. It's equally hard to give good quality feedback, so treat it as a gift, whether it's positive or negative, and make it easy for the giver.

Many people are very reluctant to give negative feedback, and get very upset if forced into it. This applies to colleagues, and sadly, to managers too, so bear this in mind when asking them to be completely honest with you. Make it easy for them to say negative things nicely. Asking them where you could improve is far better than asking them to tell you where you are failing. Offer them prompts on a plate:

'I have this feeling that I could sharpen up my presentation skills. Do you think that would be a good idea?'

Do not say 'I feel I'm useless at presenting, what do you think?'

You may find that you ask different people about different aspects of your role. This puts less pressure on them if they are only required to comment on one area. You may arrange with them in advance to give you specific feedback. For example, if they are running a client meeting with you, you could tell them beforehand that you would like detailed feedback from them afterwards. Providing that they are not too involved themselves in the proceedings, they will be able to find specific things to comment on, and to give you actual examples of what you did.

Receiving feedback

Just as giving feedback is a skill, so is receiving it. The best way to view feedback is as pure data, neither good nor bad, which you can choose to accept or reject at your leisure. To be avoided at all costs, is the acceptance or rejection of the giver. Almost as bad, is to accept or reject the feedback as it is given.

For example, Lisa asks Sue for her comments on a report she has written. Sue tells Lisa her report writing could be improved. Lisa responds immediately, 'Well, I just didn't have time to do it justice, really ...'

Lisa has asked for feedback. Sue has done the difficult thing, and given Lisa some negative feedback. Now Lisa starts defending! She is rejecting the very thing she asked for. How likely is Sue to co-operate in future? Of course, Sue may be one of the minority of people who enjoy criticizing, in which case Lisa can go back to her for more.

Insight

When someone tells you your report writing could be improved, the only response to give is to ask in what ways. When receiving feedback, stay in receiving mode, and just ask questions, if they need asking. Mostly, just listen, and always thank the giver for this useful information.

Most people find giving feedback hard, and giving negative feedback very hard, so bear that in mind as you are suffering at the receiving end! All you need to do is receive it, make sure you understand it, and then take it away to examine later. No denials, excuses, defences and certainly no emotional response from you towards the giver. You thank them for doing you a favour, which you know they find difficult.

You ask if they will give you more feedback later, when you have had a chance to work on improving whatever it is. It is vital that they feel that you appreciate and value their input, in order to encourage them to give you more. This is a time when you think of them; you can focus on yourself later, when, alone with a box of tissues or a bottle of wine, you think about what they have said and feel the pain!

When you have felt the pain, you can then move on, and decide what you are going to do with this information, because, as you know, there is no failure, only feedback, and it is there to help you learn and improve.

POSITIVE FEEDBACK

It is just as important to receive positive feedback well. In fact, although giving positive feedback is easier than negative, many people still struggle to do it, so again, it is important to express your appreciation. It is also important to receive it gracefully. If someone tells you that you are a brilliant presenter, do not brush it aside, with a dismissive 'Not really ...'. Instead just say a straight 'Thank you!' with an expression of pleasure, if not enthusiasm.

If you would like to make a resolution to change here and now, an excellent one is to look for an opportunity to give someone positive feedback every day of your life. Your resolution will also be that if you do not find something that merits a positive comment, you will not give it – you will only ever be sincere. Now this positive feedback need not be a life-changing piece of information. It might just be to make a pleasant comment to the receptionist on your way into the office. It is often in the small things of life that we can give a great deal, and receive even more in return.

Insight

Think what a difference it makes when someone says something nice to you, no matter how trivial. Anything from, 'I like your tie' to, 'I really enjoyed your blog last week.' It costs very little to say these things, as long as they are sincerely meant. Usually the biggest challenge is to remember to say them. We often think things that go unsaid.

And what does this have to do with being a consultant? Well, people who regularly pay sincere compliments to people are usually fairly popular and likeable individuals, and their success with clients is likely to be enhanced, although the sincerity issue needs careful attention here, since many clients assume any compliment from a supplier to be a 'buttering up' process.

The other product of this behaviour is that it tends to generate reciprocal behaviour, and people are more likely to give you positive feedback in return. If they give positive feedback, it is also easier for them to give the negative too, because it becomes a balancing act, which is easier for them to cope with: 'You are brilliant at this Paul, but if only you could just do this other part as well ...'.

Building on your strengths

When you have gathered all the feedback you can, first take stock of your strengths and celebrate them. Do not dismiss them as 'the bits you do not need to work on'. Allow yourself to enjoy your prowess for a while, and to gain confidence from it. This is the final stage of fixing and reinforcing the foundations before you start to build. It is vital that your base feels entirely secure.

Now you are ready to build. If you feel in any way daunted by the task ahead of you, as you are preparing to run your first client meeting, for example, or give a major presentation; if you get those scary feelings that are often associated with taking a major personal step, then think back to your firm foundations. If you have come this far, then you can go further – you are completely committed to a clear outcome, so away you go!

Closing thoughts

Where talent is a dwarf, self-esteem is a giant.

J. Petit-Senn

Use what talents you possess: the woods would be very silent if no birds sang there except those that sang best.

Henry Van Dyke

STEPS TO SUCCESS

▶ *Seek feedback, both positive and negative, about you as a consultant.*

▶ *Pay special attention to the process of getting this feedback, as it is precious, and people find it difficult to give.*

▶ *Give positive feedback whenever you can; it will generate feedback in return.*

▶ *Celebrate your strengths, and recognize them as your secure base.*

▶ *Identify the areas you will work on, to build from your solid foundations.*

7

Tools to make it happen

This chapter covers:

- *acting as if*
- *using positive energy*
- *checking your language*
- *sight, sound or feelings?*
- *knowing your learning style*
- *taking the best from role models*
- *finding good mentors*

You now have a secure base, and your clear outcome, which you are fully committed to achieving. 'So can I get on with it now?' you are probably asking.

In this chapter we look at some techniques you can use to get there. This is the final 'knife and fork' section. In the next chapter you will reach the contents: what is actually being offered to you on the plate.

So what else do I need in the way of tools? You already have one toolkit – your set of presuppositions, particularly those around your personal resourcefulness:

▶ *There is no failure, only feedback.*
▶ *If someone else can do something, so can you.*
▶ *Everyone already has everything they need to achieve what they want.*

Act as if

A particularly useful extension of these presuppositions is not only to hold them for a while, but also to act as if they are true. You therefore act as if you can be as good a presenter as Nigel, or you act as if you know you will build strong rapport with a customer.

If you do this, two things will happen. First, because you know you are only acting as if, it is easier to do than trying it for real. Secondly, the brain responds to physical signals, so if you really smile, as opposed to a plastic grin, this sends a positive signal to the brain, which will then create a feeling in your head that corresponds to that smile, even though it knows you are only acting as if. To quote Peter Honey: 'Most people smile when they feel happy. I smile in order to feel happy.'

When Kay stands up to give her presentation, she is acting as if she is as proficient and relaxed a presenter as Nigel would be. She is not trying to be Nigel, far from it, she is just taking on the easy confident way that he has, and she finds that as she is acting relaxed, she actually feels easier in herself, and can relate more easily to the audience. Afterwards a friend compliments her: 'That really went very well, Kay. You seemed relaxed, and that made for easy listening.'

Kay smiles and thanks her friend for the feedback. She might have said, 'Well although I looked relaxed, I was still fairly tense inside – though much better than before.' She does not need to say this, however, because her audience has a different view.

> ### Insight
> How could 'acting as if' be useful to you? If it seems too big a step, find something small to practise on. If you want to reduce the risk, try it in a safer environment first, or perhaps with a trusted colleague to give you feedback.

To quote Peter again, 'So far as other people are concerned, you are your behaviour; so far as you are concerned, you are your thoughts and feelings.' We know who we are, what we think and feel, but it is easy to forget how little of that we share with others. We imagine it seeps out through osmosis, but although some of it may, it is our behaviour that people see, and if Kay gives a relaxed and confident presentation, then she is a confident presenter in their eyes. This means that acting as if can have immediate and very real results.

Positive energy

Another technique to enhance your resourcefulness is to think of a time when you were highly successful. Step into that experience and feel what you felt at the time. When you are really there, and enjoying the success, create a little mnemonic device to remind you of how it felt – something like just touching your two middle fingers – it can be anything that is not an everyday gesture. Practise it a few times, so that it becomes familiar. When you are facing a new challenge, touch those fingers together again to bring back those feelings of success, so that you can take them with you into the new experience.

If you think that this will not work, you probably use the technique regularly, but only in the negative. Imagine the sound of a dentist's drill – does that trigger an immediate response? Or think of a time when you were turned down for a job you really wanted – perhaps remember reading the rejection letter. Do those feelings come flooding back? Not surprisingly, you can do just the same with positive feelings as you can with negative ones. It is interesting that many people seem to become proficient in the latter, dragging their ever-present negative history around with them like a ball and chain, but many never discover the benefits of carrying the positive energy of the past into the present, as you can now.

Insight

It really is a mystery, why we perfect the technique of negative recall so well, and hardly ever bother with the positive! Recognizing the effectiveness of negative recall is the fastest route to using the positive version.

Check your language

It is really helpful to check your use of four letter words, like 'can't' and 'must'.

Equally damaging are 'should' and 'ought'. If you find yourself using these words, in expressions like 'I should do something about that report' or 'I ought to rehearse my presentation' it means that your commitment is in question. Who is telling you to do these things? It sounds like you are hearing the voice of your annoyed parent, telling you to do your homework!

If you are truly committed to something, then you will say, 'I want to do this', 'I'm going to do ...', 'I shall be ...'. If you find yourself slipping into musts and shoulds, ask yourself the question 'Is this what I really want?' If it is, and you still feel a 'should' coming on, go back to the chapter on commitment, since getting this bit right is fundamental to your successful outcome.

Sight, sound or feelings?

The next tool relates to the way you absorb data, which will be significant for your learning of any new subject. The majority of people prefer to gather information visually, hence the saying 'a picture is worth a thousand words'. If you can easily form pictures in your head, use that facility when you learn something new. Try drawing a mind map (see Figure 1), possibly in different colours, to aid the assimilation process. Use pictures wherever you can to reinforce your learning. (If you are not familiar with mind maps, there is more information in the section on report writing in Chapter 12.)

A different group of people assimilate information primarily through what they hear. They may or may not form clear mental pictures, but sound is easily recalled, with clarity and fine distinction. If this applies to you, a tape or CD of a new subject

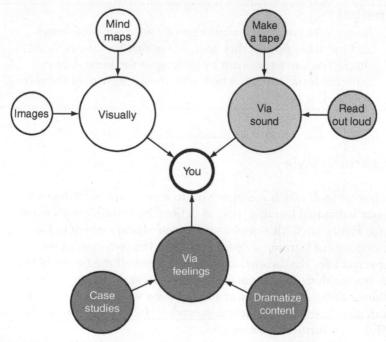

Figure 1 Mind map showing how you absorb information.

might be an excellent way of reinforcing your learning. Consider making your own, if the subject is important enough, and the method really works for you.

Finally there is a group of people for whom feelings are their strongest sense. This does not mean they are emotional, just that they are finely tuned to people's feelings, including their own. Sounds and pictures may well be part of the assimilation process; pictures are often unclear, with feelings attached to what they see.

If you fall into this category, a priority when learning will be to associate feelings with the subject matter. This may not appear to be an easy thing to do with business or technical subjects, but a good way for you to learn would be through case studies, where problems arise and are solved, and you can associate with and remember the feelings of those involved in triumph or disaster.

Learning style

Another tool, which you may wish to investigate, is to discover your individual learning style, as defined by Peter Honey's matrix (see Figure 2). With a questionnaire you identify which of four categories of learning style fits you best. The two ends of the spectrum are the theorist, who likes to learn all the theory before doing anything, and the activist, who prefers to plunge in and try things without any theory at all. Knowing which suits you best can greatly enhance the learning process. Details are provided in 'Taking it further', page 303.

Role models

As the Duke of Wellington said, 'Wise people learn when they can; fools learn when they must.' Actively seeking role models is a great aid to the learning process, and we have included a selection in this book. Sadly, role models are not always in plentiful supply, and sometimes we need to learn from the negative, as much as the positive. Ideally, every manager should be a role model, but this is not the reality. In fact, you can learn how not to do things, as well as the right way to do them. Take every learning opportunity that you can, and most people have something to offer, either to emulate or to avoid!

When you find someone to learn from, try to understand their attitudes and beliefs, as much as their behaviour. For example,

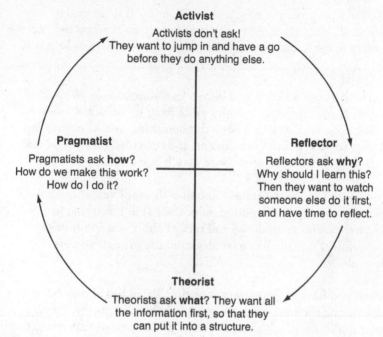

Activist
Activists don't ask!
They want to jump in and have a go
before they do anything else.

Pragmatist
Pragmatists ask **how**?
How do we make this work?
How do I do it?

Reflector
Reflectors ask **why**?
Why should I learn this?
Then they want to watch
someone else do it first,
and have time to reflect.

Theorist
Theorists ask **what**? They want all
the information first, so that they
can put it into a structure.

Figure 2 Learning styles.

if you see someone delegating well, find out what they believe about delegation, how they view the people they delegate to, as well as what steps they go through in deciding what to delegate to whom.

If you have difficulty in delegating, it is less likely to be because you don't know how to, but more because you do not have faith in the people you would be delegating to. If you could take on the beliefs of a good delegator, and act as if they were true for a while, you might find this would produce a result, whereas just studying the methodology might not do very much at all.

Be open about your learning in this context, in order to get as much information as possible. You will have observed the skill for a while, so you will have some information, but do not treat your role model as if they are a creature to be observed at a distance.

Ask for a personal meeting with them, and tell them exactly what you want. They are sure to be flattered, since imitation is the sincerest form of flattery, and they will therefore be very willing to help you.

Insight

Think about a skill you'd like to learn or enhance. Who do you know who does it really well? Even if you don't know someone very well, it's not a difficult thing to ask, as they are sure to view it as a compliment, and provided they choose the timing, you can be pretty sure they'll agree.

You could broach the subject like this: 'Brian, I've noticed how effective you are at delegating, which is a skill I'm trying to acquire. Could we sit down and talk about it when you have some time, I'd really like to understand the process you go through.'

When you have your meeting, at a time Brian has chosen, so that he has time for you, make the most of this opportunity. Prepare some questions in advance, and keep them open so that you get as much information as possible, such as:

▶ *Can you tell me about the process you go through?*
▶ *What are your beliefs about delegation?*
▶ *How do you view the people you delegate to?*
▶ *Have you had problems with delegation in the past?*
▶ *What mistakes do you see other people make when they delegate?*
▶ *How do you know what to delegate and what not to?*

Make your list as long as possible. You may not use all the questions, but they are there if you need them, and more importantly, they have helped you think the process through.

If you have the luxury of more than one role model, you might be able to go through this process again, and compare. One of the things that has become apparent from the research for this book is that a wide variety of people have responded to the same questions with a great level of consistency. This reinforcement makes the messages very clear, and the learning very easy.

Mentors

The final item in your toolkit is very obvious, but often under-utilized; it is the ability to know when and from whom to ask for help. Many people think that there is some great virtue in doing things unaided, but you might consider it as arrogant not to wish to benefit from the experience and knowledge of others. 'Learning from experience is the most important of all the life skills', to quote Peter Honey again.

If you do not feel that your negotiation technique is working, yet you have been on the courses, and think you know all the theory, then it is time to ask for help from someone you trust and respect. Often what you most need from them is feedback on what you are doing. Pearls of wisdom are to be valued, but commentary on your performance is going to provide you with a rich source of learning.

Consistent in the career development of almost every consultant in this book is the mentor. Whether in the business or the personal context, they have all been important.

Mark Brown, himself a distinguished professor, author, and public speaker, spoke with great enthusiasm about a famous personal mentor: 'Tony Buzan [best known as the inventor of mind maps], has been an inspiring mentor for me. He has a fantastic view of human potential. He taught me how to present and inspire and enthuse people.'

Leon Sadler spoke in the same way about his skiing coach, John Shedden. But mentors do not have to be famous or wise people to sit at the feet of. A friend, or someone junior to you may have a particular skill or insight, or just the ability to listen, which will meet your need. After all, as Peter Honey says, 'Life is just one learning opportunity after another.'

Closing thoughts

They can conquer who believe they can.

Virgil

The real voyage of discovery consists not in seeking new landscapes, but in having new eyes.

Marcel Proust

STEPS TO SUCCESS

Now you are committed to your outcome, use these tools to get there:

- ▶ *Act as if your presuppositions are true.*

- ▶ *Use the positive energy from your past achievements to help you in the present.*

- ▶ *Use your language as a commitment check.*

- ▶ *Assess your most effective learning method and style.*

- ▶ *Make the most of role models, positive and negative.*

- ▶ *Find personal mentors and nurture their feedback.*

Client project management

This chapter covers:
- **the role of the project manager**
- **scoping the project**
- **setting the specification**
- **creating the project framework**

In this chapter we look at key aspects of managing the client interface of a project. Project management, with its associated software tools, is a subject all on its own, which is covered by a number of books, including one in this series. Here we will focus on the client skills of a project manager, particularly in relation to the critical areas of setting specification objectives and communicating with the client on project issues.

Two project managers met on an interpersonal skills programme:

One asked, 'What are you doing here?'

The other replied, 'I'm here because no matter how perfect the project plan is, it's always the people side that goes wrong!'

'Funny you should say that – I was sent here for that very reason!'

The project manager

What are the skills needed in a project manager? Steven Hunt, the Client Services Manager for MWH, speaks from long personal experience:

'You need to understand people and be able to delegate well. It's important not to be afraid to let go of the technical detail, and increasingly I see projects in the widest focus. I never underestimate other people, but nor do I overestimate them either.

'When I delegate, I work out what people are capable of, and what they really want to do, then I delegate work accordingly, always ensuring that they have what they need to perform really well. Delegation has a double benefit: it has given me the space to develop and progress, and it is immensely satisfying to see people grow as you give them more challenge and responsibility.

'Trust is also a critical factor. I need to develop trust in the team, and I need to earn their trust so that they know that I'm there to support them. They need to trust me and know that if something should go wrong, I will help them to recover the situation without apportioning individual blame. If something fails, it is normally a systems failure, rarely the fault of one person.'

He went on to describe a project management challenge he faced early in his career: 'I left school at 16, having become frustrated with A levels, and found a job with a local council as an Engineering trainee, which gave me day release to do an HNC.' One more council job later, Steven decided to go to university at the grand old age of 25, and he loved every minute. He graduated from Newcastle three years later with a first in Civil Engineering. Steven described himself as very surprised as well as delighted by his achievement.

He then joined Binnie & Partners, a long established firm of consulting engineers, and on his first day he worked on site as the Assistant Resident Engineer, supervising major construction work. Eighteen months later, he had completed all of the training objectives required to become a member of the Institution of Civil Engineers.

'I was then asked if I would go and work in Kuwait, shortly after the Gulf War. A number of people had already turned this job down, but I saw it as an opportunity, and off I went, at 29, as Senior Design Engineer to manage a project team of Poles, Syrians, Lebanese, Pakistanis, and Indians, many of whom were in their 50s. It was a challenge to win the respect of these people, but I did it through being confident of my own technical abilities, and through dealing with everyone in a very professional manner.

'It was a cultural challenge, and the most difficult situation arose when I asked a Lebanese engineer to check some of my calculations. This man was excellent, but did not have formal degree qualifications. I was astounded when he told me he could not do it, and became very upset. The next day he came in and said that as he was not qualified, he would no longer do design work, just draughting jobs. He was immovable on this, so I went along with his wishes until I contrived a situation where I had sketched out the very basics of a design, which I gave to him and asked him to draught what he could, as I had to rush back to London for a week. I returned to find the job completed – design and drawings – and after that the relationship was restored. I had obviously infringed some cultural taboo in relation to hierarchy which I was completely unaware of, and had felt my way back to restoring the relationship. To date I've always been fortunate with the people I've worked with, and I have experienced very few major problems on projects.'

Steven is not the only consultant to have made that remark, and this 'good luck' seems to stem from a high level of interpersonal skill, combined with a very open and honest manner and a high degree of personal integrity.

Added to this is the ability to see the upside: 'I always focus on the positive, which means I have the ability to move on quite quickly from any situation.'

On the worst sins of a project manager, Steven began with blame.

▶ *'Blaming people if something goes wrong. I start by looking to see what I did wrong.'*
▶ *'Failing to accept responsibility is another sin. The buck stops with the project manager, and you must accept that.'*
▶ *'Not putting the client first – if the client can see that you are driven by personal or corporate interest which conflicts with their needs, you are in serious trouble.'*
▶ *'Failing to plan is the last one, this can result in having to make unreasonable demands on people, which is unacceptable.'*

Insight

Sign seen over an IT manager's desk: **'Your failure to plan does not constitute my emergency.'** This is exactly the point that Steven is making, seen from the other end of the telescope, but if it is your boss who is failing to plan, you can hardly use that response in reply!

David Mitchell had a slightly different angle on the subject: 'There are two key types of project manager. If you consider a project to be a big rock, some are good at cracking it into boulders, and then get bored at the thought of gravel. Some are great at turning boulders into gravel, but can't break the big rock to start with. They are the ones who will happily tick off every tiny task. If you take a £100 million project, it would be rare to get someone to span the lot, so we play to the strengths of the individual to meet the project need.'

Another characteristic of a project manager is their ability to drive a project to meet deadlines. This is normally a strength, but Mary Hill of Pecaso, a software consulting company, described some difficult project managers her organization had had to deal with, and this one took drive to an extreme:

'She was the best and the worst project manager! She was determined to meet the project deadline at all costs, so she did everything to make it happen, pushed things through, and made so many compromises. She met the April date very precisely, and off she went. Then because we are very committed to a long-term relationship with a client, not just doing hit and run projects, we spent several months afterwards working with the client to unpick everything and make it really work.'

She concluded, 'Sub-contract project managers hired by the client can present real problems. They are only as good as their last project, and so they feel under pressure to get a result at any cost. It's vital to sit down with them and make it clear that we must work together, otherwise we will all fail.'

Leon at SAP had similar problems: 'I can think of two or three instances where the client hired someone – particularly in the project management role – who did not have the skills needed for the job. What then happens is that the project manager needs to cover themselves, and in order to avoid being exposed, they may not make good decisions, and indeed they may end up blaming us for things, in order to maintain their image with the client.' There is a real-life example of this at the end of the negotiation section (see Chapter 17).

KEY MESSAGES

▶ *Be clear on the project needs for big picture versus detail, and match individual strengths accordingly.*
▶ *Drive the project forward, but not at the cost of project quality.*
▶ *Take full responsibility – the buck stops with you.*
▶ *Plan, plan and do more planning – make it your aim never to make unreasonable demands on people as a result of your failure to plan.*
▶ *Set a personal example to create team values of trust, respect, loyalty and commitment.*

Scoping the project

This section covers the earliest stage of a project, before the specification is agreed, and looks at how you decide what it is that you are going to deliver.

THE READY-MADE SOLUTION

One of the most consistent messages from experienced consultants, is the need to empty your head of preconceptions when you are briefed by a client. Mark Brown said: 'I read an Economist Intelligence report on TQM [Total Quality Management]. They said that everything that worked was tailored, and the more off the shelf it was, the more likely it was to fail.' Often we think that standard solution X, with a few variations, will do the trick, but we are trying to convince ourselves that this is tailoring, when it is not. It is very easy to produce standard solutions, which may not deliver the result you expect.

This was beautifully illustrated by Peter Honey, who told a story about a very early experience in consulting with a manufacturing company in the north of England. They produced sensitive equipment, which required skilled assembly work in calibrating a fine metal bar. They had discovered over time that men could not perform this task nearly as well as women, and that it was only a select group of women who could do this task well. The women worked on piece rates, and it was the highest paid job in the factory. Any woman could apply for this job, and they would be given three months' trial in a training area, where they were given little instruction, since no one could work out what skill was needed, and then left to sink or swim. Mostly they sank.

The owner of the company was very keen to devise an aptitude test for this task, and this was Peter's brief, which he accepted with alacrity, being already sure that a simple hand/eye co-ordination test would do the trick. He was lucky in having control groups all set up for his purpose. He had the existing team, and a group of current employees who had tried and failed. It would therefore be easy to compare results between these groups.

He duly administered the hand/eye co-ordination test, and it did not produce a result. Some of the 'failures' scored as well as the successes. Bemused by this, he decided that the differentiator could be intelligence, administered the tests, and discovered that it was not. Now seriously worried, he decided that personality must be the factor he was looking for. He discovered that it was not.

By now Peter was very concerned indeed. He had run out of options and had discovered nothing at all. He was contemplating admitting defeat, and went to the pub with a friend for some sympathy and commiseration. His friend provided more than this, and asked him if he had tried the dotting test. Peter had never heard of it. It consisted of giving the individual a page of small marked squares, and asking them to put three dots in as many squares as possible in 60 seconds.

Peter tried this, and to his great relief and surprise, it worked. The women currently on the production line entered far more dots than the failure group. He took his solution to the Managing Director, who was delighted. He now had a really simple aptitude test, which would make huge savings in training time, as well as removing the demotivating 'three month failure' syndrome.

KEY MESSAGES

Peter was left with a number of conclusions, the first being that he should not have assumed that he had the hand/eye co-ordination answer ready-made in his portfolio of solutions. It was mainly luck that saved him from failure in this instance, although you could argue he influenced his luck by choosing the right drinking partner!

His other conclusion is very interesting. To this day, he does not know why the dotting test works – only that it does work very well. It is easy to be mesmerized by the why, but in many business situations, it is the what and the how that really matter.

The presenting versus the real problem

Another of Peter's fundamental tenets is never to accept the presenting problem without investigation. This is demonstrated very well by a client's requirement for a training course. It is often the case that running a training course is seen as a solution to other, more fundamental problems.

Peter's client had asked him to design and run a course for the senior management team on chairing meetings. Although he probed for what was behind the need, nothing further was forthcoming, and so he asked to sit in on three meetings chaired by different managers, in order to help him to specify the need and tailor the course precisely to their requirements. The client considered this an unusual request, but they agreed, and Peter duly attended the first meeting, which went relatively well.

The second meeting, however, was a complete disaster, and the manager concerned made every mistake in the book. He was an overbearing individual, and no one dared to tell him anything he might not want to hear. He would regularly get angry and shout at his team, and a few moments before he did this he would tap his pencil sharply on the desk. Peter observed this consistently over the morning, and when the meeting broke for lunch, the Director went off, and Peter ate with some of the team. They moaned about their boss, saying how unpredictable he was, and Peter said, 'He's very predictable in one thing, which is that he always taps the desk with his pencil before he loses his temper.' No one had noticed this, and all were keen to observe it for themselves.

Not surprisingly, when it happened again in the afternoon, there was a reaction from the team, which the Director noticed, and asked about, but no one would say anything to him at the time. At the end of the meeting, he asked for a private word with Peter, who was expecting to see the pencil come into action, but the man simply asked for feedback, as well as an explanation of the team reaction. Peter explained about the pencil, and gave him some very straight feedback.

Peter expected to be thrown out, but the manager received the feedback well, and was, Peter realized, grateful to get it. He commented, 'Everyone is starved of feedback, people do not get enough of it, and if you have an aggressive manner, you are likely to get even less.'

Peter attended the third meeting, which was uneventful, but the reality was that he had done the work the course was designed to do, far more effectively, on a one-on-one basis.

KEY MESSAGES

Obviously the presenting problem, the need for a training course, was not the real problem, as is often the case, and it is crucially important to examine the client's stated need, to check that their diagnosis of their own problem is the right one.

A second, and just as vital message here is client confidentiality, and thanks go to Peter for his openness in giving this example, which was a very early career experience.

Peter said, 'I committed a cardinal sin in discussing the Director with his staff. In theory it was only an observation about the pencil, I said nothing else, but it was still a breach of confidentiality, which became apparent in the meeting in the afternoon, when some of the staff reacted to the pencil tapping. As it happened, the situation turned out well, and the Director was happy to get the feedback, but it was an object lesson to me, and I have been absolutely rigorous in my client confidentiality rules ever since.'

Insight

It is so easy to breach client confidentiality without intending to, and the consequences can undermine the whole relationship. If you are told something personal or controversial, check if it is public knowledge or not. Be aware that some clients may set you a test in this area, so always be on your guard, no matter how well you know the client.

NEEDS VERSUS WANTS

A different problem arises when what the client asks for is not, in fact, what they need. David Mitchell told the story of a European utilities company, who commissioned Unisys to manage one of their networks. 'It had gone wrong, and the client called in

Coopers & Lybrand, ostensibly to do an audit, but in reality to find reasons to sue Unisys. I was called in to work with Coopers and protect our position during the audit. The findings were that we had delivered what the client asked for, even though it was not what they needed. The project continued and they paid us.

'Three months later, I left Unisys and joined Coopers. The utilities company then asked me to do another audit, and give my view from the other side of the fence. I did so, and told them, "The advice I gave you then is still the advice I would give you now." What originally happened was that the client had given the local Unisys office a detailed specification, and they had stuck to it to the letter, because the people there had a purely technical background – they were content consultants, not process consultants. When the client said, "but what you've given us does not enable us to manage our network!" they replied, "but it's exactly what you asked for."!'

Insight

There's a danger of being mesmerized by a detailed specification from the client. As in this case, they appear to know exactly what they want, but it's your job to look at the big picture, and see beyond the detail. 'What do they really want this for?' can be a useful question.

This highlights the dilemma for a consultant – do I give the client what they want, or what they need? Obviously as far as possible, you go for the need, which may take some courage on your part. Sometimes, that may be just too big a stretch, as in this example given by Mary Ahmad, of Corporate HR Partners:

'Clients with a hidden agenda or a fixed idea of the root of the problem are a big challenge. I did an audit for a client, and showed him the result. He told me I hadn't got it right, so I went away and rewrote it differently. This still didn't satisfy him because he had worked out the answer before he started, and was going to reject anything else.

'Another client brought us in to look at new HR benefits, as staff morale was low. We came up with some proposals, but they asked for more creative solutions from us, although in reality the culture and management style of the organization were so demotivating to staff that the introduction of duvet days or in-house massage was going to do nothing to address the real problem.

'The reality is that you can't solve the issue when the client is the issue. There is the added problem that everyone can do HR, that's easy, but how would you, an HR person, know how to run a business?' If you read Chapter 21 on starting your own business, you will realize that Mary knows all about this particular subject!

KEY MESSAGES

▶ *Listen really well to all the client's needs, and then tailor your solution to fit.*
▶ *Check that the client has diagnosed the real problem.*
▶ *Satisfy client need, rather than want, whenever you can.*
▶ *Identify a hidden agenda, and tailor your work accordingly.*

The specification – setting objectives

Now that we have defined the project scope, this section covers how we nail down the specification tightly. To quote Penny again: 'Agree with a client exactly what they are expecting. Both the deliverable and the way you will work with them. It is in this area that most litigation takes place, so it cannot be agreed at too granular a level – almost down to storyboards of the project.'

The reason why these problems happen is that setting objectives seems to be an unnatural human characteristic. We generally do not like doing it, and yet we are very unhappy when we suffer the consequences. For example:

> Client: *'I said that we needed this urgently, so where is it?'*

> Consultant: *'We're working on it now. We're just in the final stages. We were targeting the meeting on Friday, when we're due to discuss it.'*

> Client: *'But I want to look at it today!'*

Does this sound familiar? The client's definition of urgent just is not the same as the consultant's, but they both agreed in the meeting that the work was needed urgently, and neither of them checked when 'urgent' was to be.

Insight

Are you thinking that setting objectives is the boring bit you can skip? That everyone knows SMART is what you aim for, so why bother? In reality, people (maybe you!) don't bother to set objectives, and this results in all sorts of problems with clients that could have been avoided.

What stops us setting good objectives? Is it that we do not want to be pinned down? By checking, will we discover that we have less time than we would have hoped for? If we do not check, we deny ourselves the opportunity to negotiate, but secretly we hope that we will not have to engage in the somewhat unsavoury task of negotiation.

You may not feel this way, in which case, you will not have a problem in pinning down goals very tightly. If you do have difficulty with this process, then think consequences. Think what happens when the client says, 'Where is it?' and you have not even started!

OBJECTIVE MEASURES

The whole secret is in thinking things through to the end
result. The key question to ask is, 'How will we know if we've
succeeded?' And the 'we' means you and the client separately.
If the only way you know is when the client tells you, then you are
in trouble. Find objective measures at all costs. Objective measures
are tools that you and the client have equal and open access to,
such as calendars, production statistics, and expenditure reports.
The latter will not qualify if the client controls them and you
cannot verify them independently.

The classic mnemonic for objectives is that they should be
SMART:

> *Specific*
> *Measurable*
> *Achievement focused*
> *Realistic*
> *Time bounded*

Everybody knows the theory, applying it is a different matter. Start
with a date, and remember that is only the start. It is only too easy
to think that if something is dated, it must be an objective.

Now find that objective measure – cost and quantity are great –
you will be home and dry with these. If it is quality, beware,
because that usually means someone has to decide on the quality
level, and if that someone is the client, who it almost certainly
will be, then you will have the same potential problems we
began with.

> *'The report is not comprehensive enough.'*
> *'But it covers all the areas we agreed.'*
> *'Yes it does, but not in enough detail.'*
> *'It's already forty pages long …'.*
> *'Yes because some of the content belongs in the appendix –
> in any case I didn't need all this background stuff …'.*

It is easy to see all this with hindsight, and so the best way is to imagine the conversation you might be having with the client down the line, and anticipate the problems that may arise.

Insight

You may not like the thought of it, but test how good a judge you are of objectives by reviewing these three examples and deciding if they pass the SMART test, or, thinking of it another way, deciding if you'd be happy to shake hands over them with a client.

TEST OBJECTIVES

Grit you teeth, and test out these examples:

1 *System to be fully operational by 30 June, and to meet standards set in internal financial manual.*
2 *Online tutorial to be completed by 1 March. Untrained users to be able to access the system and retrieve personal data by using the online tutorial only.*
3 *Proposal for restructuring to be presented to the Board on 7 September. Proposal to take account of new business plans, and to identify current skill deficiencies in organization.*

Comments
1 System to be fully operational by 30 June, and to meet standards set in internal financial manual.
The first objective depends entirely on what is in the internal financial manual. If it is all neatly defined with dates and reporting tables, you might be lucky. The chances are that it will have some grey areas, ripe for disagreement with the client.
'But we can't complete all the management reports, because you haven't included the sub-code breakdown.'
'No one asked for sub-codes. The detail is all there in each code heading.'
'Yes, but we use sub-codes – it's all in the manual.'

You look in the manual. There is a reference to sub-codes, but their significance to the management reports is not at all clear. So do you argue with the client, or go back and put them in?

2 Online tutorial to be completed by 1 March. Untrained users to be able to access the system and retrieve personal data by using the online tutorial only.
This looks a reasonable objective, in that it is very clear what the end result is – except that we do not know what data it is that they need to be able to access. If that were specified, then you would have an objective measure. Otherwise, you may be happy that they can access bank account details, when your client wants them to be able to access and modify all variable data on their personal file, such as next of kin and home address. It is very easy to imagine what would happen if you had not covered this in detail.
'The access is fine, as far as it goes, but they can't access all the areas, and nobody has managed to do any modification yet.'
'The tutorial doesn't cover modification at this stage.'
'What's the point of having access if you can't change anything?'

3 Proposal for restructuring to be presented to the Board on 7 September. Proposal to take account of new business plans, and to identify current skill deficiencies in organization.
The third example gives lots of scope for disagreement. First, it is vital to identify the source of the information – where is the data on the business plan and the skill deficiencies to come from? In writing from the client is the only acceptable answer, unless the client tells you, and then you write it up and present it back to them for approval.
Having done that, then check that there are other criteria that the client has not mentioned because they may be too obvious to them, although not to you, otherwise you may be faced with something like this at the end of your presentation:
'That's fine as far as it goes, but what about the product obsolescence issues?'
'We do cover the implications of substitutional sales ...'

'That's all very well, but there are much bigger problems associated with discontinuing two of our product lines, which need to be reflected in any future organization plans.' So there you are, back at the drawing board, because you missed a key criterion, even though you had checked out the new business plans and the skill deficiencies most carefully.

The point of these examples is not to depress you, but to encourage you to think through to the end result of the objectives you set. Ask yourself the following questions:

- ▶ *What is the objective?*
- ▶ *When does it need to be completed by?*
- ▶ *What will it 'look' like when it's finished?*
- ▶ *How will we know if we have succeeded?*
- ▶ *What can go wrong with the end result?*

Insight

There's a limit to how much you can do to refine an objective looking forwards. What is also helpful is to look backwards and imagine how you will judge the work when it's done, and to list all the things that could go wrong. Use that information to reassess your objective.

Let us use these questions to test out objective 2 again:

- ▶ **What is the objective?** *Online tutorial to be completed by 1 March. Untrained users to be able to access the system and retrieve personal data by using the online tutorial only.*
- ▶ **When does it need to be completed by?** *1 March.*
- ▶ **What will it 'look' like when it's finished?** *Users able to retrieve some personal data without help other than from the tutorial.*
- ▶ **How will we know if we have succeeded?** *They can access the data without difficulty.*
- ▶ **What can go wrong with the end result?** *They need help to gain access; they cannot access the data they require; they require access to different data; they want more than just access.*

- **Review objective again:** *Online tutorial to be completed by 1 March. Untrained users to be able to access the system and retrieve and modify the following personal data using the online tutorial only: Personal data: Address, Next of kin, Marital status, Bank details.*

This revised objective is much tighter, and offers far less scope for disagreement.

GO INTO THE FUTURE

As you are thinking through an objective, it is helpful to take your client with you.

'So can we just imagine for a moment that we have achieved this objective, and you can see your staff, happily accessing the system, having learned from the online tutorial. They can now see their bank details. Are you happy with that?'

The chances are that the client will then tell you that he doesn't just want bank details, and that access on its own will not be enough.

KEY MESSAGES

- *Take time to create a tight specification – it will pay off.*
- *Make your objectives SMART.*
- *Find objective measures whenever you can.*
- *Apply the test questions to every objective.*
- *Project yourself, and your client into the future, to test out your measurable results.*

Creating the project framework

Let us now look at how we manage the project through to a successful conclusion. Maintaining a continuing informal communication with the client is normally the basis of any project, but a formal structure is absolutely essential. The project framework specifies the formal communication processes for the project. As a minimum, these will be:

- ▶ *Project milestones.*
- ▶ *Key delivery dates.*
- ▶ *A set programme of review meetings based around the above.*
- ▶ *A timetable for formal written reports.*
- ▶ *An escalation procedure, to deal with problems.*
- ▶ *A change management procedure, to cover all changes, whether chargeable or not.*

Critical decision-making points for this framework are firstly the client requirement. They may prefer to be briefed frequently in detail, or less often with a high-level view. Sometimes a client may request less briefing than you feel is right for the project, in which case you may need to suggest more meetings/reports in order to meet your responsibilities to the client.

The other factor to consider is where the project milestones fall, and the timing of key deliverables. Taking the above factors into account, you can then determine a sensible timescale for meetings and reports, which doesn't overload you, and keeps them well informed, according to your standards as well as theirs.

Let us now assume that this complete project framework is in place. We have a project with measurable outcomes, set milestones, and a formal communication process. This is now the basis of your relationship with the customer. Your relationship can be far more than this, but it can never be less.

Insight

It's so easy to be lured into a false sense of security by what you think is a good client relationship. You haven't fixed a complete meeting schedule, because after the first few, things were fine, and then the client discovers something you have not told them about, and you're in trouble!

Even if you are doing a tiny part of a huge project, you still need to know the project framework at the highest level, in order to fully understand your part within it. It forms the basis of the customer's expectations, and project management is all about setting and meeting those expectations. Any resetting of expectations should also be part of the formal process.

Closing thoughts

Plans are only good intentions unless they immediately degenerate into hard work.

Peter Drucker

Spectacular achievements are always preceded by unspectacular preparation.

Roger Staubach

STEPS TO SUCCESS

▶ *Listen to the client – really listen!*

▶ *Be sure you are addressing the real issue.*

▶ *Create a tight specification.*

▶ *Project yourself and your client into the future to test out the measurability of the objectives set.*

▶ *Create a project framework designed to ensure the right level of communication with the client.*

▶ *Recognize that the project manager must take ultimate responsibility for the project.*

9

···

Managing client expectations

This chapter covers:
- *over-commitment*
- *handling project delays*
- *meeting deadlines*
- *handling client delays*
- *agreeing completion*

The perils of over-commitment

Leon Sadler of SAP made the most telling comment on this subject:
'Not managing your client's expectations is a cardinal sin, if you are
a consultant. You are the person who sets the expectations, not the
client, so if you don't meet them, it's entirely your fault – no one
else's.' We are at the core of the consultant's world here. Expertise is
all very well, but if you cannot set and manage expectations effectively,
your career as a consultant is likely to be fraught with difficulty.

CASE STUDY: OVER-COMMITMENT

Noel is a young and inexperienced consultant, keen to impress. The
short project is going well, and he is even a little ahead of schedule,
although the client is not aware of this when she asks Noel to fit in
just a small piece of additional work. Noel knows that this work is
not in the original specification, but it seems a very small thing,
a couple of hours at the most, so with time in hand, he readily agrees.
It is not worth bothering with the change control procedure for this.

Sadly, Noel rapidly discovers that this is not a small thing. He struggles with it for three days, by which time he is well behind schedule. He finally tells his manager, who gives him the predictable response: 'Noel, you should never have agreed to this – it's not a trivial task.'

'I know that now, Sara, but at the time it looked like a couple of hours work.'

'Never agree to anything outside of the specification without talking to me first. You don't have to say no to a client, just tell them you'll check and come back to them. That's not a difficult thing to say, now is it?'

The most extreme case of this is illustrated by a software company, who described one of their worst client nightmares. A bank had decided to do away with the debit and credit designations on one of their systems, and to have the negative figures shown in red. This seemed a simple change, and the project manager readily agreed, with no extra charge. What he did not realize was how deep in the code this change would have to go, and it took eight weeks of programming time to achieve it!

WHY OVER-COMMIT?

So why do we get this so wrong, so often, when we are not under pressure from the client? If this is a problem you suffer from, think about what it is that drives you to say yes, rather than no, or maybe.

There are a number of drivers – let us look at the list:

1 *Optimism*
2 *Inexperience*
3 *Lack of planning*
4 *Need to please*
5 *Need to prove competence*

Now let's examine each of these in detail:

1 *Optimism is an innate characteristic that some of us have which is usually a blessing! In the context of project management it is a positive curse. Discipline yourself to come up with your natural optimistic estimate, then label it as such and add a factor – like two or three times, or add in lots of contingency. Create a formula and make it a habit!*

2 *If you do not have the experience, and simply do not know, then ask! Memorize the saying: 'I think that might be possible, but I'll need to check. Let me get back to you.'*

3 *Lack of planning is the easiest sin to commit of the five. Instead of listing all the details of the requirement and working through them to arrive at a time plan, you just take the main items, do an estimate and add on a bit. Perhaps you feel that the bit you add on is quite generous, and will cover it all, but in fact you may find that when you make a detailed plan, you have used up your entire contingency and more.*

Insight

Sometimes we just don't know how long things take. You may quote for a whole job, but not measure all the elements that make it up. It can be a surprise, if not a shock, to discover that something you thought was a little job actually takes half a day.

The rule is therefore to think through every element of the task, and time each one, and then add on a generous contingency. As a general rule of thumb, no task on its own takes less than half a day. This may all sound obvious in the context of producing a full project plan, but we are talking here about the additional requests, and the add-ons that people tend to ask for in a casual way, and we are therefore tempted to respond just as casually.

4 *The need to please will lead you down dangerous roads with clients. The way to combat this is think consequences. You*

may please the client now by saying yes, but that may mean making them unhappy later. So better to delay saying yes, so as to be sure that you will keep the client happy in the long term. Again, you need the words: 'Let me just check and come back to you,' on the tip of your tongue.

5 *If you are out to prove how competent you are, you will do better to think long term rather than short. This was part of Noel's problem. Saying yes to the client made him look good at the time, but was it worth it when the client saw that he could not deliver? Noel had done double damage; saying he could do something when he could not, and failing to do it. He would have appeared more competent if he had said no in the first place.*

INVOLVING THE RIGHT PEOPLE

Another aspect of setting expectations is to make sure that you set them with the right people. Penny Stocks described a project where expectations had been set, but at too high a level.

CASE STUDY: CAP GEMINI ERNST & YOUNG

'A few years ago, we were working on transformation on a global scale in a very large multinational, as part of a huge project. The team had been there since January, and I suddenly got a message that the HR director was seriously concerned as he felt that they had added no value for the past two months. He was proposing to put this work out to our competitors for tender.

'This happened in May. I went to see him, and had one of the most difficult client meetings of my career. It was a case of allowing him to give full vent to all his anger and complaints, some of which were very valid. The team had one or two weak links, and had not had the best leadership. There were good reasons for this (around health and problems at home), but not ones that I wanted to present as excuses to the client. Also, we had made the fundamental mistake of setting expectations with his boss, but not with him. He had been missed out of the loop.

'We then had an open and honest discussion, and it came down to a personal commitment between him and me. He then gave us four weeks to turn it round. Now this is where the support of a big firm around you makes all the difference. I was able to go back to the office, and demand 100 per cent from our top people to turn this project round, and we did! We worked really hard; went more than the extra mile; we were open and honest with the client, and delivered above expectations. In this process the client did recognize and acknowledge that he was also part of the problem, and waiting for two months to say anything at all was not in the spirit of good supplier management. This experience had been demoralizing for the team, but this result restored their self-respect and engaged great team spirit.'

It is so easy to think that because you have a good relationship at the top level, the rest will follow. Often it is the awareness of this top-level relationship that generates more resentment towards you lower down the organization, so work hard to build positive links and set expectations at all levels.

KEY MESSAGES

▶ *Never over-commit!*
▶ *Take time to respond to any customer request.*
▶ *Say, 'I'll get back to you', when in doubt.*
▶ *'Under-promise and over-deliver!'*
▶ *Build good relationships and set expectations at every level.*

Project delays

Having carefully produced and agreed the project plan with the client, what do you do when, despite all your best efforts, the project goes off track, and it is entirely your fault?

If you are part of a larger organization, this is where you ask for help, and probably for more resources. If you are on your own, maybe you call in an associate, or start weekend working. The critical point is what to tell the client? Assuming that you have no formal progress review meetings set up in the near future, do you advise them of the delay, or hope that you can make it up, and say nothing?

Insight

When things go wrong, it's very tempting to say nothing and hope for the best. Think consequences at times like these, because often the short-term pain you get from telling the client immediately is nothing to what you will suffer if you hide the problem from them, and are forced to tell them later.

From the client's perspective, you are denying them the opportunity to take corrective action, assuming that they need to. If they do not need to, they would still prefer to know exactly what is going on, although, of course, you will lose face if you tell them. There is a very fine line between keeping the client informed and preserving your image of competence in these situations, and you are making a continuous judgement about whether you will get back on track, in which case no need to tell, or whether you definitely will not, in which case you will want to tell the client sooner rather than later.

CASE STUDY: PROJECT DELAY

Alan and Mike have been working together on a project for the past two months, and things were going well, but Mike's wife has just walked out on him, and this has seriously affected his work. Alan has tried to cover as much as possible, but he cannot do all the work for two of them, and now they are a week behind.

They have a milestone review meeting next week, and Alan wants to tell their manager the situation. Mike does not get on well with their manager, and resists this. 'I'm going to work long hours next week, and all day Saturday. I'll soon catch up, Alan, no need to tell David.'

'That's all very well, Mike, but you know how hard you're finding things at the moment. I think it would be much more sensible to ask for help. I'm sure Susan has some spare capacity at the moment, and she's got just the right skill set.'

'I thought she'd been put on that major project with the electricity company. She wasn't in the office last time I was there. Anyway, I just don't want David to know. He doesn't like me, and he's looking for reasons to give me a bad review. If you could just work extra hours with me next week, Alan, I think we'll get there easily.'

'I'll do what I can, Mike, but my MBA exams are coming up, and I have a big essay to submit by the end of next week. I'm already behind with it because of working longer here, and I really can't leave it any later, as it counts towards my final exams.'

'Oh well, more work for me then! I'll do it Alan, I really will!'

Alan now faces a dilemma. He does not believe that Mike will catch up in time for the milestone review meeting. He wants to discuss this with David, their manager, but he cannot do this without betraying Mike. If he tells the client, that would be even worse for everyone. If he says nothing, then unless Mike performs miracles, they will be in a very difficult position at the milestone meeting, and both their boss and their client will be very unhappy. This will reflect very badly on them both.

Alan is therefore faced with a choice between loyalty to his colleague, his company and his client, with some career self-interest thrown in for good measure. You might want to take a moment to reflect on what you would do in his place – no need to write an essay on the subject, but the mental exercise of working it out for yourself will always enhance your learning experience before you find out what he actually did.

In fact, Alan decided to go back to Mike that day: 'Look Mike, I've been thinking about all this, and I really don't want to be sitting in front of the client next Friday, explaining why we're behind schedule, and even worse, why we haven't told anyone. So I'll give you this weekend to do some serious catching up. I'll work Saturday morning with you. That's all I can manage, I'm afraid. So then we'll have a review on Monday morning. If the situation looks good, I'll say nothing. If it doesn't, then you or I will ring David and ask for help. Is that a deal?'

Mike protests, but in the end, accepts what Alan says, on condition that he rings David with his version of why he has not been able to contribute as he should. Alan is now satisfied that he has not betrayed Mike, but not let down his company, or the client.

By Monday, although some progress has been made, it is clear that there is still a problem, so Alan stands by Mike's desk as he makes the call to their manager. It turns out that Susan is available to help, and all ends well for the project. Although Mike remains nervous about his review, he accepts that they have done the right thing.

KEY MESSAGES

▶ *Tell the client if you know the problem is irretrievable, and tell them as soon as you are sure of it.*
▶ *Tell your manager early about delays – you will get into far less trouble that way, and may get help!*
▶ *Maintain good relations with colleagues, management and client – balance your loyalties carefully.*

Meeting deadlines

If the project plan is working well, then deadlines will not be an issue. They become a problem when expectations are not reset and agreed. If you know that you cannot meet a deadline, then tell your client immediately, and take a revised plan to show the corrective action. This gives the client the opportunity to participate in the re-planning process. They may have an alternative that you could never have anticipated.

If the client is not meeting deadlines, then you have a different set of problems to address, but immediate action is still needed, to discuss the problem, and advise them of the consequences. In the next section we look at examples of this.

Handling client delays

Sometimes clients drag their feet. It may be because of lack of resources, which is more straightforward to address, but it may be lack of commitment – they know what they need, but they are reluctant to get there. Sir John Harvey Jones summed this up:

'The art of consulting is to tailor advice to the optimum of what the outfit will take on board. I would always tell it as close to the bone as I thought they would accept. In my time doing *Trouble shooter*, I was invited in because people believed they had a problem, and the fact that it was a TV programme acted as a blackmailing process on all of us, because it was in everybody's interest to achieve a satisfactory outcome.

'Even in this situation, all too often one misjudged how keen they were to resolve the problem, and there was a continuing cajolery to get them to do things. Where people had an open mind, and accepted the steer from me, then it was a real joy to see them taking the problem away and working on it in a way that you knew would deliver the right result.'

Insight
Clients offer many challenges, but changing their minds about a project is one of the hardest things to cope with. Delays, vagueness, cancelled meetings – all are signals something is wrong and are best dealt with sooner rather than later.

Frank Milton described similar experiences. 'Clients are very reluctant to make the brave decision, and often they don't, despite all our efforts to convince them that it's absolutely right.

'One client had over 20 warehouses across Europe and another one about to open. We were a joint project team, with a Board member heading the client side, and everyone was completely committed to the team's findings, which were to go to a two-warehouse model, and close all the others. We managed to persuade the European Board, but the American Board said no. The client team was just as frustrated as we were. Eventually though, the company did go to the model we had recommended, but they could not make the brave decision in one hit.

'Another client was going to implement massive organization change, and install a new corporate software system. We had been working there for nine months, and the time came for the client to provide the staff to work on the new software. None came. Eventually I went to see the managing director, and asked him if he was serious about the project. After some straight talking, he told me that he was not committed, and we stopped the project, which was the right thing to do, though painful. We were paid for the nine months' work, but the sales effort to get the deal was not recovered. I'm glad I forced the issue when I did, otherwise we could have gone through a very long and messy period, which would have soured our relationship very badly. This was a clean finish, but it needed my initiative to make it happen.'

Both Frank and Sir John emphasized how much interpersonal skill is needed to handle these situations. 'You need a combination of charm and grit,' Frank said, 'and humour helps a great deal, if used in the right way.'

'Humour is the shortest distance between two people', to quote Peter Honey, and it is particularly relevant in situations like these.

KEY MESSAGES

▶ *Identify the real reasons why a client is holding back the project.*
▶ *Address the problem quickly and openly.*
▶ *Accept that there are limits to how far you can push a client, and make a clean exit if there is no more to be done.*

Agreeing completion

The project is finished; you have submitted your final report. You go and see the client for signoff, and he tells you he is not happy. 'But the project has gone really well. We've finished two days ahead of schedule. Everything is working fine. What's the problem?' you ask, amazed. To which he replies:

'You may think everything's working, but I'm not satisfied with the financial reports.'

Avoid a knee-jerk reaction here! This is not the time to point out that you have checked these reports against the very detailed specification. Your role now is to thoroughly understand the objections, and unless there is an obvious misunderstanding, to take them away and consider your next step. You may decide to argue, or you may make some changes just to keep him happy. You will probably want to discuss this with your manager or a colleague.

You want a satisfied customer, who views the signoff sheet with positive, not reluctant acceptance. However, some customers make dissatisfaction a vocation, or will play that game in order to squeeze more out of the project. The trick is to know who deserves a little extra effort to make the difference, and who will never be satisfied, no matter how much extra you give away.

KEY MESSAGES

▶ *Know your client!*
▶ *Balance the cost of concessions against the cost of disagreement.*
▶ *Set the project criteria so tightly, that scope for different interpretations is as limited as possible.*

It is so easy to say yes to a client, and by doing so to create problems that need never have existed. Clients usually manage to create enough problems for you all by themselves, so do not add to them by over-committing, or leaving gaps in the specification for misunderstanding to fill.

Closing thoughts

Here is a simple but powerful rule ... always give people more than they expect to get.

Nelson Boswell

The only real mistake is the one from which we learn nothing.

John Powell

STEPS TO SUCCESS

▶ *Build relationships and set expectations at every project level.*

▶ *Under-promise and over-deliver.*

▶ *Reset expectations early if something changes.*

▶ *Identify lack of client commitment and act promptly.*

▶ *Be clear on the benefit to you of making a concession to your client.*

▶ *Ensure that signoff will be a fait accompli against your tight specification.*

10

Avoiding project pitfalls

This chapter covers:
- *agreeing the specification*
- *contract renegotiation*
- *contract cover*
- *reading the signs*
- *prevention plan*

Having looked at the overall project process, let us examine some of the key elements, to see what can happen when these things go wrong, and you end up in court!

Gill Hunt, an independent consultant who is often called as an expert witness in court cases, gave some very real examples of this. She described the legal process, which is lengthy and expensive. She also pointed out that during this process, most cases settle without actually going to court, which reinforces the point that resorting to law is really only good for lawyers, rarely for anyone else!

She added, 'If you ever find yourself faced with a threat of legal action, there is a recognized alternative, set up for each business sector, in the form of a mediation process or ADR (Alternative Dispute Resolution), which is the next obvious step to take when you find that you cannot sort things out between yourselves.'

Gill described examples of three of the most typical cases. Although Gill operates in the IT field, the examples she gives can apply to almost any commercial project.

> **Insight**
> Don't dismiss this chapter as technical or legal stuff. Most
> of it is completely straightforward common sense. When
> you agree terms, take a forward view, and then step into the
> future and look back on what you have agreed. What can go
> wrong? How could terms be misinterpreted?

Agreeing the specification

The first is about a dispute over the specification, and she stresses
that it is at this point in a project, more than any other, that the
seeds of a court case are sown.

'I was a witness for a manufacturing company, who sued a software
supplier because their product could not deliver on one key part of
their requirement. It was a large corporate system, running across
several departments. The implementation had initially gone well,
but then this deficiency was discovered, and instead of raising it
immediately, the supplier tried a million workarounds. Eventually
they failed, and the client threw them out and sued successfully.'

The burning question here is: how did this get past the original
specification stage? 'What happened was that there was a long tick
list at tender stage – can your software do this, that and the other,
and they ticked everything, because at that general level, their
software could perform, they were not making dishonest claims.
What did not happen was a detailed examination of what was meant
by each of those generic statements, so the problem was unknown
to both sides until that stage of the implementation started.'

There was clearly fault on both sides here, but the supplier came
off far worse in legal terms. This was a case where neither side had
taken the time to clarify what exactly was needed. In fact the client
had requested a workshop from the suppliers at tender stage, but
the three suppliers who were competing would not spend the two
days needed unless the client paid for it, and the client would not

pay. In fact, the client paid very dearly later, because, as Gill put it, 'What they won in court was nowhere near enough compensation for the disruption caused by having to replace the system that didn't work, and the management time soaked up by the dispute.'

Contract renegotiation

Gill's next example was around the need to renegotiate contract terms early in the project lifecycle.

'This case involved a software supplier and financial services company. The contract was to deliver a working system by July 1999, which was Year-2000 compliant. This was the requirement when the contract negotiations began in May 1998, and nothing was changed in the contract, which was finally signed six months later, in December 1998!

'The supplier had decided to start work in parallel with the contract negotiations to save time, but at no point suggested a change to the deadline. It was therefore not surprising that the code they delivered in July did not work – they had simply run out of time. The customer then put their own contingency plans into place, threw out the system, and successfully sued the software supplier.'

Gill commented, 'You'd think it would be an obvious thing to do, to renegotiate that date, especially as it was the client who dragged out the contract signing process. I suppose they thought they might lose the business if they changed anything, but they lost it anyway, in more ways than one!'

Insight

Fear of losing business can drive some very poor decisions, like this one. At the time, it may seem that the risk is worth taking, but some realistic planning can soon tell you otherwise. Think through the long-term consequences, not just the potential short-term gain.

Contract cover

The last example is one where the contract did not cover all aspects of the project. 'There were two suppliers involved in the project, which was to provide a very specialized application in the entertainment business. The prime contractor delivered 99 per cent of the software, but a very small, very specialist piece was provided by a company with only one employee.

'Initially all went well, and then a problem arose, which was found to be in the specialist software. By this time the individual concerned had left the country, taking his source code with him, and could not be traced. The prime contractor had not covered this relationship contractually, so they had no rights at all to this software and no access to the source code. This proved such a critical issue that in the end, the client threw out the whole system, and successfully sued the prime contractor.

'These things seem so obvious when you're standing in court,' Gill commented, 'but at the time people don't think. Usually there are huge time pressures, the specialist software is just a detail, and is therefore overlooked. It was very unlucky that this should have had such an impact on the whole system, but that's life!'

Reading the signs

Gill also made the point that many companies do not spot the problem early enough.

'Unfortunately a lot of companies don't notice until the problem is staring them in the face, by which time any or all of the following will be happening:

- ▶ *Previously friendly customer staff won't talk/return calls.*
- ▶ *The project is way over time and budget.*

- *Staff from your competitors are visiting.*
- *Payments for services, maintenance or other items are overdue.*
- *The customer keeps finding new faults.*

'The final, undeniable sign of a serious problem is the letter from a senior figure on the customer side (and we are definitely talking about "sides" now rather than "partnerships") or from a lawyer. By the time it has reached this stage it's going to be very difficult to resolve things without the application of money and serious amounts of effort.'

Insight

Be honest with yourself about changes in the client relationship. Sometimes you know that things aren't right, but you do nothing, ostrich-fashion, because you don't want to face up to the problem that you suspect is heading your way.

Closing thoughts

Words have a longer life than deeds.

Pindar

He who asks a question is a fool for five minutes; he who does not ask a question remains a fool forever.

Chinese Proverb

STEPS TO SUCCESS

▶ Don't sell what you can't deliver – try to avoid unrealistic deadlines, get a delivery specialist involved as early in the sales cycle as possible, who really understands how to estimate timings.

▶ Pay attention to the contract. Don't allow material to be added to the contract unless it is clear and unequivocal, for example, using the responses to an ITT (invitation to tender), when a proper specification would be better. Whatever it says in the contract is what the courts will expect you to have done. Don't rely on any understandings, gentleman's agreements or assumptions.

▶ All customers will do their best to get a good price. Make sure that any discount given doesn't detract from the level of service that will be provided.

▶ Specification – get a good, clear specification of what is to be delivered and when. If the project includes the work to produce a specification (as in an R&D project) make sure all changes are minuted and that there are opportunities within the plan to stop and take stock before ploughing on.

▶ Change control – make sure there is a process and that both sides use it. Don't allow the project to be pressurized into 'just doing this' to keep things sweet. Even if you decide to do a change for free, go through the process so the customer knows you are serious about keeping control.

▶ Communicate frequently and clearly with everyone involved. Make sure that people know what has to be done to make the project work. If there is a problem say so. Make it clear what the consequences of a particular problem are, and also what will happen if a decision is not taken.

▶ Monitor the project closely, and look for any signals from the customer that all is not well.

11

Image

This chapter covers:
- *messages that image conveys*
- *what is image?*
- *matching the client*
- *the image consultant's view*
- *image from the inside*

Image is a subject that can create a great deal of angst, especially in these days of casual dress codes. Here we examine the issues, and a prominent image consultant gives some advice.

Sam joined one of the big consulting groups straight from university, and was carefully briefed on the matter of his appearance. The rule was always to dress smartly, but there were special graduations in smartness. When working in a regional manufacturing company, where many people would be in casual dress, the rule was to wear a suit, but nothing obviously fancy or expensive. When working in the City, however, anything less than a designer label suit would look positively inferior, and the rule was never to appear inferior in any sense to a client.

Insight

Dress codes have become much more complicated at work, with a much wider range of clothing being considered acceptable. What then becomes tricky is to match your client's style, but keep your professional edge as a consultant.

You may feel that you do not want to appear superior to a client, and if they all wear jeans and a T-shirt, so can you, in order not to appear out of place. You are working with them, you want to be seen as part of the team. This is a complex subject, and to reach the right conclusion you need to be very clear about your outcome, and very clear about your client's expectations.

Messages that image conveys

Most people make judgements about appearances. Many people make a judgement that if you have dressed up (whatever that means), to meet them, you have made an effort. This effort means that you regard them as important, and this importance means that you value and respect them.

This story from a Marketing Director illustrates the point:

'I always remember the first request I received for a business interview from a trade journal. I was wearing normal business dress; the journalist (male) arrived to see me in jeans, a T-shirt and an earring. I vividly remember feeling deeply insulted that he had not even bothered to put on a suit to visit me in my corporate environment. I later realized that he was wearing the journalists' uniform, and that he was absolutely conforming to the rules of his trade. However, the message stayed with me, "I make no concessions to you. I meet you on my terms, not yours. Take it or leave it." The fundamental arrogance of this is what sticks in my mind.

'This was some time ago. Today I might have been in casual dress, surrounded by people in jeans and earrings. He would have looked less out of place, but I would still have been disappointed that he had made no effort at all; still have felt that he did not place any importance on me as an individual.'

These views are not shared by everyone. There are people who say, 'I don't care what they look like, if they can deliver what I want.'

This may be true for some people, but remember that although your project sponsor may not care, his boss might, or her boss's boss might, or some political enemy of your project might use it as ammunition.

All in all, it is not worth taking the risk. Make it clear that you have made an effort, that you consider the client important and worthy of respect. Do not overdo it, so be sensitive to the style of the organization you are working in, but err always on the side of being smart, and never scruffy.

Insight

It's so important to keep asking yourself what the client will expect, and how they will interpret your appearance. Do not assume that dressing to match your client will be the safe solution.

If you are working long term as part of a project team with the client, and everyone else is completely casual, then you would begin very smart, stay smart for any formal meetings, but match the rest of the project team the rest of the time in order to fit in, and be seen as part of the team.

As a project manager, you might be called to formal meetings at any time, therefore casual dress is probably too risky for you. Unless the client requests you to dress down, do not bother to ask their permission. Current social pressures will almost guarantee that they will say yes, whatever they really feel, so do not put them in this position.

What is image?

Yes, of course it is the way you dress, but image has other aspects that we can easily overlook. You can wear a very smart outfit, but if it, or you, are not very clean, then your designer label will count for nothing.

Hair and fingernails can also ruin a good impression, both in cut and cleanliness. Cheap perfume and a harsh voice will offend other senses, and do not forget your accessories – a briefcase full of rubbish, a dirty car, a chewed pen, can all count in different ways.

'I never notice details like that,' a consultant commented, 'it's what I deliver that counts.' Many people do not notice these things, but they are very important to others. Also, although we say we do not notice if shoes are shiny or not, we often form a subconscious impression of these things, so although when we meet Bob, we may not consciously register the slight stain on the tie, the dirty fingernails and the grubby shoes, we are left with an impression of a slightly scruffy individual.

This subconscious impression can then lead to other conclusions. Sue has just met Bob, and is reporting back to her boss. 'I don't know, there was something unpolished about him. I didn't feel he was really sharp and on the ball. I wonder how focused he will be, how good his attention to detail is …'.

If you think this is far-fetched, then take a look at all the research that has been done on first impressions at recruitment interviews. People reach an astonishing number of conclusions about an interviewee in the first five seconds of the meeting.

Insight

If appearance is not very important to you, then scuffed shoes and a tired suit won't bother you. If your client sees (or rather doesn't see) things the same way as you do, then no problem. Your client could, on the other hand, be visually very sensitive, and the scuffed shoes might be the very first thing they notice.

My professional uniform

There is one perspective on image which we can usefully consider: the need for the consultant to wear a 'uniform of office', and this is usually very far from what we would normally think of as a uniform.

This is illustrated by this story, told by record producers, who live in the depths of the countryside, coincidentally close to the lead singer of a famous rock band. In the nature of relationships like this, as they had never worked with his group, they knew him by sight, but he did not know them. They would often meet him in the local village, or out walking in the woods, and were on nodding acquaintance.

One day the record company asked them to go and see him, as he wanted to make a solo album. They duly went to his house, and were shown into a spacious hall with a wide staircase, down which the rock star came, in full stage regalia, as he wore very elaborate costumes. Imagine his embarrassment when he realized that they had seen him weekly in Barbour and gumboots, walking the dog. He expected to meet strangers, and so had donned his professional uniform for the occasion.

You may not be a rock star making a grand entrance, but you might be a creative designer, and want to create a distinctive image with your client. In this case, will it not be right to go for the fun T-shirt and the earring – these things symbolize the creativity that the client is paying for?

Probably not, is the answer. It may be that the client wears that kind of dress at home, but that is not how he appears in the office. He conforms to corporate standards. If he does it, so will you. Now there are degrees of conformity, and your tie need not be boringly conventional, but do not stray too far from his norm.

Here the Marketing Director's view is useful: 'I have worked closely with various advertising agencies, and met some delightful "creatives". Lenny was a good example: he had shoulder length hair and a source of clothing that appeared totally original and very colourful. I observed this when I met him at his agency on a tour of their offices. He was not expecting to see me, so I met him on his home territory, dressed accordingly. The agency won the contract, and duly came to my office to present. Lenny's hair was in a neat ponytail, and he was wearing a jacket, trousers and tie. Not what I would describe as a suit, but certainly respectable. It was very obvious to me that he had made an effort to conform to my environment, and I was happy with this. On other occasions when I met him at the agency, he would dress in this same "formal" way for any scheduled meeting. If I simply called in, he was dressed in his normal attire, and that was fine by me.

'Lenny did not have his hair cut and go out and buy a business suit. I did not expect that. However, he dressed smartly, and minimized the effect of his hairstyle. He made the effort, and met my standards more than half way. Had he been an IT consultant, however, I would not have been happy. Creative designers do have an image that people are prepared to make concessions to. IT consultants like to think they do too. Some people may think so, but it is a risky assumption.'

Insight

Dressing to suit yourself can be seen as a form of arrogance. If you are confident that clients will buy your skills, however they are packaged, then go ahead. The message it gives is 'take it or leave it', and that is a very strong negotiating position, suggesting you don't need their business. For some, (not all), this can make you seem a more desirable asset.

The image consultant's view

Irene Nathan is the Managing Director of the Interpersonal Relations Group, and founder President of the Federation of Image Consultants. If you are thinking in terms of lipstick and hairstyles, forget it! Irene founded this organization precisely because she wanted to create a 'non-cosmetic' image for the work that she and many others do, and to set standards of best practice for the image profession.

Irene says, 'If you start off in the image consulting profession, you can go one of two ways: you either stay with the looks and the superficial, or you develop into a consultant for far more than the colour of a tie or a suit. Image is about who you are as a person, and most consultants in the profession deal with a much bigger picture than someone's mode of dress.'

IMAGE ADVICE

'Consult an image consultant!' was Irene's first suggestion. 'If you can't afford that, then you can volunteer to be a model on a training course for image consultants. They are often looking for people, and of course there would be no charge.' The Federation website has details of recognized training providers. All this can be found in 'Taking it further', page 304.

When Irene meets a new client, she spends time finding out who they are. She prompts them and then listens objectively. She will home in on their values, and find what is really important to them. When they both understand who they are building the image for, then she can begin.

'It is not unusual for the individual to be unclear about who they are or how they want to be perceived, and that is often the underlying reason why they might call in an image consultant, although they may not have recognized it consciously.

Insight

Are you quite clear who you are as a consultant, and how you want to be perceived? This may be a question you have never asked yourself, in which case you may find the image you are projecting is not one you have chosen, or worse, it's not the one you think it is!

'For example, someone might say to me that they are looking to project more gravitas. Everyone has substance, but sometimes, when they are in a new situation, they may feel vulnerable and this can show. Often people like this will be high achievers, but they do not place a high value on what they have accomplished. If I can help them to value themselves more, then the gravitas tends to follow, and clothing is really a thin decorative veneer on the solid wood of self-esteem. It is this change in self-esteem, which really delivers the image change. I can't make someone acquire self-respect, but I can be persevering and tolerant enough to help them find things in themselves of worth and value so they are able to project in a confident manner.

'If I were advising you as a new consultant, I would suggest that you find an outfit that you not only look good in, but you feel good in too. These two things are quite different, and the feeling good is the important point. When you are sure that you have found this feeling, then slowly build a few similar items on the same theme. No need to spend a great deal of money, the important thing is that you retain this feeling, which will enhance your performance in whatever consulting role you perform.'

Irene's advice on casual versus formal dress is very specific. 'The important thing is not to look sloppy or incomplete. People think, whether consciously or otherwise, that your sloppiness may well translate into other areas of your work. Similarly, always look current – if you appear to be out of date in your dress, they might think that also applies to your thinking.

Insight

Two critical messages: Look smart, not sloppy. Look current, not out-of-date. You do not want clients to think that your work is sloppy, or your thinking is out of date. You may not make that link yourself, but others might.

'Do not over-dress or under-dress – always choose appropriate dress, and when the culture demands casual dress, go for smart casual, avoiding any suspicion of that sloppiness mentioned earlier. You are aiming, as far as possible, to look like yourself, as a business professional.

'I do not play God with clients. If they tell me they will only wear designer labels, that is what I will advise them on. We can help people move from being self-obsessed to self-possessed, but knowing when to stop is a key skill in this field, because it is so personal, and I am not there to be a psychiatrist. A good consultant becomes a catalyst – someone who identifies areas that can cause a positive chain reaction.

'If I feel that the individual is really unhappy during a session, then I will stop it, and suggest a delay. Whilst running a corporate programme recently, I was coaching a senior manager and I could see he was very uncomfortable, so I said to him, "Shall we delay this session for a few months, as I think you have other priorities at the moment." He was obviously relieved, and asked me if I'd spoken to any of his business colleagues. I assured him I hadn't, that I simply sensed that he was uncomfortable and distracted in talking to me. He then told me that his wife had walked out on him two weeks before. He needed to talk but certainly not about his business dress.'

CASE STUDY: NEVER DISMISS FEEDBACK

'My advice to other consultants is to take careful notice of every detail and not to ignore anything. It is easy to dismiss a piece of negative feedback as someone having an "off" day. I ran a group session in a company a while ago, and it seemed to go well. When I received the feedback forms a few days later, most were very positive, but I was dismayed to see that one person in the group had given me negative, indeed, insulting feedback.

'I rang my contact in the company, who told me she was very happy with the forms and not to worry, since this lady could be very negative. I then learned that this lady had been dieting for many months, and had lost three and a half stone. She had just bought a new suit to celebrate her success, and, not knowing any of this, what I had said to her on the course was that the suit did not fit – she should go up a size. I now realized the enormity of those words, so I asked if I could go and see her. This was duly arranged, and I began our meeting by telling her that I was surprised that she hadn't given me a black eye on the spot for what I had said! I was then able to put right the great wrong I had unknowingly done her, and she did in due course slim down to fit the suit I had criticized. I was so pleased that I had not just dismissed her comment, as the client advised me to do, and the learning for me was invaluable.'

GENERAL ADVICE

'My advice to the aspiring consultant is that you will need to demonstrate huge amounts of integrity and honesty. You are also in the "service" industry; if you say something, keep to it. If you promise something, deliver it. Never be lured into doing something you are not qualified to do. It is very easy when a client says, "Can you help me with this too?" If money is important to you, it is easy to be tempted, but you are only creating problems down the line. To say "I know a man who can!" is a much better answer, if you really do! Another key skill is to listen well, and generally not to talk too much about yourself.

'I view my professional career as a continuing learning process. It is easy to get stuck in your own time warp, and think that you have the perfect solution worked out. It is important to acknowledge your own change too, and the impact that has on the work you do. If I were hiring someone to work alongside me, I would be looking for someone hungry for growth and development, so that their needs would be a positive driver for me too, rather than me having to think for them.

Insight

Are you in a rut? When was the last time you refreshed your thinking on your specialism, or had someone challenge the techniques you use? If yesterday is the answer, you are likely to be in that state of continual learning that Irene talks about here.

'I often consult other consultants on different subjects, as part of my learning process. I believe you need to keep yourself fresh and alive and learned and knowledgeable – that is the most important thing you can offer, whatever your subject.'

Irene's comments are very much in line with those we have heard from other consultants. This reinforces the commonality of consulting skills across different contexts, as well as perfectly illustrating Irene's point that image is not a superficial subject.

Closing thoughts

When you are content to be simply yourself and don't compare or compete, everybody will respect you.

Lao-Tzu

What lies behind us and what lies before us are tiny matters compared to what lies within us.

Oliver Wendell Holmes

STEPS TO SUCCESS

▶ *Avoid looking sloppy in your dress – clients may think that is how your work will be.*

▶ *Be sure that your dress is current, to match your thinking.*

▶ *Wear clothes that you feel good in, as well as knowing that they look good.*

▶ *Match the client's dress code as far as you can, but retain the edge, and avoid straying beyond smart casual.*

▶ *Recognize that image can convey messages (intended or otherwise), about how much respect you have for a client.*

▶ *Be aware of all the physical aspects of image – your car, your shoes, etc.*

▶ *If you are unhappy about your image, consult an image consultant!*

▶ *Image comes from within, so pay as much attention to your state of mind as to your dress. Self-belief, enthusiasm and conviction will shine through the dullest of outfits.*

12

Writing a client report

This chapter covers:
- *how to change your attitude to report writing*
- *an easy method*
- *your readers*
- *structure*
- *mind maps*

Does your heart sink at the thought of writing a report? Is it something that you put off until the very last minute, and then grapple with in desperation?

Well, the first thing you need is a reframing of your view of this subject, rather than a course on literary excellence – that is not a priority. The important thing here is that you lose that glowering black cloud feeling that reports give you. If you procrastinate over them too, then we need to add another step in the process.

Your attitude to report writing

What do you find so alarming about the blank page? How is it that you can dash off an email without thinking, but the thought of a report fills you with dread? Length may have something to do with it, but have you ever plunged into an email, and been surprised by how much you have written? It is probably as long as a short report, but because it is 'only an email' you do not think twice about it. Because it is 'only an email' you do not put it off for days or weeks, you just do it!

If that is the way you think, then start thinking that a report is the equivalent of 'only a long email'. If you can approach a report with the same mindset, you are more than half way there, and that mindset will mean that you do not leave it until the last minute either! If you are one of those rare people who quite like writing reports, just bear with this, and we will come to technique very quickly.

So how do you convince yourself that this very important document, that you have to present to the client by next Thursday, can be treated in the same way as an email?

Insight

It is rare for a report to be difficult in itself, but there can be an association with exams in your mind, which is another piece of baggage to get rid of. Most of the difficulty is in your head, not in the reality on the page!

First, examine how you view the size of a report. Do you see a thick volume – practically a book – involving hours and days and even weeks of work? What would you do if someone presented you with such a document? Would you sit down and devour every word, cover to cover, or would you look for the summary page and hope you would not need to read any more than that? Not surprisingly, the majority of recipients of a report hope it will be short, so why do many of the writers of reports think that it should be long?

Discard that image of a thick volume. Think instead of a slim document, perhaps only a page or two, which is tightly targeted to its subject. If you need to include back up information, put it into one or more appendices. They come under the heading of optional reading, which is less work for the recipient. Now you have a clear slim document in mind, associate that with a happy reader, and you have a new perspective on the task that faces you. As long as you cover the essentials, you will make your reader happier by giving them less, not more.

The next step in this process is to think of this slim document as a series of fairly short emails, linked together to form a coherent whole. You can write the emails at different times to suit you, and so you do not have to lock yourself away for a week. You can do it in stages.

If we take a metaphor for this process, it would be to say that most people view writing a report in the same way that they would see making a wardrobe by starting with a solid tree trunk. It looks like a massive task, and they will have to sit for hours, carving away. It is something they will put off for a long time, and worry about.

Insight

A lot of your energy may be applied to worrying about the report. Transfer that energy to planning it, and to getting other people to give you input, and your worrying will reduce in direct proportion to the amount of timely preparation that you do.

The alternative view is that your slim report is more like a wardrobe made from a flat pack assembly kit. You choose the components, and the biggest challenge will be fitting them together in the right order, which is a much smaller problem than a solid tree trunk!

So what components will you need? Each piece will be a section of your report, and we will spend some time on structure shortly. You will also need some glue or other fixing to hold the pieces together. This need not be elaborate. A report does not need to read like a novel. In fact, people often prefer bullet point headings to flowing prose, so if you are worried about the quality of your written English, the challenge is not as great as you think. This is well illustrated by Ray's report.

CASE STUDY: COURSE REPORT

Ray has just returned from an expensive project management course, and has told his manager it was a complete waste of time. Through his manager, the HR Director asks for a full report.

Apparently the course was run by someone he knows well, and Ray gathers that this is not the feedback he expected. He tries to persuade his boss that he does not need to do this, but his boss views this as an important exercise, for some reason.

Ray sits at his desk and chews his pen. Then he jots down some notes on various aspects of the course. Finally he makes a list of the elements he wants to comment on:

- *the course tutor*
- *the course content*
- *the practical exercises*
- *the other delegates*
- *the handouts*
- *the location*
- *what he learned*

He reviews this list against his comments, and finds that it covers all the things he wants to say. He therefore has all the elements of his 'flat pack'. Some will be bigger than others: he has little to say about the handouts or the location, but a great deal about the tutor and the other delegates.

He decides to use bullet points to keep the report short and punchy, so he begins:

Course tutor:

- *No practical experience of project management*
- *Lectured us at length in a boring tone*
- *Not familiar with MS Project!*
- *Did not allow discussion*

He continues in the same vein for the other topics, and decides not to use bullets for the conclusion, but to write a simple paragraph at the end, expressing his great dissatisfaction. He does this because he thinks that the change in style will have more impact. His report runs to just two pages, and takes him an hour to produce.

Can you feel the sense of relief, now that it is finished? And it was not nearly as difficult as it seemed, when he sat down to it. Perhaps you have found the same yourself – that something you have been dreading doing has turned out to be far less of a problem than you expected. This is almost always the case with writing reports.

Insight

Did that happen to you the last time you wrote a report? You worried about it, but when you finally did it, it wasn't nearly as bad as you had expected! Can you remember and hold that feeling of ease and satisfaction, to replace the unnecessary worry?

This is the secret – think of reports as short documents, as a series of tasks, not just one; as occupying short periods, therefore you do not need to set aside a long period of 'tree trunk carving' time. This means that if you have a report to write, you can start now, just for a little while. Then you can stop, and do something else.

In fact, it is almost essential to start on a report before you intend to start writing. Often you will need to check things, gather information from other people or assemble facts from files. If you work out what you need immediately, it will enable you to plan when to obtain it, and give other people time to deliver.

Have you ever come close to a deadline, and then discovered that you need data from a department that works on a one-month lead-time? You usually find yourself scrabbling through their files late one evening, because they have refused to help you, or else bribing or upsetting someone into delivering to meet your timeframe, only to find that they have missed something vital, either deliberately, or in their haste to meet your deadline.

SUMMARY

Here is the recipe for changing the way you think of report writing:

▶ *You see a happy person receiving a short report, and an unhappy one laden down with a heavy volume.*

▶ *You see this slim report as a series of short tasks that can be done quickly, not as one big one.*

▶ *As soon as you know you have a report to write, you will want to sit down and work out what you will need before you can start writing. The more you get from other people, the less work for you, so the sooner you tell them what you need, the better. This will also help you to plan your series of short tasks, and when to start them.*

STILL WORRIED?

That is all very well, you say, but I am no good at writing. I really find it hard to string words together on paper. Will you also say that you have trouble holding a conversation with a friend? Unlikely, so unless you are one of those very rare beings – a truly inarticulate consultant – then you are quite capable of being fluent, you have simply not learned to apply your fluency to paper, and we will deal with this problem now. As in the example above, the use of bullet points can be a great help – to you and to your reader. You do not need to write a novel, and your readers do not want to read one. If you cannot use bullet points, then try writing as you speak. Do not use literary language. Your readers want quick access to facts, not complex linguistic contortions.

> ## Insight
> Unless you know your audience contains professors of English, your report does not need to be perfectly written. People like short sentences and bullet points. They prefer simple words to abstract labels. That's not so hard, is it?

If you really feel that you have no confidence at all in your written English, then find yourself a buddy or a mentor. This can be anyone you know, inside or outside of work. If they are talented in written English, they will be flattered to be asked, and often very willing to spend time explaining things, rather than just wielding the red pencil. It will be worth your while to understand your most frequent mistakes and learn not to repeat them.

Creating the report

Now that you are feeling more calm and relaxed about report writing, we will cover the process of creating a business report.

YOUR READERS

We start by switching our attention to the reader. Who are they, and what do they want? A small wardrobe for a spare room, or acres of space for a big collection of designer clothes? If you were actually building a wardrobe, you would ask them, so do the same with a report. Find out what they are expecting, and get the equivalent of precise measurements, not just a vague generalization, for example:

'John, this report on the bridge – do you want full structural data?'

'Shall I include coverage of all the planning objections, as well as the environmental issues?'

Ian went through this process the other day, and rapidly discovered that what he thought was to be a lengthy analysis, turned into a high-level review, with a key criterion of two pages maximum!

STRUCTURE

Now you know what your readers are looking for, you can structure the report to meet their requirements.

Summary

If the report is more than two pages long (excluding appendices), it needs a summary page. If the body of your report is long, then bear in mind that the summary is the only thing that some people will read, especially as it lives at the beginning of the report, and not at the end.

Introduction and conclusion
Most reports contain these two sections, with the conclusion being the crunch piece: 'We therefore recommend the purchase of A rather than B.'

Sections
These are the individual pieces of your flat pack, and there are often a number of ways of covering the same topic. Mind maps can be invaluable here, which we shall examine shortly. If you do what Ray did, and jot down the key points you want to make, and put those into groups, this is one way of arriving at the sections you need. If you have a key point that does not fit into a group, you may need a new group, or perhaps you could re-label one of the groups you have already identified.

Section headings
However short a report may be, break it up with headings for the different sections. Just as your reader will be happy with a slim report, so they will be happy with lots of white space on the page. You may feel proud of producing a whole A4 page of closely typed script, but your reader will feel daunted by the look of it.

Links
You do not need a great deal of fixing material for your flat pack. If the pieces appear in the right order, all you do is refer to their sequence in your introduction, and possibly again in the conclusion. Let us look at Ray's introduction. He has not wasted any words.

Introduction

This is a report on the project management course run by ABC Training on x date. The report has six sections covering all the key aspects of the course, plus a final section, which details what I learned. In my conclusion I make recommendations regarding our future use of this course.

He then goes straight into the first section:

> Course tutor:
>
> ▶ *No real practical experience of project management*
> ▶ *Lectured ...etc.*

His conclusion is equally brief:

> Unless we have potential project managers who wish to
> learn through monotonous lecturing from someone with no
> practical experience, I cannot recommend that we use this
> course again.

In effect Ray has used very little glue to hold the pieces together: a few words to open and close, with bullet points between. There is no need for anything more, his report is short and to the point.

There is another major virtue in brevity: what you put in print to a client can be used in any kind of dispute, therefore extreme care is needed when committing to paper. The less you write, the less there is to be vigilant over!

Mind maps

You may be familiar with the concept of mind maps. If not, you will find that although they appear initially to be a slightly unusual way of working, you will soon get the hang of them and appreciate their value. This takes a matter of minutes to achieve. The concept was originated by Tony Buzan, and if you want to explore the subject in depth, read one of Tony's books (see 'Taking it further', page 304).

For now, all you need to know is that instead of linear thinking, in list form, you create a map of your ideas, and can link them together in different ways.

Don't be put off by mind maps, and think you need to learn a special skill to use them. Do a quick trial. Take a blank piece of scrap paper, and put a word in the middle – say 'Holiday'. Circle it, and then write all the ideas about your holiday that come to you, in circles around it. All this can be scribbled in one or two minutes – simple!

Taking the subject of the report on the training course, Ray produced a list – which is based on linear thinking. If he had gone for the mind map approach, he would have started with the subject 'Project Management Training Course' in the centre circle. Then projecting from different sides of that circle would be the key subject areas: the course tutor; the course content; the practical exercises; the other delegates; the handouts; the location; what he learned.

What will happen as you put these in place would be that alternative structures would begin to suggest themselves to you. Practical exercises could be a subsection under content, for example.

When you have the inner ring of circles in place, you then look for the next ring. For example, overnight accommodation might be a subsection of location.

Figure 3 shows how a mind map can offer you different ways of structuring a report, in a way that a list of headings will not. And Figure 4 shows that list of headings, in a different mind map version.

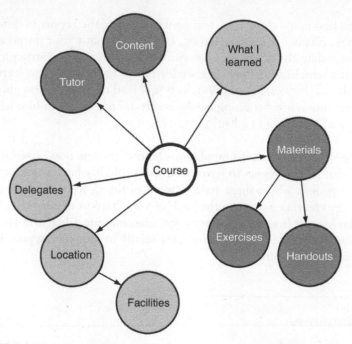

Figure 3 Mind map course report 1 – project management.

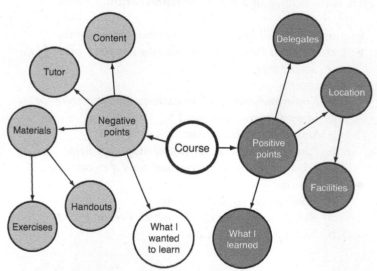

Figure 4 Mind map course report 2 – project management.

The two maps show how you could structure the report in different ways. Neither is right or wrong, but one may suit your purpose better than the other, and you can see from the second structure that a new heading has suggested itself: 'What I wanted to learn'. This is a very useful addition, as it will lead to a discussion about Ray's unsatisfied training needs, and it did not occur to him when he was just making a list.

If you have never used mind maps before, try one now. Even if you do not have a report to write, you will probably have some aspect of a project where there are a number of things to be dealt with, so try creating a map on the back of your napkin or proverbial envelope. It is as easy, if not easier, than making a list, and you will soon see what benefits it brings, especially in sequencing your flat pack components.

Summary

Here is the outline of a report on report writing:

- Summary: *Will be a list of key points from below.*
- Introduction: *Process like wardrobe flat pack assembly, not carving tree.*
- Main steps:
  - *Know audience you are making the wardrobe for*
  - *Identify pieces they need*
  - *Size of pieces they need*
  - *List all pieces in order (mind map may help)*
  - *Glue or attach them together only if necessary.*
- Conclusion:
  - *Much easier to write in bits*
  - *Results in shorter report, which people prefer*
  - *Not a big deal!*

Closing thoughts

> There is no such thing as a long piece of work, except one that you dare not start.
>
> Charles Baudelaire

> Writing is the best way to talk without being interrupted.
>
> Jules Renard

STEPS TO SUCCESS

▶ *Find a positive attitude to report writing, and you are over your biggest hurdle!*

▶ *Start planning at once, to give other people more time and to save you work.*

▶ *Be crystal clear on your target audience – ask them what they expect.*

▶ *Divide the work into small tasks, to make them manageable.*

▶ *Find a mentor or buddy, if you are worried about your written English.*

▶ *Use mind maps to define the structure.*

▶ *Aim for a short report, and a happy reader!*

13

Giving a client presentation

This chapter covers:
- *dealing with nerves*
- *knowing your audience*
- *style and delivery*
- *use of language*
- *creating images*
- *structuring content*
- *getting good feedback*

For many people, this can be one of the biggest challenges they face as a consultant. This chapter will take you a good way along the road to giving a good client presentation. If you combine it with live training and/or coaching, with lots of practice and feedback, your route to success is guaranteed. If that sounds like an ambitious promise, then you may wish to remind yourself of some of the presuppositions that the learning in this book is based on, which apply very well to this subject.

▸ **The meaning of communication is in the response you get.** *No matter what message leaves you, it is what the client hears that matters.*
▸ **There is no failure, only feedback.** *It is vital to believe this as you learn to improve your presenting skills, if not, you are likely to end up with:*
▸ **If you always do what you always did, you will always get what you always got.**

▶ **If someone else can do something, so can you.** *Usually, inspiring presenter role models are not difficult to find, which is helpful in the learning process.*

▶ **Everyone already has everything they need to achieve what they want.** *You have within you everything it takes to be an excellent presenter – all you have to do is release that potential.*

Insight

You may be thinking that you can't learn how to present from a book! Although this is true, this chapter can give you useful tips to use in combination with other ways of learning.

There are many excellent books on the subject of presenting and public speaking, and most of them will start by telling you that the written word is not the best way to learn how to deliver the spoken one. However, there is much to know about giving a good presentation, and some of it can easily be taken from a book. We will focus here on the most likely scenario for a client presentation, which will be to a smallish group (from two to twenty people), in an office/meeting room environment.

As we look at each element of presenting, we will refer you to other forms of learning at each step.

Dealing with nerves

Have you ever thought about what happens when you get nervous about something? You know all the symptoms only too well, but what are they the result of? Usually there are two answers:

▶ *Worrying about how well you will perform.*
▶ *Fear of failure in front of a group of people who are important to you.*

These are natural fears, and they thrive when the focus of your thinking is on yourself. If you are concerned for others, you will have less emotional space to worry about you. The natural conclusion to this is that the best way to get rid of nerves is to think about your audience, not about you.

That sounds like a very glib statement, but if you think about being nervous, or being shy, they are very self-centred emotions. People rarely accuse a shy person of being self-centred, but that is the root of their shyness: they are so preoccupied about what people think of them, that they cannot deal easily with others. Being nervous falls into a similar category. If you can put yourself in your audience's shoes, and think about how they are feeling, then you will stop being so self-obsessed, and give a better presentation as a result. It is also vital to remember that an audience does not want to be bored – who would want to inflict that on themselves? They want you to be interesting – that is what they are hoping for. Therefore you start with a great deal of goodwill from the audience – even when they are clients!

CASE STUDY: FINDING A HOT BUTTON

June is about to give a presentation on personal image to a small group of sales managers. She has been told that they are an outspoken bunch, who will tell her exactly what they think, and this has put her on edge. However, she has done her research and knows that behind the gruff exterior are some fairly insecure people. She joins their conference two sessions before her own, to get to know some of the issues they face. She talks to them at coffee break, and tries to understand their thinking and preoccupations. When she starts her presentation, it is with an introduction that flows naturally from what she has learned that day.

After a brief introductory sentence, she says: 'I know that you are planning a major thrust into the IT industry this year, which is new territory for most of you, and a critical part of your business strategy. Well, the bad news is that image in this sector has a set of rules of its own, but the good news is that I've spent a lot of time working with senior IT people, so I can make sure that your image will be a positive factor in the sales process.'

June is so focused on the needs of her audience that she is able to modify her presentation very easily. She has identified their top issue, and related her presentation to it in a way that would not be possible for someone who is busy worrying about how well they are going to perform. Because she knows she has hit a 'hot button', and can read their non-verbal signals of interest, such as leaning forward and nodding, she becomes even more confident and fluent.

With a small group, it is also easy to ask if people want more information on this topic or that, and to tailor accordingly. In fact, the more you question your audience, the more feedback you will get, and the more natural your presentation will be.

BREATHING DIFFERENTLY

The other way to banish nerves is to learn how to breathe deeply.

Insight

Most people dismiss deep breathing as a waste of time, largely because they think deep breathing involves taking a few deep breaths! In fact, it is a special technique and it is unlikely that you will know how to do this, unless you have specifically learned it, so forget all your normal breathing habits. It has been physiologically proven to have a calming effect, so it is worth giving it a try, since the technique is very simple, it is just not what you are used to.

This is how to do it:

▶ *It consists of inflating the abdomen (home of the beer gut, just below the navel!) when you breathe in, and deflating it when you breathe out.*
▶ *Ignore anything higher up, and focus below the navel.*

- *It is easier to remember to IN-flate when you breathe IN, because you might be inclined to do the opposite!*
- *A good way to practise is in bed, flat on your back.*
- *Rest your hands gently on your abdomen, finger ends touching and thumbs pointing up towards your navel.*
- *Now breathe in and feel the area inflate, then exhale and feel it deflate.*
- *Practise a few times, as it may not come naturally! It's a good idea to do this regularly, since it will have the effect of helping you go off to sleep.*

When June first tried this in bed, she was not convinced that it was working, except that she eventually realized that she could not remember anything after she did her deep breathing.

Practising the technique is important, not just to get it right, but to learn to believe in it. It is physiologically proven that this technique relaxes people, but there is nothing like seeing, or rather feeling for yourself, and the more you believe it works, the better it will work for you. In the end, just the thought of doing your deep breathing will have a calming effect.

ACTIONS

- *Practise deep breathing, and enjoy its effects.*
- *Practise thinking about your audience, and forgetting yourself.*

Knowing your audience

Find out as much as you can about your audience, and stay focused on them as you plan your presentation. If you start with questions like: 'What is the purpose of my presentation?' you may lose audience focus before you start, and tell them what you want to tell them, rather than what they want to hear. Instead, ask yourself who the audience is, and knowing that, then the key question is: 'What do they want from me?'

CASE STUDY: MEETING YOUR AUDIENCE'S NEEDS

Gerry was planning a detailed talk on the structure of the new bridge that was to be built as part of the docklands development project. He was busy producing handouts of structural calculations, when Dennis passed by his desk.

'What's all this for, Gerry?'

'Client presentation tomorrow. They want full structural details on the bridge. It's not the most challenging bridge I've ever worked on, far from it, but they seem very concerned about …'.

'Who are you presenting to?'

Gerry explains to Dennis that he will be presenting to a group from the client's structural engineering department.

'I heard that Jack is going to be there – in fact, I think it was Jack who requested the meeting.'

'Nobody told me that!'

'I'd check if I were you.'

Gerry checks and discovers that Dennis is right. The meeting is for Jack, the project manager. The structural engineers are there to back him up technically if he needs it. He immediately modifies the technical content of the presentation, and it becomes very high level, with lots of back-up documentation to refer to, but not to talk about. It also focuses on potential construction problems, which he knows is always Jack's hot button.

KEY MESSAGES

▶ *When preparing a presentation, start your thinking with your audience, not with your subject matter.*
▶ *Who are your audience?*

- *What do they want from your presentation?*
- *What form of presentation are they expecting?*
- *How long have you got?*

Style and delivery

The best way to work on style and delivery is through practice and feedback. This could be in a training course, with video, or with a friend or coach.

Insight

It is important to practise in a safe learning environment, and get good quality feedback on your performance, preferably including video at some point.

To help with this process, here is a checklist that you may wish to give to your 'coach', to help them give you good feedback.

- **Content:** *Was it clear, structured, convincing, interesting, relevant to my audience?*
- **Visual aids:** *Were they clear, helpful, interesting, understandable, distracting, necessary?*
- **Delivery style:** *Did I appear – confident, arrogant, in tune with you, nervous, uncertain, fluent, sincere, convincing, passionate, unfeeling, wooden?*
- **Voice:** *Was my voice interesting, monotonous, audible, grating, loud?*
- **Language:** *Was my language understandable, patronizing, lively, boring, active, passive, inclusive, exclusive?*
- **Body language:** *Was I stiff and wooden, over-dramatic, natural, annoying. In tune with my words and my voice?*
- **How did you feel?** *Were you bored, patronized, interested, fascinated, amused, confused?*

Good delivery is fundamental to a good presentation. It is a sad fact that your content may be brilliant, but if your delivery is poor, it will have a deeply negative effect, far worse than if your content were poor, and your delivery brilliant. It is possible to give a presentation which people think is wonderful, and also happens to be content-free. Happily, as a consultant, your content will matter far more to your client audience than it would in many other contexts, but even so, delivery is still a key factor.

Insight

Jane listed every fact, all totally accurate, in the way you might read out the telephone directory with a hangover. Joe's information was scant, but his style was lively and amusing. Who would you prefer to listen to?

Much research has been done into the way we communicate, and into the relative importance of the verbal versus the non-verbal messages. If you have not seen these figures before, you may be surprised to learn that in any face-to-face communication, the words we use count for little. The way we say them is far more important, and most important are the non-verbal signals that we send out with them. Where there is a mismatch between content and delivery, the percentages are as follows:

> *The words we use – 7 per cent;*
> *The way we say them – tone, volume, etc., 38 per cent;*
> *Non-verbal signals – 55 per cent.*

So a staggering 93 per cent of your ability to influence is coming from things apart from the words you use. Now you can see how a speaker can appear brilliant, without saying anything at all! Conversely, a speaker with wonderful content may not succeed in conveying it, if the delivery is very poor.

ACTIONS

▶ *Practise, practise, practise your delivery, with someone primed to give you the very best feedback, every time.*

Use of language

It is vital, when giving a presentation, to use the spoken, rather than the written word. The previous sentence is in written English. If you were to deliver this same message out loud, it would probably be something like: 'When you are presenting, speak naturally, don't sound like you're reading from a book!'

This difference is enormous, and is probably the single most vital thing that will make you sound like a confident presenter who is talking to the audience, rather than an inept one who is nervously reciting a memorized script into the air.

The spoken word has a number of characteristics which distinguish it from what you would write in a report, and you may find it helpful to understand what these are, in order to use them to best effect.

It helps to get into this subject by thinking about the different qualities language has.

Here is a list of descriptions, which contrast opposite types:

Abstract	Concrete
Active	Passive
Boring	Fascinating
Understandable	Confusing
Patronizing	Makes the audience feel intelligent
Lively	Lifeless
Inclusive	Exclusive
Vivid	Unclear
Sensuous	Devoid of feeling

(Note sensuous means appealing to the senses, not to be confused with sensual, which has a different emphasis!)

Contrast Jeremy's presentation:

> *'So, gentlemen, it appears that an unsatisfactory conclusion has been reached, in that no one solution could be found. However, it does seem probable, according to the experts, whose input I will not trouble you with here, that there may be a way of overcoming our construction difficulties.'*

with Ted's, on the same subject:

> *'So I have to tell you that we were pretty disappointed that we couldn't solve the problem. But we consulted our most experienced structural engineers, whose report is available to you at the end of this presentation, if you want to see it, and we are delighted to tell you that we think we've found a way to get the bridge built after all!'*

Insight

When faced with something new, do you prefer to dive in at the deep end, or is experiential learning your preference? This is the same question, differently phrased: the first in Ted's style, the second in Jeremy's.

If you refer back to the list above, you will see that there are many differences in these two extracts, but two areas stand out above the others: these are the use of active as opposed to passive, and abstract rather than concrete. For example:

- ▶ *'has been reached'* and *'could be found'* are examples of passive voice.
- ▶ *'I have to tell you'* and *'we couldn't solve'* are examples of the active voice.
- ▶ *'a way of overcoming our construction difficulties'* is an abstract expression. The concrete version (almost literally!) is *'a way to get the bridge built'.*

The consequence of Jeremy using the abstract and the passive is that his presentation becomes boring and lifeless. If you actively use concrete words, as Ted did, you sound much more lively, and more interesting.

Jeremy was also patronizing and exclusive, as he referred to experts, and implied that the audience would not be able to cope with their input. Ted, on the other hand, told us who they were, these mystery experts, and offered us their report to read, if we wished to. Even if we are not structural engineers, Ted assumes that we can understand their report, and we feel included as a result.

Ted also tells us how he feels: 'disappointed' and 'delighted', whereas Jeremy's passive voice does not permit any expression of feeling, and is more lifeless and boring as a result.

To summarize then, Jeremy's use of passive, abstract, exclusive, patronizing and unemotional language, means that his presentation is boring, harder to understand, and lifeless.

Ted, on the other hand, tells it straight with feeling to people he assumes are intelligent. He talks about concrete things, like the bridge, and he includes people in what he says.

Ted is therefore much more interesting to us, and his lively, direct style is easy to understand.

You might be tempted in Jeremy's direction because you think it is sophisticated and professional, compared with Ted's straightforward, down-to-earth style. If you have any last doubts, imagine yourself again in the audience, and think who you would rather deal with – distant, cold Jeremy, or warm, enthusiastic Ted. As a client, how much value would you place on a straight-talking consultant? There really is no contest.

Imagery

Another way to make your presentation more lively and vivid is to use imagery to bring your words to life. This includes visual aids, but give your audience mental pictures and let them share your feelings too. Use **simile** and **metaphor** as much as you can. A simile compares two things and usually begins with 'like' ... 'She has a neck *like a giraffe.*'

A metaphor generally uses a concrete word to represent something abstract: e.g. 'He sank into *a well* of pain.' So, 'This project has had its setbacks' becomes:

'We've had a bit of a *roller-coaster ride* with this project. We've felt pretty uncomfortable at times, but we've also had great fun. It really has been *like a runaway train* at times, but *we are now moving at an orderly pace into the station.*'

The more senses you can include in your imagery, the better. Most people are able to create vivid mental pictures, if you give them the opportunity. Some people prefer to deal in sound and feelings, and everyone will get a more vivid impression if you add these too: 'So if you were expecting to *feel the shock and hear the crash when we hit the buffers,* you'll be disappointed, I'm afraid!'

Insight

Don't just expect metaphors to roll off your tongue at the right moment. Where you want to convince a client of something, you might work at the language well in advance. 'Shall we opt for the longer, smoother route, or risk a bumpy ride if we take the short cut?'

The other kinds of visual aids to a presentation are ideally that – visual – and not just a list of the key words you will be reading from the screen. An ideal format is to have lots of imagery in the words you say, and very few words in the pictures you show.

KEY MESSAGES

▸ *Think active: begin with I, you, we. Not 'the silence was broken' but 'we broke the silence'.*

- *Think concrete words, not fancy abstract labels. Not 'communal leisure facilities' but 'a new swimming pool and golf range'.*
- *Treat your audience with respect, as intelligent people.*
- *Include your audience – bring them into your presentation.*
- *Use verbal imagery (or rather, word pictures!), to make your content vivid and memorable.*
- *Make your other visual aids truly visual.*

THREE MESSAGES TO REMEMBER

Think about presentations you have attended. Can you remember much about them? Research has shown that people rarely recall more than three key points from a presentation, whatever the length. Often, they do not manage even three items.

With this in mind, focus hard on your audience: who are they, and what do they want from you? With this information, you can answer the key question – what are the three things that they would most want from your presentation?

This will be the core of your structure, and you will probably want to repeat those three things in different ways as you present. Still holding firmly to your audience and their needs, you can add other information, which ideally, will reinforce your core three points. Do not slip into the 'what do I want to tell them?' mode, when you are making outline notes on your content, but keep that tight audience focus on what they want from you, and, provided you know your audience, your content will flow from that.

Structuring the content

When you have made your notes on content, which will probably be in the form of topic headings, you can address the structure. Here the same method will apply as for report writing, and it will be easier, because you can happily deal in bullet points throughout.

You will not be writing a script, because unless the subject matter is very sensitive and controversial, you will lose all rapport with a small audience if you read to them, as well as sounding inept and boring.

Instead, you will have the elements of your 'flat pack' identified as major headings, and then put them in the sequence that makes most sense to those listening. Refer back to the section on report writing for more on the subject of structure.

One key difference is that unlike a report, they will not be able to refer back to an earlier section, so build in repetition. This will also allow for concentration lapses, which are very frequent for some people. The most acceptable way to repeat things is to follow the old adage:

> *Tell 'em what you're going to tell 'em!*
> *Tell 'em!*
> *Tell 'em what you've told 'em!*

Otherwise known as:

> *Introduction*
> *Key points*
> *Conclusion*

This structure also serves as a road map of your presentation, so that people know what to expect, and are therefore in a more receptive frame of mind.

KEY MESSAGES

- ▶ *Keep your focus on the audience.*
- ▶ *Identify the core three things they want from your presentation.*
- ▶ *Build the structure around those three, with repetition.*
- ▶ *Give the audience a road map, so they can anticipate the journey.*

Getting good feedback

We have already reviewed the kind of feedback you will request from your 'coach', be they a trainer, colleague or friend, whilst you are practising and rehearsing. Continue to request that same feedback whenever you give a presentation. Ideally, brief someone beforehand and ask them for specifics taken from your checklist. Even if you do not have someone in the room who is pre-briefed, you can still ask colleagues what they think. If they are too polite, press them a little with specific questions, and even if they say very little, there is usually something to be gleaned from 'Is there anything I could improve on, or do differently next time?'

Do this consistently, and treat every presentation you give as a learning opportunity.

KEY MESSAGES

▶ *Ask for feedback every time you present.*
▶ *Practise helpful prompts, which make it easier for people to give you their views.*

Closing thoughts

Grasp the subject, the words will follow.

Cato The Elder

Success is not the result of spontaneous combustion. You must set yourself on fire.

Reggie Leach

STEPS TO SUCCESS

▶ *Design your presentation to deliver what your audience want from it.*

▶ *Create a clear structure and use vivid language.*

▶ *Prepare well, so that you feel confident that you are in tune with your client's needs.*

▶ *Practise your delivery style, and get lots of feedback.*

▶ *Practise true deep breathing, so that you believe in its effects.*

▶ *In the moments before you start your presentation focus entirely on the client, and what they need from you.*

▶ *During and at the end of the presentation seek non-verbal feedback from everyone, and then specific verbal feedback from appropriate people.*

▶ *Expect to learn and improve every time.*

14

Running a client workshop/
project meeting

This chapter covers:
- *assembling the right people*
- *briefing the essentials*
- *facilitating a discussion*
- *dealing with awkward questions*
- *winning commitment*

Definition

Some organizations call them workshops, others project meetings, but whatever the label, we are referring to a meeting which is designed to gather data from the client, usually at the start of a project. Note that we are not referring to the type of workshop which is essentially a training course. Designing and running training courses is a quite separate skill, which we have not attempted to address in this book.

Objectives

Be absolutely crystal clear about your objectives for running a workshop, and when you have them written down in front of you, you can decide who the participants should be.

Here is a sample set:

1 *Gather specified project information from the client.*
2 *Get everyone's views on the table.*
3 *Give enough information to the client in order to get 1 and 2.*
4 *Discover any issues or obstacles to implementation.*
5 *Win commitment of participants.*
6 *Give a positive impression of your organization.*

The participants

You will want the people in your meeting to be those who are best able to give you the data you need. It is worth spending time discovering who are the people to target. Organization structures can be misleading. Sometimes more senior people do not know enough detail, sometimes junior people do not have the big picture. Be careful that the organ grinders do not send their most junior monkey. The way to avoid this is to ensure that the client staff fully understand the benefits of investing their time. You may wish to arrange a briefing session for key staff as a preliminary to setting up the meeting.

Insight

Do not underestimate the importance of briefing senior staff in advance. Getting them on board can prevent problems arising later, and is a good investment of your time.

Running the workshop

This is a hybrid activity, requiring skills in several areas at the same time. The key objective of a workshop is to gather data for a project, but in doing that, there are some fairly critical sub-objectives to be met, such as winning the commitment of the client team, and discovering any obstacles which may lie in your path.

It is critical to share your main objectives with the people in the meeting, and give them a plan for the meeting, so that they can see what is required of them and identify with the outcome. This is best presented to them in written form – on a flip chart, for example, so that they can use it as a reference point in the meeting. It is generally not appropriate to share with them your secondary goals concerning obstacles and politics, although sometimes this does emerge, as in this example.

CASE STUDY: THE ROOT PROBLEM

Julie is an HR consultant who was called in by Donald, the managing director of a company to review their compensation and benefits package. She ran a small workshop with the HR team, and soon discovered that the package the company had was already pretty competitive. It was not the best in the market by any means, but it did not require radical surgery. In the workshop she discovered that the real problem was Donald himself, who was highly autocratic, and a very poor communicator. People operated in a climate of fear and uncertainty, which meant that the good ones did not stay for very long. Donald put this down to a poor benefits offering, and told HR to fix it.

Julie then used the workshop to come up with creative solutions to fix the problem, but sadly the best solution was to replace the managing director, which was not a practical option. They did devise a plan to counteract some of the poor communication problems, at least for the staff lower down in the organization, who could be protected from Donald to some degree. They also came up with a plan of what to present to him, to show that the consulting project had been worthwhile. The HR team told Julie, 'It's no good just telling him that the package doesn't need much changing. He's hired you to change it, so you need to do what he asks.' They devise a plan together.

It is clear that Julie will not be able to fix the root problem here, since he was the person who hired her. However, she has achieved a number of key objectives by using the workshop approach:

▶ *She gained a rapid understanding of the current situation, and the real problem, with its political implications.*

- ▶ *She won the confidence of the HR team.*
- ▶ *She has come up with a damage limitation plan, and a proposal to give to the managing director, all with the full commitment of the team.*

If you can achieve the same objectives as Julie, you will be doing well, as, in your case it is unlikely (we hope) that you will be facing the impossible challenge of the managing director being the root of the problem.

Insight

If you can discover that your client is the root cause of the problem before you take on the work, it may be wise not to accept the commission. Julie managed her way round it – think if that will be possible for you.

Let us review the workshop objectives again here:

1 *Gather project information from the client.*
2 *Win client commitment.*
3 *Give enough information to the client in order to get 1 and 2.*
4 *Find out how the political land lies – especially if there are any opponents to the project, or controversial issues.*
5 *Create an action plan the client group in the meeting buys into.*
6 *Give a positive impression of your organization.*

To do all those things, you need the following skills:

a *chairing a meeting;*
b *facilitating a group discussion;*
c *giving a presentation;*
d *political awareness;*
e *influencing skills and winning commitment.*

This may look like a long list, but in fact it is just a breakdown of skills you are almost certainly already using to some degree. It is more helpful to break them down as much as possible, and then put them back together again. Items (c), (d) and (e) are covered in depth in other chapters, so we will pay most attention to chairing and facilitation skills.

Briefing the client

Let's look first at objectives 1 and 3. You want project data from the client – that is your key purpose. To get it, you may well need to give some information. This is where your presentation skills come in, and you can refer to the previous chapter for more information on that, but the key point for a workshop is not to get carried away. Your main aim is to gather data, and you will want to give as much information as necessary to get that data and no more. You will not want the presentation to take the form of a monologue from you. Instead, break it up with questions, and test people's understanding as far as you can.

For example, 'Is everyone clear on that point? I know it's a bit convoluted, so I can give another example if that would be helpful?' Just the slightest nod from one person in response to this should tell you that you need to give further explanation. Usually, for every one person who indicates they are not clear, there are at least three others with the same problem!

Insight

Stay tightly focused on this aim: give them the minimum information they need in order to give you the maximum information you need.

You may also wish to deliver the information in small chunks, so that you cover one area at a time. This is preferable, except where input would not make sense unless it is delivered in one piece. It is really important to put yourself in the client's shoes, and think what would make life easiest for them. In this example, participants have different levels of knowledge.

Sarah is about to run a workshop to gather data for a new product tracking system, and she is planning what she needs to present. There are three different departments involved in the workshop, and she needs specific information from each of them. They also need to understand particular aspects of the system constraints and capabilities, as well as the departmental interfaces. It is because of this last point that she is seeing them together, otherwise she might have seen them separately.

She has thought through the information she needs to give them, and decided that she will need to deliver most of it at the start, because they will need the complete picture from the beginning. There are a few specifics that she can cover when she asks for detailed information, but these things are minor. In case she forgets them, she decides to include them at the beginning too.

What she is not entirely sure about is precisely how much they know already. There have been various briefings and meetings, and some may therefore know more than others. She decides to be very open about this from the start:

'Thank you for coming to the meeting. Our objective today is to gather the information we need from you to set up this part of the system. Now I know that some of you have already been briefed on this, so could you tell me what aspects you are already familiar with?'

The clients then brief each other, at Sarah's careful prompting. She then fills in the gaps, and no one is bored to hear the same thing twice.

Getting a contribution from everyone

It is critical that you get contributions from everyone in your meeting – assuming, of course, that you have the right people there. Spend time discovering precisely who the participants are, and even if you find that you have people who are superfluous, it is still important to get their contribution, not for your benefit, but for theirs. If you have done all the right preparation, and you still do not get the right people, they are still your clients, and you need to win their commitment. Your aim will be that everyone leaves the meeting feeling that they have contributed something useful to an outcome that they understand, and are committed to. They will therefore feel motivated and impressed by you.

Insight

It can be as hard to encourage the silent to speak as it is to keep the talkative quiet! These case studies show you how to achieve this, and build good client relations at the same time.

CASE STUDY: SILENT PARTICIPANTS

Keith is running a workshop with six people. He has checked on precisely who they are before the meeting, and has discovered that Graham has been sent at the last minute to stand in for Terry, who has an urgent problem to deal with. Keith also knows that Susie is very junior, and was not on his original list. The other four people are as planned.

The meeting has been going well, but part way through Keith realizes that Graham and Susie have said nothing. Keith gently invites Susie to comment on a point of detail in her area, which she does very easily. He then asks her a bigger question and she looks uncomfortable: 'I'm not really sure about that. It's not really my area.'

Keith does not want Susie to feel inadequate. 'Sorry, Susie, I should have known that. Will you be able to ask Mark for that information? I think that is Mark's area, isn't it?'

Susie confirms that it is, and that getting the information will be no problem. Face is saved, Susie relaxes, and is then able to volunteer some useful comments.

Keith now turns his attention to Graham. 'Graham, are you happy that the specification will meet your needs on this issue?'

Graham shrugs and says, 'Looks OK, I suppose.'

'Are there areas you would like to explore further?'

'Not really ...', he trails off.

'Are there any other points you'd like to make, Graham? I really don't want to move on unless you're completely satisfied.'

Graham shrugs and says nothing.

Keith now has a problem. Graham is clearly not happy, but is also not prepared to say why. Keith suspects that Graham does not feel confident to comment, but does not want to confess to this. He decides it would be best to leave this until the end of the meeting, when he will suggest a follow-up session with Terry and Graham together. He moves on, and takes care to ask for input from Susie and Graham at intervals, but without putting any pressure on them. He asks Susie less often, since she does volunteer the occasional comment. Graham says nothing at all unless prompted, and so Keith will occasionally say, 'Are you happy with that, Graham?' to which Graham usually replies with a nod and a shrug.

Keith is lucky here, in that the other four members of the group are positive and helpful contributors, but not overly talkative. Consequently no one dominates the meeting, and Keith does not have to police their input.

CASE STUDY: AVOIDING RED HERRINGS

With the group he had last week, Keith had a completely different set of problems. There were eight people with a lot to say. The person who said most, Colin, knew least, and Keith had to be very careful not to be rude to him and just tell him to shut up! What he did was to ask the others if they wanted to hear from Colin on specific issues, and he could be sure of getting a unanimous reply.

'Colin, could I just stop you there a moment. Does everyone want to hear the detail on this item from Colin, as it's not really relevant to ...' Keith did not need to finish the sentence, as a chorus of 'No!' and 'Not now!' drowned his words. Another red herring bit the dust!

Using the power of the group
What Keith is doing to remove this red herring is using the power of the group to silence Colin. Instead of saying, 'Colin, I don't think what you are saying is relevant ...', he asks the group for their view, and he is pretty confident of what they will say. If someone strikes you as annoying, or nit-picking, or overbearing, then the chances are that the group will think the same way. It then becomes much easier for you to say, 'Does everyone agree that we can close down the discussion on location now?', rather than trying to control the individuals yourself.

Needless to say, it also avoids personal animosity. Colin knows the group did not want to hear; you were merely their facilitator.

Maintaining control
The other problem was that everyone would talk at once, so Keith had to establish some rules. 'It's great that you all have so much information to give me, but I can only take it in from one of you at a time. Can we agree that when I hold my hand up you'll all stop speaking, so that we can restore a little order to all this enthusiasm?' This is really telling them to shut up in the nicest way he can manage. They won't all see his hand, of course, but he has set the scene nicely and they will be ready to accept his good intentions in silencing them, when he has to resort to saying, 'Stop for a moment now please ...', as he waves his hand in the air. In doing this he is both controlling the discussion, and maintaining the focus on the workshop objectives.

> **Insight**
>
> Be alert to political issues in any context. Make sure you
> know if anyone opposes your work, and the names of their
> team, as Karen does here.

CASE STUDY: HANDLING POLITICS

Karen finds she has an unexpected visitor to her workshop – one of
Gerald's team, who arrives uninvited, and sits quietly in a corner.
She knows that Gerald is opposed to the project, and that Naomi
will be there to gather ammunition, and possibly to disrupt the
meeting. The other staff do not seem to be aware of any antagonism,
and there are friendly greetings between them all. Karen will treat
Naomi in just the same way as the others, even though she does not
need her input. At intervals she asks check questions of any non-
contributors, of which Naomi is invariably one.

'Is everybody clear on that? Mark? Brian? Naomi?' She gets nods
from each and continues. Then she reaches what she knows is a
controversial point: 'So this change will affect all the departments
listed. Does anyone see any issues with that?'

Naomi becomes very animated. 'It absolutely won't work for our
department. You'll have to do it some other way!'

'What is the specific issue you have, Naomi?'

'The whole thing! It would be a disaster if you go down that route.'

Karen now has a choice, and looking around the room at bemused
faces, it is clear that now is not the time to have a debate. Instead,
she says 'This is clearly a big issue for you Naomi, so I'd like to
meet with you separately and discuss it. Can we defer this item
until that has happened?'

The group murmurs assent – Naomi is alone in her objections. Had
she not been, Karen might have allowed some debate, although
knowing Naomi's political motive, this could have been dangerous.

As a general rule it is best to take politics out of a workshop, as Karen has just done, particularly where the other participants are unaware of the political situation. Often the root of the problem lies outside the control of the people in the meeting, and so any debate will remain unresolved in any case. Karen will report on the meeting to her project manager, and together they will decide what to do about Gerald, rather than Naomi, who is just the messenger. How you might deal with this problem outside the workshop is covered in the section on politics (see Chapter 16).

Reaching decisions

When you chair a meeting, one of your key responsibilities is to help the group reach a conclusion. This may also be required in a workshop.

'So are we all agreed on Option A?' Karen looks round and sees general assent. 'That's fine, then, I shall record that as our conclusion. Now what about the location – I think the Brighton office is favourite?'

There are some murmurs of agreement, but Clive says 'No Karen. John and I are firmly in favour of Bradford.' John nods agreement.

'Is there any way we can agree on location today?' Karen perseveres.

'Sorry, but we need more information, so I think we will have to discuss it again.'

From her knowledge of previous discussions with the project board, Karen is pretty clear that Brighton will be the final choice, but she resists the temptation to impose a decision, or to suggest a majority vote. It is critical that she wins commitment from all her clients, and for the sake of a small delay, it is not worth alienating John and Clive.

She knows it is deeply frustrating to an individual to be asked for their view, and then to have it over-ruled – particularly by someone outside the organization. A majority vote is more acceptable, but the person will still be dissatisfied. The worst thing of all is to pretend to consult, and then announce the decision that has already been made, with little or no regard to the discussion that has just taken place. People see through this very quickly, and view their contribution as a charade. If the decision has been made, it is better just to announce it, and not pretend you are interested in people's views, when they are clearly not being taken into account.

DEFERRING AN ITEM

The other thing that Karen did well here was to 'park' the item for later discussion. She made it very clear that it was not going under the carpet, but would be deferred to another meeting. It often happens that an issue which is of vital importance to someone cannot be dealt with in the meeting. They need to be told how and when it will be covered, so that they are able to let it go, and the meeting can continue. Often it helps to write it down on a flip chart, so they can see it has been recorded. If they think it will get lost, then they are likely to keep on raising it, and hinder the progress of the meeting.

Insight

'Parking' is a useful technique. Write down the item to be parked very visibly, so that everyone can see it. Refer to the follow-up action to be taken in your closing summary.

CASE STUDY: HANDLING DIFFICULT QUESTIONS

Kevin's workshop has started well. He has the right people there, and they all seem keen. He has just finished outlining his 'route map' for the meeting, when Ann asks, 'Kevin, before we start, I'd like to be clear on something that's bothering me. I understand you've never done this type of project before, is that right?'

Kevin has been with the company for six months, and this is certainly his first time. He decides to be honest: 'You are quite right, Ann, this is my first time on a project of this type, although I have done quite similar work.'

'I didn't actually mean you, Kevin, although thank you for telling us, I meant your company.'

She is right, and he decides to prevaricate. 'Can I just ask where you are going with your questions, Ann? I'm happy to answer them, but I'm not sure what purpose ...'

'I just want to know who I'm dealing with. If it's a load of novices, then the information I give and the amount of checking I do will be greater than if I know you are seriously experienced in this field.'

The rest of the group nods assent, and Kevin is back in the hot seat. 'Well, I think it comes down to degrees of similarity. I cannot give you a definitive answer here, but what I do know is that our company is very experienced in managing projects that are similar, and have been consistently successful. I think it is the way we work, our attention to detail and our project management skills that will deliver for you. And that is more important than whether we have done exactly the same thing for another client.'

Kevin sees a positive response from the group to his words, but Ann still looks doubtful. 'If you want a more precise answer, Ann, I can find out more detail after the meeting. Shall we talk then?'

Ann shrugs, and this is Kevin's cue to move on swiftly, and hope that she does not follow this up afterwards. If she does, he will refer the problem upwards.

Here, Kevin has succeeded in doing two key things – he has maintained integrity, by not lying about his own, or his company's experience, and he has maintained credibility, by placing emphasis on their working methods and track record, rather than their specific project experience.

The group was clearly happy with this response, and when he saw that Ann was not, he offered her precise detail after the meeting, which made it difficult for her to continue the debate with him. She would have appeared to be nit-picking, and her shrug acknowledged that.

Insight

Do I lie to a client? You want to keep your reputation for integrity, so lying should of course be avoided. Usually long-term ethics win over short-term gains.

When faced with this type of question, it is always a balancing act between honesty and credibility. If in doubt, honesty wins, because if the client discovers you have deceived them, the relationship will be severely damaged. Better to tell the truth, and lose credibility. On the other hand, there is no need to rush to the client and tell them that this is your first time, when you have not been asked. It goes without saying that you would not take on a project that you were not competent to complete, so you are justified in maintaining as much credibility as you can.

Closing the meeting

Karen concludes her workshop like this: 'I'd like to thank everyone for their contribution. We have achieved all the objectives on the flip chart except for item three, location. There will be another discussion on this topic when we have more information.

'Now, is there anything else anyone wants to raise? No? Well then, I'll be writing to you all by the end of the week with a summary and action points. Thank you all very much for coming. I think we've made an excellent start.'

The conclusion is brief, no need to go over any detail, but useful to summarize so that the participants feel a sense of achievement. It is vital that any deferred items are mentioned. Karen knows John and Clive will be poised to complain if she forgets. She thanks the contributors, describes the next step, and ends on a positive note, all designed to reinforce commitment, and leave a positive impression of her company.

Closing thoughts

Whether you believe you can do a thing or not, you are right.

Henry Ford

I hear and I forget. I see and I remember. I do and I understand.

Confucius

STEPS TO SUCCESS

When setting up and running a client workshop or project meeting:

▶ *Be clear on the objectives.*

▶ *Invest time and effort to get the right participants.*

▶ *Give them a 'route map' for the meeting.*

▶ *Check their knowledge levels.*

▶ *Brief them well, but only give them the information they need, and check their understanding.*

▶ *Get contributions from everyone.*

▶ *Use the power of the group to control the discussion.*

▶ *Win commitment to decisions, never impose them.*

▶ *Identify political issues, but keep any political discussion outside the meeting.*

▶ *If you defer an item, record it, and mention it at the end, to reassure its owner(s) that it is not forgotten.*

▶ *If faced with awkward questions, put integrity before credibility when you reply.*

▶ *Before closing the meeting, do a final check that you have met your objectives.*

▶ *Summarize what the meeting has achieved, and define the next step.*

▶ *Leave your participants with a sense of achievement and a positive impression of your company.*

15

Building client relationships

This chapter covers:
- *listening*
- *creating rapport*
- *filters and styles*

Building client relationships is a fundamental skill, and perhaps more important if you have not been part of the sales process. In converting a prospect to a client, you are bound to have built a relationship, but when you walk into the client offices for the first time to begin the project, you are starting from cold.

Building a relationship begins with effective communication, and listening, not talking, is by far the most important skill of the two. Everyone interviewed for this book was unanimous that listening was a vital skill in a consultant, and they all had stories to tell about the consequences of not listening. However, just using your ears will not make you an effective listener. Let us examine what is involved in this activity, which everyone believes they can do, and most people take for granted.

Insight

How well do you listen? Be honest in your self-assessment, so that you can work on improving, if you need to. It should be easier to listen to a client, because what they say really matters to you, but if they ramble on in a boring tone, you will have to make a real effort, and this is where a new technique is useful.

Whole body listening

Being proactive when you are listening is a skill you need to work at, and it involves using your whole body. If this seems a strange concept, welcome that response, because a fresh approach to this subject is helpful.

Working from the top down, your mind will need to be completely focused on the person you are listening to, not on what you might say next, nor on tomorrow's problems.

Your *eyes* will be collecting lots of information about the person you are talking to, from their dress to their emotional state – you will be looking for all those non-verbal signals. Your gaze will stay with them, and not wander around the room.

Your *ears* will be busy not just hearing the words, but also the tone of voice, hesitancy, and everything about the way something is said.

Your *mouth* will generally be shut, but will open occasionally to offer encouraging words and sounds, such as 'Oh?', and 'Mmm'.

Your *body* will reflect the posture of the person who is talking. If they are sitting, do not stand over them. If they are relaxed and laid back, so will you be. Do not mimic them slavishly, but match their style, so that they can see that you are in tune with them.

ACTIONS

This skill needs practice, so you might want to surprise your family or friends by trying it out in a social context. A good exercise is to take a social situation with someone you do not normally talk to very much. Perhaps you have little in common. Give yourself twenty minutes to find out what they feel passionate about. It might be jam making or sky-diving – the point is that you do not get distracted by the subject, and can focus on listening rather than talking. Consciously check what all the different parts of your body are doing. If your ears are working well but your eyes have found an interesting distraction, then bring them back to your subject, and see how differently the person responds when you look at them.

Insight

The key is to treat this as a whole body exercise. Be aware of every bit of you, and work out if all these parts are helping you to listen, or providing distractions!

Building rapport

If someone feels that you are really listening to them, then that is a great start to building rapport. There are three steps in this process, called:

1 *Match*
2 *Pace*
3 *Lead*

Matching means getting in tune with the person you are talking to. For example, Henry loves cooking. He talks of it with expansive gestures, and great enthusiasm for the creative expression he finds in the kitchen. You respond with animation, and frame your questions with expressive gestures.

Sally adores sky-diving, and to your surprise, speaks of it in distant dreamy tones, describing a sense of peace that she finds in the silent air. You respond in tones of quiet interest, so as not to interrupt her dream. She speaks slowly, and so do you.

These are examples of matching and pacing. When you are in tune with someone like this, operating at their pace, then you can start to lead them where you want to go.

In Henry's case, it might go like this:

'Just give me some chillies and a wok, and I can do anything!'
(Arms thrown wide!)

'That's fantastic, Henry! I can taste those flavours now! Is Chinese your speciality?' (Hand gesture.)

'I do the best stir fry ever!'

'Have you ever cooked for ten?'

In Sally's case, the pattern will be the same, although it will look and sound very different, since instead of animation and excitement, we have calm and quiet.

'It's such a peaceful experience, up there, so calming.'
(Closes eyes.)

'I can sense how you feel, Sally – complete serenity.'

'Mmm.' Sally's eyes are still closed.

'Is it always like this?'

'Every time.'

'Even the first time?'

'Not quite the first time.' Sally's eyes open. 'There's a lot to think about the first time.'

'I thought so. How would I feel, doing it for the first time?'

Note how well Henry and Sally have been matched and paced before they are led in a new direction. The listener is there, tasting the food, and feeling the serenity.

Let us now look at a case study where matching does not happen.

CASE STUDY: MISMATCHING

Phil goes to see the client project manager, Raj. They have been
working together for several weeks now, and have a reasonable
working relationship.

'Raj, do you have a minute?'

'Well, actually …'

'It's just that something urgent has come up.'

'What?'

'Diana has just told me she has to work on a different project
as of tomorrow. That will create a serious problem.'

'Can we talk about it later?'

'I really need an answer now, Raj.'

'Sorry Phil, I just can't deal with this now, come and see me
tomorrow.'

It is very clear that Phil was oblivious to Raj's needs and feelings in
this interchange, and therefore did a mismatch. Let him try again:

'Raj, do you have a minute?'

'Well, actually Phil, I've just had a big bombshell land on my desk, so now is not a good time.'

'Okay – I hope it's nothing to do with the project.'

'No – it's just that the Board has decided to pay us a State Visit from Canada next week, so that means mountains of work.'

'I know just how you feel. I had the same problem with our Group Managing Director last month. It's out with the PowerPoint and everyone on parade!'

'Exactly! And no time to do any real work.'

'Speaking of which, Raj, I do need to talk to you about a project issue. I know at a time like this you will just want the project to run really smoothly so that you don't need to think about it. If we can just iron out this problem, I can leave you in peace to get on with the state visit.'

'Absolutely right. Let's get it out of the way now.'

Phil did an excellent job of matching and pacing Raj the second time. He empathized perfectly over the 'state visit', and was able to make his request a natural progression to lead Raj where he wanted him to go.

KEY MESSAGES

▶ *Practise match/pace/lead in a safe – probably social – situation.*
▶ *Use your whole body listening skills to assess the state the person is in.*
▶ *Match that state and pace them. For example, if they speak slowly, so will you.*
▶ *Then adjust the pace to lead them where you want to go.*
▶ *If they do not follow, go back to matching and try again.*

Rapport breakers

Having examined some of the elements in building rapport, it is worth looking at some of the things that can break it, particularly as they are everyday expressions that we may use without realizing their impact. Take a look at the following interchange, to see if you can identify the problem phrases.

'Do you realize that this is a serious project issue, James?'

'I know that, Murray!'

'You should be making contingency plans. It seems to me that the whole project depends on how you manage this crisis scenario. If you take my advice, then a group crisis team could formulate some alternative outcomes, and ...'

'Thank you, Murray, I know what I'm doing,'

'But with respect, James ...'

'I said I know what I'm doing! Now can you just ...'

'I hate to say this, but ...'

Insight

At this point we can imagine that James might hit Murray! Can you identify why – just from the words he uses? You can imagine the tone that goes with them, but for now, focus on the words themselves.

Below we repeat that same conversation and highlight the 'red rags' which are guaranteed to alienate and upset people.

'<u>Do you realize</u> that this is a serious project issue, James?'

'I know that, Murray!'

'You <u>should</u> be making contingency plans. It seems to me that the whole project depends on how you manage this crisis scenario. <u>If you take my advice</u>, then a group crisis team could <u>formulate some alternative outcomes,</u> and ...'

'Thank you, Murray, I know what I'm doing,'

'But <u>with respect</u>, James ...'

'I said I know what I'm doing! Now can you just ...'

'I <u>hate to say this, but</u> ....'

These 'red rags' fall into the following categories:

- ▶ **Assumed deficiency:** *'Do you realize ...'* or *'Have you thought ...'* assume that you have not! This is insulting.
- ▶ **Parental language:** *'You should ...'; 'You ought ...'; 'You must ...'.* All of these are prescriptive instructions that parents often give to their children. This is not recommended between adults! Similarly *'If you take my advice'* is thrusting the unwanted onto the unwilling.
- ▶ **Pompous or formal language:** *This is generally a real turn-off. James does not want to hear about Murray's plan to 'formulate alternative outcomes'.*
- ▶ **Insincerity:** *'With respect' means the opposite! 'I hate to say this' means, 'I'm going to enjoy saying this.'*

KEY MESSAGES

If you find yourself using any of these expressions, there is a solution. It is called respect. If you have respect for the person you are talking to, these rapport breakers just will not happen.

Imagine that this is a person who is extremely wise and talented, who you look up to and admire. If you see them in this light, respect follows automatically. Then you will find that there is no danger of assuming deficiencies, or speaking to them like a child.

Filters and styles

Another key element in building rapport is recognizing different filters and styles in other people. Some people are easy to get on with; they seem to be immediately on your wavelength. Others feel like very hard work.

The chances are that the people you get on with have similar filters and styles to you. An example would be someone who is laid back, and does not take things too seriously. Everything is done at a relaxed pace; time is not important. If this describes you, then you will be off to a good start together. If, on the other hand, you are someone who is impatient for results, who eats and talks quickly and likes to use time efficiently, then you may have trouble relating to our relaxed friend.

If you ask someone what is important to them about a business presentation, for example, you will get some consistent remarks, such as it must be interesting and relevant, but other aspects may vary; for example,

'I like a presentation to give me the big picture. If there's too much detail I get bored very quickly.'

'I don't agree. I like a presentation to be thorough, and you can't see the big picture unless you have all the detail there too.'

These are examples of two very different filters – the preference for detail, or lack of it, and the need to see things on the grand scale before dealing with any detail.

Think of a current client: can you identify their key filters? This can be useful in many ways. If a client who likes big picture suddenly asks for detail, treat this as an alarm bell. It may indicate they are uncomfortable about something and are looking for reassurance in detail.

There are many different filters that people apply to their map or view of the world, but here are some major ones:

▶ Focus on detail   or on the 'big picture'
▶ Focus on things/systems   or on people/feelings
▶ Focus on being proactive   or being reactive
▶ Focus on looking for similarity or for difference
▶ Focus on the past   or on the present or the future.

If you imagine a client called Adam who loves detail and similarity, and has a focus on things rather than people, then that knowledge will have a major impact on how you present a report to him. You might say: 'This is very similar to other successful implementations in parallel environments. It covers all aspects of the topic in full detail, with complete systems information included, and additional references as appendices.'

This would be the opposite of what you would present to Graham, who is very focused on people, dislikes detail, and looks for new ways of doing things: 'This implementation has very special features which will be unique to your organization. The report covers all the top line information you will need, so that you have a complete over-view of the system. The impact on staff is highlighted throughout.'

STYLES

Then there are different styles – such as:

▶ *Pace – fast or slow, relaxed or pressured;*
▶ *Manner – formal or informal.*

Styles tend to be easier to spot than filters, but if you are wondering how you find out about all these things, then the best way is to ask. This sounds so totally obvious, but it is something that we rarely think of doing. If the client asks for a presentation, instead of saying yes and rushing off to prepare, you could say: 'Could you run through quickly what you are expecting from this presentation?' You can also check length, and style: 'How long have we got, by the way, and what medium shall we use?'

If the client has no preference, that tells you something, but if they are speaking for someone else, it is better to check about them specifically: 'Do you know how much time the MD has? Does he prefer formal presentations? How much detail … etc.'

Insight

It's not difficult, asking questions like these about a presentation or report, as opposed to asking someone 'Do you like detail?' which is a much more personal question, and one to which you may not get a straight answer.

The more information you have, the better you can tailor what you deliver. If your audience is mixed, then you will be addressing the politically significant client(s), and matching their requirements as your priority. If you know that there are detail freaks in the meeting, but they are not your prime audience, then tell them that they can read detail in the notes, or that you can cover detail with them separately.

KEY MESSAGES

▶ First of all, identify your own filters and styles. Ask someone who knows you well if you are not sure.
▶ Now think about key clients or prospects, and see how much you know about them. If the answer is not a lot, then you might want to practise on someone reasonably 'safe' before you start in earnest. Think of someone you know, but do not get on with particularly well. Take an opportunity to meet

*them informally, and work on your questions and observation.
It is often easier to question someone about what is important
to them regarding a specific work issue, rather than asking
general social questions.*

▶ *It is likely that you will find that you get on more easily with
people who share your styles and filters, but it is an interesting
exercise in itself to test this out. If they are different, you can
then experiment to see what effect matching them will produce –
you may be surprised by the positive response that you get!*

Closing thoughts

Listen or thy tongue will keep thee deaf.

American Indian Proverb

**Everyone is kneaded out of the same dough but not
baked in the same oven.**

Yiddish Proverb

STEPS TO SUCCESS

▶ *Listening is a critical skill for a consultant: practise it actively, with your whole body.*

▶ *Practise match, pace, lead – it gives you immediate feedback – use it to improve next time.*

▶ *Think of your clients with respect, to avoid using language that could break rapport.*

▶ *Identify and match your clients' filters and styles.*

16

Handling client politics

This chapter covers:
- *political structure*
- *political intelligence*

Politics viewed from inside an organization can be challenging. The challenge increases when you are dealing with client politics, and often a major project will generate its own set of politics. It will involve change, and change normally has its initiators and its enemies.

Political structure

Most organizations have some level of politics, and the first thing to understand is the political structure. This comes in three levels, which it is easiest to think of as concentric circles (see Figure 5).

This method of analysing politics was originated by Target Marketing Inc., now part of Oracle Corporation.

The inner circle consists of the real movers and shakers, who set the culture and make all the key decisions. Note that the published hierarchy may not always map neatly onto these circles. The PA to the Managing Director might be a central figure in the inner circle, as might the wife of the Chairman. An excellent example of this was Nancy Reagan during her husband's presidency.

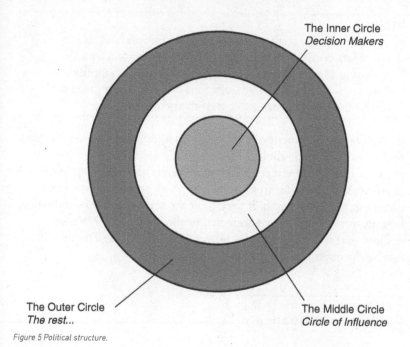

The Inner Circle
Decision Makers

The Outer Circle
The rest...

The Middle Circle
Circle of Influence

Figure 5 Political structure.

The middle circle is called the circle of influence, and consists of people who understand the political structure, know that they are not in the inner circle, but have ways of influencing one or more inner circle members, and are quite well informed by their contact as to what is really going on. They are usually the key implementers of inner circle decisions.

The outer circle consists of people who may not know that there are circles at all, never mind which one they are in! They are the people that things happen to.

If you are in a position to draw the three circles, and name the key players in the first two, you have an excellent understanding of your client, which will be a great help to you in project implementation. It would be exceptional to have all this information before you start your project, but work on gleaning whatever you can, and stay alert to political issues in any situation.

If you find an opponent of the project in a meeting you are holding,
find out which circle they are in, who they are allied to, what the
political history is between their most senior ally and your project
sponsor. It is also vital to know where your project sponsor sits –
ideally in the inner circle. If they're in the second circle of influence,
how powerfully are they connected to the inner circle? Never
assume that seniority bestows power. The Managing Director may
not be the most powerful person on the Board.

Political intelligence

The way to discover all this information is to listen for clues in any
client interchange. If someone says, 'We can't do that, x would never
agree to it.' That suggests 'x' has power, and a few follow-up questions
from you can prove very fruitful. People often have a lot to say about
those in power, usually because they are nervous of expressing their
own feelings to the individual concerned, so they tell others instead.

The other way to find out about your client's political structure is
to ask your tame allies within the client organization. Every project
will have at least one dedicated supporter, and there is your ally.
Sit down and ask them to describe the power structure. Who are
the key people to convince, who will put obstacles in the project's
path, etc.? You can do this openly because it is all in the interest of
the project's success, and again, people are often very forthcoming
on this subject – if they are politically aware.

If your prime ally is someone who does not take much notice of these
things, then find another ally, or ask them to recommend someone to
talk to. Take greater care with your questions now, unless you are sure

that they are truly on your side, since you risk getting misinformation, or alienating someone who does not wish to answer this type of question. Your project needs allies and supporters, so if these are thin on the ground, you need to set about winning some more! If unsure, save your political questions until you feel you are on safe ground.

CASE STUDY: DIVIDED LOYALTY TO CLIENT

Clara has been having weekly meetings with Toby, her main client contact. She started the project three months ago, was enjoying the work, and all went well to begin with, but then Toby came to ask her to make a very minor change. Clara agreed, as it was only minor. However, after that there was another, equally minor, and several more, and now Clara has realized that the cumulative changes add up to something substantial, and the project is now off track. Her manager, James, knows about the changes, they are all in her weekly report, but she is fairly sure that he has not realized what the implications are yet, and gives him a call.

They are due to meet Toby and his boss next Friday for a milestone review, and Clara asks James how they should handle the meeting. They know that Toby's boss is new, and Toby is not getting on well with him – Toby appears very stressed and insecure.

They discuss the options. Clara asks, 'Shall I sit down with Toby, explain the whole situation, and then let him decide how to handle the milestone review?'

'I'm not comfortable about that,' James replies. 'He might want to cover up the whole thing. How about if I have a word in his boss's ear, tell him the problem, and ask how he'd like it handled?'

'That would really put a knife firmly in Toby's back if you do that! Although, of course it protects us. Suppose we just wait for the meeting, tell it straight, and then let things sort themselves out between Toby and his boss?'

'If both of them are taken by surprise, that will reflect badly on us. I think I'd rather ring his boss.' James sounds impatient.

'If you do that it will destroy our working relationship with Toby – he'll never trust us again. I see him practically every day, and I don't want us to appear so disloyal to him. Give me a couple of hours to think about it and I'll ring you back.' Clara puts the phone down and heaves a big sigh just as Toby's boss walks by.

'You look very worried, Clara, is there a problem with the project I should know about?'

Insight

You might now want to put yourself in Clara's place, and decide what you will say to Toby's boss. She hardly ever sees him, certainly never without James, and this is a very rare invitation to discuss the project, and begin to establish a working relationship.

Here are the options which Clara considers:

▶ *be non-committal*
▶ *ask to go into his office and tell him the whole story*
▶ *say everything is fine*
▶ *say it would be best if he discusses the project with James.*

Clara decides that she must remain loyal to Toby, even though she fears his days may be numbered in the organization. She tells Toby's boss that she is just about to prepare a project review to discuss with James, that there is a lot of analysis to be done, and that everything will be ready for the milestone review next Friday. He frowns, but says nothing more and goes off. She has missed her chance to impress. She rings James and tells him what has happened.

'Well, you've set things up very nicely for Friday, Clara!' James is very annoyed. 'Apparently everything's fine today, and then we hit them with a major bombshell. And you realize I can't ring him either now – that's very clever. I'll call him in two days' time, after we've had this theoretical review meeting you told him about.'

'I'm sorry you see things that way, James. I've decided that the best thing I can do is to sit down with Toby and go over everything, so that he's prepared for what's coming. If he wants to do a cover up, I'll tell him you won't wear that, we have to tell it straight, and he has to find a way of handling that in the meeting.'

'Is he capable of handling it, Clara?'

'No, I don't think so. There's going to be trouble whatever happens, but at least we won't be going behind his back. Shall I call you after I've seen him and let you know how it went?'

James sighs. 'Okay Clara, let's hope Toby stays in his job long enough to appreciate your loyalty.'

Insight

Imagine how you might feel if you were in Clara's shoes now. You've upset your boss, and potentially created a big problem with the client. This is a complex conflict of loyalties.

In fact Toby coped far better than Clara expected, he came up with some creative proposals at the meeting which solved the immediate problems, and he did so well that he was promoted at the end of the year. He is just in the process of commissioning a third project from Clara's company. James congratulates Clara on her astute handling of the client, as he takes all the credit for the new business!

Things might have gone very differently, of course. Suppose Clara had succumbed to the temptation of seeing Toby's boss, and had spilled the beans. He might have said something like this:

'I'm very alarmed to hear about all this, Clara. What does Toby have to say about it?'

'Well, I haven't actually told him yet,' Clara stammers.

'So why are you telling me, when you should be telling Toby?'

Toby's boss immediately sees the disloyalty, and views this as an improper conversation, in hierarchical terms, despite the fact that he initiated it. On the other hand, it might have been just the information he was looking for to complete his case for dismissal. You are dealing here with client politics, and it is so important that you do not get drawn into them, as you may well end up on the wrong side!

CASE STUDY: THE BLAME CULTURE

Politics can be very difficult to handle when they are embedded in a company culture. Mary at Pecaso described an exceptional case. 'Pecaso specialize in implementing SAP HR systems, and we won this contract with a very traditional company in the North West of England. This company had a number of small subsidiaries, and the implementation was complex because they had lots of small groups of staff on different terms and conditions. A previous implementation by a different supplier had failed. Two of the main board directors, although apparently very positive, played a constant political game of nice cop, nasty cop, with the nice cop providing the nasty cop with all the bullets.

'Soon after the project began, there was clear lack of commitment on the client side, and John, the Managing Consultant put the project on hold, and then renegotiated the terms of engagement. The situation improved for a while, but as time went on, it was clear that the client did not have the energy or the resources needed, which meant even more effort from us. When a meeting was called to discuss an issue, the priority was to allocate blame. John explained: "I would tell them not to waste time finding fault, but just to get on with fixing the problem, but it wasn't any good, until they'd found someone to blame they couldn't go forward, it was so much part of their culture."

'The whole situation was made feasible only by the project sponsor, the Finance Director. He would regularly receive a list of complaints about us, and call in John to discuss them. John would go through them, and almost invariably find that none of them had been raised with him by his project manager. The implications of this were that the client staff were breaking the agreement with us, where issues should be raised through the project structure, and were simply sending secret complaints to the sponsor direct.

'Fortunately the sponsor's view of this was the right one – and he refused to accept any complaints unless it could be shown that they had come through the agreed channels, and this eliminated almost all of them. Because of him, the project did reach a conclusion, based on the terms of engagement we had renegotiated.'

KEY MESSAGES

▶ *This case study illustrates the kind of client you might want to avoid completely, if you can detect the culture problems early enough in the sales process.*
▶ *Often this is not possible, in which case, identifying the political structure and building a really solid relationship with the project sponsor is vital. Without this, the project would have been impossible to complete.*
▶ *When the client demonstrated lack of commitment early on, a renegotiation of contract terms was absolutely the right thing to do. Just to soldier on would have given the client lots of scope to blame you, as things went further off track.*
▶ *Having a really tight complaints procedure, agreed up-front with the client, was also vital in this situation, where politics are going to work against you. In fact, all operating procedures, especially change control, need to be dealt with in the same clear and firm way.*

Closing thoughts

Man is by nature a political animal.

Aristotle

Nearly all men can stand adversity, but if you want to test a man's character, give him power.

Abraham Lincoln

STEPS TO SUCCESS

▶ *Analyse the political structure of your current client(s).*

▶ *Identify your allies and any opponents.*

▶ *Ensure that your project framework is strong enough to withstand political attack.*

▶ *If you hit a political problem, ensure that you have someone outside the client organization to help you to solve it.*

17

Influencing and negotiation

This chapter covers:
- *influencing techniques*
- *negotiation skills*
- *managing conflict*

Influencing techniques

Sitting at the core of influencing skills is a critical value which underlies all relationships: trust. Without trust, influencing skills will not work. Here is the basic equation:

$$No\ trust = No\ influence$$

People see the application of influencing skills without trust as manipulation, and react accordingly. If you are thinking this is very obvious, then can you honestly say that you have never tried to influence someone without having established trust, and discovered that it does not work?

When asked about building client relationships, Leon Sadler said: 'I endeavour to create opportunities and give them reasons to trust me.' Clearly this is not something you do to the client – they choose whether to trust you or not. This means that learning all the persuasive words in the book will not win you influence, unless, for a short while at least, you have also won trust. 'Would you buy a used car from this man?' is a well-worn cliché, but is another way of saying 'Do you trust him?'

So why should the client trust you? Trust is normally built over time: you keep your promises; what you say is seen to be accurate and truthful; you are open about what you do, what you know, and also what you do not know.

Insight

You can build trust in very small ways: being punctual for meetings, always doing what you say you will do. Saying you don't know can build trust, as long as the knowledge is not central to the project!

In addition to this objective verification, people also detect non-verbal signals which they associate – not always correctly – with trustworthy people. These include the classics, like looking people in the eye, sounding confident, and relating strongly to the other person's needs. The unscrupulous used car salesman succeeds largely through doing this well. They also have qualities of apparent openness, and might appear to confess to something minor, in order to build a reputation of honesty.

This can all be summarized as building rapport, which was covered in the previous chapter. If you have not read it, do so now, as it is fundamental to influencing skills.

In summary, to influence successfully:

▶ *build rapport*
▶ *act with integrity*
▶ *value the other person's interests.*

CASE STUDY: BEING OPEN

Jodi and Carol have been working together on a project for only a short while, and Jodi's performance is erratic. They are consequently a little behind schedule, and Jodi suggests working over the weekend to catch up.

'We don't need to do that, Jodi. If we just work a bit longer early next week, we can soon catch up. The review meeting isn't 'til Thursday, so we've plenty of time.'

'I'd feel more comfortable if we were back on track by Monday, Carol. We could do it if we just worked Saturday and Sunday morning.'

'I really don't want to do that – I've got a lot on this weekend, and it would be difficult to fit in the time. I really don't see why ...'

'Carol, you're really efficient, I'm sure you could manage at least a long half day.'

Insight

You can see that Jodi is not getting anywhere with her attempts at persuasion. Can you work out why? Think about the reasons, before you read on.

There are several reasons why Jodi is not succeeding:

1 *Carol has found Jodi's work to be erratic, therefore she questions her reliability.*
2 *Her commitment is also in question, for the same reason, and this desire to work at the weekend is therefore inconsistent with her previous behaviour.*
3 *Because of this, Carol may suspect an ulterior motive, which Jodi is not telling her about.*
4 *Jodi has not given Carol sufficient motive to work at the weekend, and indeed is not sensitive to Carol's needs in this regard.*

All this adds up to the fact that Carol does not trust Jodi, and does not feel that Jodi has Carol's interest at heart. Carol decides to play it straight with Jodi: 'Look, Jodi, you've said nothing to convince me to do this. Let's be completely open about things – tell me the real reason why you want to work at the weekend?'

After some hesitation Jodi explains that she is having problems with her partner, which is why her performance has been erratic.

He is away on business over the weekend, but they have agreed to spend lots of time together next week to sort things out.

'So tell me what's in it for me, Jodi?'

'Not a lot, I suppose, Carol, now I think about it, except some free time next week when you don't need it. I think if I work for longer at the weekend, I can probably cover for both of us, so you can forget the whole thing, and perhaps just do a little checking on Monday. I'm sorry I raised the issue at all – you just enjoy your weekend.'

Do you think that Carol will go along with Jodi's last suggestion?

In reality, she decided differently: 'Well, Jodi, now I understand the real situation, I'll be happy to help. I'll come in for a couple of hours on Saturday morning, we can divide up the work, and then I'll carry on again on Monday, and if necessary Tuesday evening – that should cover all eventualities, and leave me free to enjoy most of my weekend.'

Several things have happened to enable this change to take place.

1 *Jodi has been open about her problems and her motive.*
2 *She has satisfactorily explained her erratic behaviour.*
3 *Both of these things allow Carol to trust her to a reasonable degree.*
4 *Jodi has recognized (with some prompting) that she is not offering any incentive to Carol, and has therefore withdrawn her request for help.*

This has the immediate effect of removing the pressure from Carol. This is a critical step in the influencing process: giving people the freedom not to do what you are suggesting. When this happens, Carol decides that she will help after all, on her terms, and under no pressure, with the motive of helping out someone with a problem she understands and can identify with.

KEY MESSAGES

▶ *Honesty leads to trust.*
▶ *Seeing the other person's perspective is vital.*
▶ *Removing the pressure is a powerful tool.*

Insight

When influencing, put yourself in the other person's shoes and ask the key question: 'What's in it for me?' If you have a good answer that you truly believe will be theirs, your influencing will be to show how you can give them what they want.

The next case study shows that even when you have good rapport and trust in a long-standing relationship, influencing can still be a challenge.

CASE STUDY: UNDERSTANDING MOTIVATION

Jason has been working with Nigel for many months, and they get on well together. Jason wants to introduce some new software into the project, but Nigel is resisting.

'We don't need it, Jay. By the time we've both got the hang of it, we'll have wasted more time than we've saved.'

'But Don tells me that it will have a real impact. He's been raving about it ever since he tried it.'

'I don't have a lot of faith in what Don says. Let's just carry on as we are.'

Jason is clearly not getting anywhere with Nigel. He has rapport, and mutual trust. He's offered Nigel a good reason to change, but he won't accept it. At this point Jason asks a critical and much neglected question. It is much neglected because it is so obvious, and because it is so obvious, people feel that they should not ask it, that they need to be more subtle.

'What do I have to do to convince you about this software, Nigel?'

'I'm not sure you can do anything, Jay.'

'Is there nothing that would persuade you?'

'Can't think of anything.'

'Do you want to be persuaded?'

'No, not really.'

'And why's that?'

'I don't want to have anything to do with anything that Don has recommended. He thinks he knows it all, and I just don't want to give him the satisfaction of seeing us using the stuff.'

Now Jason knows what he's up against. If he had continued with his original line of persuasion, it would have led nowhere. Instead he asked those two vital questions:

▶ *'What do I have to do to convince/persuade you to …?'*
▶ *'Do you want to be persuaded?'*

Not everyone will give you the answer on a plate, but some will, and most will give you some useful information, so you have little to lose by asking. If you think that the question is unsubtle and will make your intentions plain, you are probably labouring under the false illusion that your intentions are hidden! Most people on the receiving end of any persuasive approach are normally only too well aware what is going on, and will almost be relieved to receive an open question.

Key steps in influencing

▶ *Find a non-critical opportunity to practise your influencing skills.*
▶ *Build rapport, so that you feel in tune with the other person, have matched and paced them, and can lead them in the direction you want them to go.*

- *Act with integrity, so that trust is established as early as possible. Above all, this means being open, and delivering on whatever you commit to deliver.*
- *See the other person's viewpoint, and identify what is in it for them.*
- *Ask how best to convince them.*
- *Demonstrate how you can meet their needs, and if you can enable them to discover that for themselves, so much the better.*
- *Take the pressure off, so that they feel they have choice, and can make their own decision. This is the most powerful form of persuasion.*

The win–win approach to negotiation

Let us first consider when you will need negotiation skills. As a consultant, you will encounter the need to negotiate in various situations, no matter what role you play. You may be involved in the sales process, where negotiation is almost always a key element. Or you may only get involved post sales, when everything is supposedly nailed down tightly, but invariably the customer will ask for something that is not in the specification, or want to bring forward a date, or make some change to methodology, which will mean that you end up negotiating with them over it. This means that wherever you are in the consulting field, you will need negotiation skills.

Insight

Recognize negotiation for what it is, especially when it comes disguised as a casual request, suggesting that a casual reply is all that is needed.

YOUR MINDSET

Your mental approach to negotiation is all. If you hold the presupposition that there is a solution to every problem, then this will help to deliver to you the key skill you need for negotiation. This skill may not be the first that springs to mind, but it is the most vital. It is creativity: creativity to find that solution, and to create a win–win outcome.

The win–win outcome sounds like a cliché, but only because it works! This will also be part of your mindset – you are not seeking victory at your client's expense. You are creatively searching for that solution which delivers victory to you both – except it is not really a victory, since no battle has been fought. You have simply found the best way to meet both your needs. Hold on to that line of thinking whilst you consider the next case study, and examine your reaction to the client's demands.

CASE STUDY: MISINTERPRETATION

The small engineering company that Judy is working for has never used a consultant before. It feels like a great extravagance to most of them, and Judy's time and effort have been monitored closely. It is only a small project, to produce an outline salary structure, and Judy is in the final week when Peter, the managing director, makes a casual remark which throws her completely.

'Will we need to invest in new hardware for the system you are proposing?'

She is uncertain how to respond, but then decides to take the bull by the horns there and then.

'I think you may have misunderstood what I am delivering at the end of next week. A new salary system is the structure you will use, I am not looking at the software to administer it.'

'But that's what we're expecting.'

'I didn't know that until this moment! It's not in the brief though, and I would not expect to ...'

'What do you mean, not in the brief! It says a new salary system, and that's what we're paying you for!'

How do you think Judy is feeling now? You, sitting calmly observing, are in the best position to tell her that she now has a negotiation opportunity to enjoy. That she will be feeling at her most creative at this moment, and wanting to make the client feel good by generating a win–win outcome.

Since you know very well that she is feeling none of these things right now, you can readily identify with the difficulty of doing a brilliant piece of negotiation on the spot, from the back foot.

She does as you advise:

'Peter, I can see that we have a major issue here. Let me go away and think about it for a little while, then I'll come and see you to discuss it. When are you free this afternoon?'

'Any time after three. The sooner the better – but can't we deal with it now? I'm very unhappy about this.'

'That makes two of us, Peter, but I need some time to put some thoughts together. I'll see you at three.'

In buying this time, Judy has been careful not to diminish the problem. Peter knows that it is a major issue, and totally unsolved at this point. She has not made any reassuring noises because she does not have a solution at this moment, but she now has time to think, and get herself into the positive and creative frame of mind she needs to find the solution that she knows is there for her win–win outcome.

The one question that we might want to ask her now is whether she has enough information about the client's expectations to find her solution. If not, she needs to get as much as possible now, before she starts working on the problem. At present, she has defined the problem as: 'Client expects recommendations for software as well as new salary system. I have not quoted to do this, and do not have time to do it by Friday. Client will not pay any extra for it.'

The definition is flawed, in that the last item is an assumption on her part, although in the context of their penny-pinching approach to the whole project, it is a pretty reasonable assumption. So the solution she sets about finding is one that enables her to offer a system recommendation, at no extra cost to the client, without her having to give more time free of charge.

Insight

Never assume that the client won't pay more. Judy's assumption is right in this case, but for some clients it may not be so: first they say no, then maybe ... Do not give yourself that disadvantage until you have tested it thoroughly, beyond their opening negotiation position, which will always be no!

At her meeting with Peter she first of all tests her definition: 'Peter, can we start with cards on the table. Tell me exactly what you are expecting from me on Friday.' Peter confirms what she suspects. She continues: 'Now, from my side, Peter, I quoted for a new system, meaning a document covering the new structure. I saw the choice of software as a next step, requiring more work from me, if you chose to commission me to do it.'

Peter reconfirms that the company will not pay any more, and indeed they feel cheated by her price, if it excludes this key element.

'So we need to find a way of delivering this extra piece, without any further costs to you or me?'

'If you want to put it like that. Your costs and time are your affair. I just want what I believe I'm paying for.'

Although the client will often push aside your needs, it is important to establish them clearly, as Judy has done here, so that they become a significant part of the negotiation, even if the client does not acknowledge this point overtly.

'My proposal is this, Peter. I can recommend an excellent software company that I have worked with before. I can't be sure that they will have an exact fit with your requirements, but they are very flexible, and reasonably priced. I could spend a long time looking at different off-the-shelf systems, and it is almost certain that they will all need some element of tailoring.

'I therefore suggest that we invite them in now, and arrange for them to work with me during the latter part of next week. As my work is completed, they will be able to put together a proposal in parallel. You will then have your system and your software recommendation on Friday, at no extra cost.'

'Suppose we don't like their quote, and go somewhere else?'

'That's your decision. I doubt that they would make a charge for producing a proposal, so you would still have no additional costs.'

'Then we'd be on our own. You wouldn't help us to choose another vendor, would you?'

'Not unless you had a very serious reason for rejecting the company I propose. But I'm sure you won't. They're good people and very trustworthy.'

'Let me have some information now. I'd like to know more about them.'

Peter will not give Judy the satisfaction of openly accepting the deal, but this last remark tells Judy that provided her software company play ball, she has her win–win outcome.

KEY MESSAGES

We can draw a number of key messages from Judy's experience:

1 *She used time well, deferring the negotiation until she could get into the right frame of mind, and giving herself time to think. The client was impatient, but she did not give in, and took the time she needed.*
2 *She checked the problem definition with the client, to ensure that she was looking for the right solution.*
3 *She was confident of finding a solution, and making it a win–win.*
4 *She was assertive and clear about what she needed to make it a win for her.*
5 *She did not behave as if the client had all the power. This enabled her to achieve 4.*

CASE STUDY: CHANGE OF TERMS

If you think that Judy's problem was easy to solve, here is a very different situation.

Kevin has just agreed the terms of a new project with his client, Colin. Colin wants a total review of his sales operation, which Kevin is well qualified to perform. It will start in six weeks, and take a month to complete, ending just before he is due to go on holiday in October. Kevin is very pleased about this, since he is about to start a five-week project with another client – this will all fit very nicely.

The next day he gets a phone call from Colin. 'Kevin, the sales review project – it's become an issue internally, so we've got to bring the date forward. Can you start it next week?'

'I'm sorry, Colin, I really can't do anything before September, which is the date we agreed. I have another project running 'til then.'

'Kevin, you don't understand. This is really critical. I need you here next week!'

'Let me come and see you, Colin, so that we can discuss this properly. Are you free later today?'

'There's nothing to discuss! But if you must, I could see you at five.'

Kevin has a little time to think about his problem. His company is small, and he is the only person capable of doing Colin's work. The current project needs him too, but he can delegate some of it – though not more than 20 per cent, he estimates. That's hardly enough to release him for the four week's work that Colin needs.

He has associates that he can call on, but no one who could really do Colin justice. His current project is for a regular client, who would object to substitution, and who are very hot on deadlines. He cannot afford to upset them. He does not have any kind of solution as he makes his way to Colin's office. However, he is clear on his goal, which is to search for variables during the meeting, and to be as creative as he possibly can.

Insight

Colin explores every avenue before he goes to see the client, then he gets all the information he needs to come up with a solution. He stays open to all the possibilities, and does not fix on a solution too soon – which is often tempting – to grab the first one that comes to you.

He begins by questioning Colin on what has changed. At first he gets very little in the way of explanation, but finally the truth emerges:

'Well, it's really the timing in the sales cycle. August is a much better time.'

'So it could wait until August, could it? You don't need me next week?'

'The sooner the better, it's really important that we have the results as early as possible.'

'For what purpose, Colin?'

'So that we have more time to plan changes and restructuring.'

'But won't everyone be away on holiday? I thought we'd agreed that October was when people really got going.'

'The VP of Sales from the USA is coming over in the middle of September. We want to have a plan in place by then.'

'Why the urgency? I thought that this review was entirely your initiative?'

'It is, but there are rumours that they want to change the reporting structure. I want to be seen to be ahead of the game.'

'And what does ahead of the game mean?'

'My spies tell me that he wants to see the same structure in the UK as in the USA, and the same commission plan.'

'Would you be happy to do that?'

'Pretty much. There are a few things I'd need to tweak, but we could do a very good cosmetic job anyway.'

Kevin has searched hard for variables, and found them. He may have lost a sales review project, but he has gained an opportunity to make his client look very good in front of his US VP.

The story ended like this: Kevin spent three half-days with Colin in the following week, to help him plan the reorganization.

He then dedicated the first two weeks of September to the commission plan, and to helping Colin prepare his presentation to the VP. This went really well, and since then Kevin has done various projects for Colin. The sales review project was not needed, but the loss of that work was more than compensated for by the gain of what followed.

KEY MESSAGES

The key lesson that we draw from this example is not to take what the client wants at face value. Kevin could have negotiated dates for the review, or tried to share the work with an associate, but he would not have been solving the real problem. In searching for variables, he was able to find a new and better solution.

This search can be applied just as effectively to a seemingly obvious negotiation item like price. A client may say they want a cheap option, but it may be that when they pay is more important than what they pay. It may be that they need to be seen to be getting a huge discount, and the starting price is therefore less important than the percentage cut they 'negotiate' from you. The key skill is to put yourself in the client's place, and see the situation through their eyes.

There are two stages in doing this. The first is just to sit where the client sits and say to yourself, 'If I were the client, what would I want?'

The second stage is to sit where the client sits and say to yourself, 'If I were this client, this person, with a different set of values and priorities from me, what would I want?'

The two are quite different, and getting into the second position is more of a challenge, since you need to know quite a lot about the client. The more you know, the better you will be able to understand what they want of you.

In the last case study, Colin originally asked for an objective review
of his organization. However, his priorities changed when his
position was threatened, and his motives became understandably
political. Objectivity went out of the window, in favour of
impressing the US VP. Kevin immediately recognized this, and at
no point did he try to persuade him to conduct the original review.

CASE STUDY: PROTECTING REPUTATIONS

The final case study on negotiation comes from Leon Sadler at
SAP, who described it as one of the most difficult client situations
he had had to face.

'We were working for a medium sized client in the communications
industry, and they had contracted in a project manager to run the
whole implementation, since they had no expertise themselves.
Sadly, we rapidly discovered that the project manager, John, was
not very skilled, and he started to create major problems. I sat
down with him and tried to build a relationship, saying that if we
didn't work together, then it would reflect badly on both of us.
John was too insecure to accept this, and went back to the client
and complained about us. This problem went on for some time,
and we tried to work around it, but in the end I had to go to the
sponsor and tell all.

'The sponsor was horrified:

"Leon, are you telling me the man's incompetent?"

"Sam, I really didn't want to do this, but I've tried everything and
it just isn't working." I gave Sam real evidence of the problem,
which he had to accept.

"Leon, if I sack John now, then I will look incompetent too, the Board would eat me for breakfast. I've practically staked my career on this project."

"I could bring in my own project manager, but that would involve significant extra cost ..."

"I can't possibly extend the budget, Leon. If I ask for more money, they'll want to know why, and we're back with the same problem. You'll just have to work with John as best you can."

"Believe me, Sam, I've tried. I wouldn't be sitting here now if I could make it work. Unless you're prepared for a minimum four-week delay on the project, something's got to give."

"We can't be even a day late!"

"I know, Sam. Leave it with me for a while, I won't leave you exposed.'''

Leon takes time to think about the problem. He is very clear on the client's needs, and understands why he cannot manoeuvre on price or timing or on the contractor. This makes a win–win outcome very hard to achieve, if he defines it as meeting the client's needs, at no extra cost to SAP.

Leon chose to define win–win differently. He would meet the client's needs, and preserve his company's reputation. He agreed with Sam to move the contractor to manage a smaller part of the project, where he had appropriate skills. Leon then brought in his own project manager, at his cost, to complete the project on time.

'I made no profit, but the project was a great success, the contractor co-operated in his new role, and the client was very happy indeed.'

Clearly, Leon made a major concession here, but he won on all other counts, even keeping the contractor on side, and he did not make a loss, so he was happy to consider this a win–win for SAP.

KEY MESSAGES

It is not a perfect world, and we do not always get exactly what we want, so be very clear about your priorities in a negotiation. Leon's were:

1 *Reputation of SAP*
2 *Successful project*
3 *Profit target.*

When he had explored all avenues, and saw that he could not achieve all three, he was very clear about which one he could be flexible on. In the long run, he may regain that lost profit, either from new business earned on the basis of that success, or from the deeply grateful project sponsor, when he moves to another company.

KEY STEPS IN NEGOTIATION

▶ *When faced with a potential negotiation, remember the presupposition: The person with the most flexibility in thinking and behaviour has the most influence on any interaction. Overt exercise of power, unless taken to extremes, will not win the battle against the flexible thinker.*
▶ *Start by understanding what the client really wants.*
▶ *Do not be pressured into negotiating before you are ready.*
▶ *Take time out to think and get into the right mindset.*
▶ *Think positively, believing that there is a solution to every problem.*
▶ *Feel an even balance of power between you and the client.*
▶ *Be very clear about your priorities in the negotiation.*
▶ *Make your needs clear to the client, so that they feel the balance of the negotiation.*
▶ *Remain assertive throughout – which means persevering and unemotional.*
▶ *Get into the client's head, and see things from their perspective.*

- *Look for as many variables as possible, and be creative.*
- *Find the win–win solution you know is there.*

Managing conflict

If you are personally involved in conflict, it can have a very negative effect on the team and the project, so in this section we will cover the fastest way out of conflict. We will not even contemplate the notion of conflict between you and the client, but if it did happen, the same principles would apply.

Ideally, it would be good to avoid conflict altogether, which is different from avoiding it once it has arisen. If conflict occurs and you pretend it is not happening, you create a festering wound which will not heal until you bring it out into the open and deal with it. If conflict has not arisen and you see it coming and can stop it happening, that is by far the best course.

Insight

Pre-empting conflict is a great skill – cultivate it well. Read negative signals, anticipate where people are heading and where they might collide. Now how can you change their course?

The difference between conflict and disagreement is emotion. If you can take the emotion out of both sides, you have a disagreement, which is much easier to handle. We will show how you can do this by reducing your own emotional level, and gradually helping the other party to reduce theirs.

When the emotion is gone, handling a disagreement is much the same as handling a negotiation: you find out the outcomes of both parties, and then look for win–win solutions. Refer back to the negotiation section if you need to, as we will not cover the same ground here. We will focus on helping you to manage your emotional responses to conflict, and giving you control.

People vary greatly in how they respond to conflict, but those who have difficulty with it generally fall into one of three categories:

- ▶ *Those who avoid it at all costs.*
- ▶ *Those who are intimidated by it.*
- ▶ *Those who get angry and aggressive, and may be conflict generators.*

A few presuppositions will come in useful at this point:

- ▶ *There is a solution to every problem. This is always a good start.*
- ▶ *The meaning of communication is in the response you get. Vital to have this clearly in focus when in conflict!*
- ▶ *If someone else can do something, so can you. This evens out the playing field, if you are feeling disadvantaged.*
- ▶ *Everyone already has everything they need to achieve what they want. Another empowering belief if you feel you might be the weaker opponent.*
- ▶ *If you always do what you always did, you will always get what you always got. Just a reminder of what will happen if you have not coped well with conflict in the past.*
- ▶ *The person with the most flexibility in thinking and behaviour has the most influence on any interaction. This is your way out of any conflict you encounter.*

HOW DO YOU RESPOND TO CONFLICT?

If you are someone who avoids conflict when it has arisen, then ask yourself why, and keep asking. Your answers will be something like:

- ▶ *'I'm afraid of losing.'*
- ▶ *'I just can't face it.'*
- ▶ *'I can't pluck up the courage to engage in conflict.'*
- ▶ *'I worry that I'll go to pieces.'*
- ▶ *'I might lose control.'*
- ▶ *'I'll make an enemy.'*

If it is a fear of losing that holds you back, you are hardly winning by ignoring the problem, are you? Imagine the worst that could happen – you lose completely; so not failure, but feedback, and the knowledge that you did not run away this time, which will make you stronger for next time.

If you cannot face even the thought of conflict, feel you lack the courage, and worry that you will go to pieces, then you are seeing yourself getting upset by it. This means that you see yourself getting emotional, and yet it is not necessary to invest emotion in conflict. You deal with conflict by being assertive. You quietly and calmly state your case, and do not respond emotionally to whatever your opponent is throwing at you.

If you think that the theory sounds wonderful, but the practice is a long way from where you are now, then it is worth investing some time in assertiveness training. Fundamental to being assertive is the knowledge that to feel emotion is your choice. No one can make you feel anything unless you let them. If this is a novel concept, think of someone you know who stays calm in the face of anger or panic. They are choosing not to invest energy in those same emotions. This choice means that they can use their energy in other ways, and gives them greater staying power. It would be hard work to rant and rave all day, but if you are calmly stating your case and exploring options, you can keep doing that for a very long time.

If the words 'but I can't help it' spring to mind, that is the essence of assertiveness – you can. The power is yours, unless you choose to give it away. Your energy is precious, think of it as money: you choose how to spend it, so you can choose how to spend your energy in the same way. People often think that assertiveness training is for wimps, but being assertive gives you power, and is just as helpful to the aggressive as it is to the intimidated.

If you worry about making an enemy by engaging in conflict, bear in mind that most people respect someone who is not afraid to speak up and express differing views. There are the few who need yes-men around them, but they are easily spotted. In any case, your aim is to find a win–win outcome, not to turn your opponent into a loser.

If your response to conflict is to become aggressive, and possibly even to enjoy it, then dumping the emotion is even more vital to a successful outcome. The same techniques apply, and the faster you get to a calm and reasonable state, the better. Aggression breeds aggression, and your opposing positions are likely to become more entrenched the longer the emotion continues.

Insight

Assertiveness training for the aggressive has other names, such as conflict handling or anger management. Just removing your aggression will not work; you need something else to put in its place, which is called assertiveness!

A TECHNIQUE FOR HANDLING CONFLICT

If you are in conflict with someone, take time out to think the issues through. To see things most clearly from the other person's perspective a special technique may help – if it appears a little unusual, do not let it stop you trying it, because it works really well!

First, find an empty room with two or three chairs. You can do this alone, or with a trusted friend who knows all about the conflict.

Now imagine that you and your 'opponent' (called John, for convenience) are sitting in opposite chairs. If your friend is with you, they will occupy the third chair as an observer – on no account should they sit in John's chair!

Now think through, or talk through your own point of view, and what outcome you want. When you are very clear on your outcome, move chairs and sit in the opposite chair. You are now in John's shoes, almost literally. Imagine you are him, with his values and his priorities, not yours. Think as he would think, express his point of view, and work out what outcome he wants. When you are very clear on his outcome, stand back from both chairs, and describe the conflict as if you were an observer: 'I see two frustrated people here, who both have the same outcome, which is a successful project, but …'

If you have a friend with you, ask for their comments after each stage of the process, but do not let them do it for you.

Insight

You may think that you could do all this in your head, or just by chatting to your friend, but the physical movement of sitting in someone else's chair and standing back from both chairs does literally give you a different perspective – try it. It is a useful tool for negotiation too.

At the end of all this, as a minimum you will have a much better understanding of the situation, and you might even have some possible solutions. It is often the case that people in conflict share the same final objective. If you can recognize this, then it is a big step along the way to resolution.

KEY STEPS IN MANAGING CONFLICT

▶ *Whether you enjoy conflict or hate it, dump any emotion you attach to it, and turn conflict into a negotiation.*
▶ *If you fear conflict, use assertiveness to gain the power you need.*
▶ *Try literally stepping into someone else's place when you are identifying their needs and outcome for a win–win solution.*

Closing thoughts

You have not converted a man because you have silenced him.

John Morley

Use soft words and hard arguments.

English Proverb

STEPS TO SUCCESS

Whether you are facing conflict, a negotiation, or want to influence someone, there are some common steps:

▶ *Put yourself in the other person's shoes, to get a good view of what they want and why.*

▶ *Ask them as much as you can, to really understand their needs.*

▶ *Keep emotion out of any interchange.*

▶ *Take time to think and plan.*

▶ *Act with integrity.*

▶ *Be creative, look for variables to find a win–win outcome.*

▶ *Believe there is a solution to every problem.*

18

Dealing with difficult clients

This chapter covers:
- *how to deal with the following types of difficult clients:*
  insecure; angry; obstructive; antagonistic; abusive

What else is a consultant's job about, you may ask yourself, other than coping with clients who change their minds but will not admit it, need everything by yesterday, and assume that your service includes vastly more than your quotation ever contained!

As an experienced consultant you learn to expect all this, and have found ways to deal with it, and often to anticipate and avoid problems completely. What complicates the issue is the small matter of client personality, which can present real problems. Your client radar system, which is permanently gathering information about the people involved in your project, may help you to prepare. Sooner or later though, you will come face to face with the full force of a problem client, and here are some examples. We will look at clients who are insecure, angry, obstructive, antagonistic and abusive. Because the case studies are based on real life, they do not always have a happy ending, but we will draw out some key messages at the end, and in some cases the value will be as much in recognizing the problem, as in what you can do to overcome it. This is very true of this first case study.

Case study: The insecure client

Insecure people can be very difficult to deal with when things go wrong. They will immediately look for scapegoats, and will make sure that they have covered themselves very carefully. Because they are not confident in their own ability, their instinct for self-protection is usually stronger than their sense of what is right, so their behaviour may not appear to be very ethical.

Malcolm was newly promoted, and clearly very uncomfortable in his new role. His manager had been taken seriously ill very suddenly, and Malcolm was thrust into the breach. Tom was leading the project when all this happened, and whilst he had a good relationship with Malcolm's boss, he had never bothered much with Malcolm, whom he viewed as 'a bit of a wimp'.

Now Tom has to tell Malcolm that one of the new functions in the software they are installing is not working properly, and there will be a two-week time delay, which he believes he can make up. More critical than that is the fact that one of Malcolm's team on the project, Mary, is not pulling her weight, and this is slowing down their progress. Mary is a large aggressive girl, and Tom is sure that Malcolm is terrified of her. Malcolm says he will talk to Mary.

Three weeks later, the software problem is not fixed, Mary is still not pulling her weight, and this is affecting her colleagues. Tom is pretty sure that Malcolm has done nothing. There is a review meeting due on Monday with the Project Board, and now he is facing a serious delay. He is told that the software will be working by Wednesday (two days too late for the Board), but they now have at least three weeks to make up.

He knows that Malcolm will heap all the blame for the delay on the software issue, but Tom believes that if Mary had pulled her weight, and not wasted other people's time by being difficult and distracting, they would be barely a week behind. He doesn't want to openly contradict Malcolm in the meeting, but he will not be used as a scapegoat either.

Insight

How would you handle this situation in Tom's place? You need to tread a fine line between protecting your company's reputation and damaging your relationship with the client.

Tom could just go head to head with Malcolm, produce the facts, and let them draw their own conclusions. He could let Malcolm make him a scapegoat, or he could try to reason with Malcolm before the meeting. He decides there is nothing to be lost by reasoning with Malcolm, so off he goes.

'Malcolm, can we talk about the Project Board meeting?'

'If you like, Tom, though it seems pretty cut and dried to me. You just have to accept the consequences of delay, and tell us when the software will actually be ready.'

'Do you feel that your team has contributed to the delay, Malcolm, because I do.'

'Well, I know Mary isn't at her best at the moment – she has problems at home, you know. But I think that's neither here nor there, the problem is yours, not ours.'

'Malcolm, I know the software is late, but not everything we're doing is dependent on that. We've been working on other things at the same time, as you well know, and if your team had done their bit, we'd be barely a week behind.'

'So it's my whole team now, is it Tom? Aren't you just looking for excuses to save your skin in front of the Project Board?'

Tom has a choice at this point, and this is the route he decides to take.

'Malcolm, can we just talk for a moment about what we're going to say to the Board. How will it look if they see us arguing like this?'

Malcolm hesitates, then says, 'Very unprofessional, but I'm not going to let you get away with blaming me for things that are entirely your problem.'

'And that's exactly how I feel, Malcolm. So what can we say that meets both our needs and doesn't make us look like a pair of squabbling school children?'

Malcolm shrugs.

Tom continues, 'Let's present a united front – I'll deal with the software delay, you explain that you've had personal issues with your team, and without allocating blame, the two add up to a three-week delay. How's that?'

'Okay, I suppose.'

'Right, that's what we'll do then, but they're going to ask whether the problems will be fixed and how much time we can recover. Any thoughts on that?'

Malcolm looks very uncomfortable. 'I'm not sure we can recover any of the three weeks. I'm hoping Mary's personal problems will have settled down soon.'

'So the delay might get worse?'

'No, I'll try to bring someone else in.'

Tom looks doubtful. 'I didn't think you had any more resource.'

'I don't, at the moment.'

'So where …?'

'I'm going to sort that out now.' Malcolm strides off.

At the Project Board meeting, Malcolm opens with his report, which places all of the blame for the delay on Tom's company. Tom prompts him a little. 'Malcolm, whilst I accept that the software delay has had an impact, I think there were other issues too.'

Malcolm flatly denies this.

Tom makes his report, and describes the situation as he and Malcolm had previously agreed it. When asked again by a Director if he accepts what Tom has said, Malcolm flatly denies it. When asked for comment, all Tom can say is that they agree to disagree. The tone of the rest of the meeting is frosty, particularly as the software is not working yet.

Later that afternoon, Tom gets a rare phone call from his manager, telling him that one of the directors has complained to him about Tom, and said that he is worried about his ability to maintain a proper working relationship with Malcolm. Tom tells him the full story, and then his boss goes to see the Director concerned. They refuse to accept that Malcolm might be at fault, and accuse Tom's company of looking for scapegoats. The project runs late, and ends on a sour note, with threats of resorting to lawyers.

Insight

An insecure client can do a huge amount of damage. They are experts in covering their backs, and blaming a supplier is such an easy route for them to take. Sometimes people above them see through this, but as in this case, they may not, or it may suit them not to.

This is a real lose–lose scenario, because Malcolm is so insecure. He is prepared to agree to one thing and say another, and he covers his back so well, and manages his superiors so well, that he gets away with it. Tom's only workable options would seem to have been either to help Malcolm with his team, or to find irrefutable evidence against him.

Helping Malcolm might have been difficult, since he would probably see accepting help as confirming his managerial incompetence. Producing evidence against him will still look like betrayal to his company, and appears very underhand, even if they accept that it is valid. If they are truly convinced, however, they will probably accept that it was a necessary step – if they are not convinced, Tom would be in worse trouble.

KEY MESSAGES

▶ *Recognize signs of insecurity in a client. Be aware that insecurity can lead to very negative behaviour, so be on your guard if things go wrong.*
▶ *If things do go wrong, discuss the issues early and fully with your manager, or a colleague, and take as much pre-emptive action as you can.*
▶ *Handle any senior client contacts with extreme caution. The insecure individual may have done a great deal of work to cover their back, and that may include negative feedback about you!*

Case study: The angry client (1)

Eddie is hard working and dedicated, but not at his best with people. The work he has been doing for Business Leasing for the past three months has gone exceptionally well, and this has been recognized by his client contact, Andrew, with whom he has built up a good working relationship.

Unfortunately Andrew's team has now hit a problem, which only they can solve. Eddie has done all he can, but now he's stuck. He cannot do any more work until Andrew's team deliver. He rings his boss, Wayne, explains the situation, and is told to leave site, as this is a fixed price contract, and he would be wasting his company's money just sitting there waiting. Wayne tells Eddie that something urgent has come up, and Eddie will be able to help out that very afternoon – it is only a three-hour job.

He goes to Andrew and explains that he is leaving. To his amazement, Andrew hits the roof. He shouts at Eddie, tells him he is not going anywhere, that he is paying for him to be on site and that is where he will stay.

Eddie is transfixed. He had no idea that Andrew could be like this. He leaves Andrew's office, wondering what to do. He is very tempted to just walk out, and go back to his company and tell his manager – his office is only a five-minute drive away. But then what would happen if Andrew came looking for him and he was not there? Eddie hates the thought of another confrontation, but perhaps he should let Andrew calm down a bit, and then go and try reasoning with him. The thought of that makes it easy for Eddie to decide. He goes back to his desk and phones his manager, who is not there. He is in a meeting for the rest of the afternoon, with instructions not to be disturbed. Eddie decides to leave. He cannot face Andrew again, and he has to get this job done for Wayne before the end of the day.

At 4 pm Wayne asks Eddie into his office. Andrew has just phoned him. His team have solved the problem, and they want to know where Eddie is.

'So what did you say to Andrew?' Wayne demands.

'I just told him I was leaving.'

'And what did he say?'

'He told me not to – got very angry. Said I must stay on site.'

'So what did you do then, Eddie?'

'I left his office and rang you, but you weren't there, so I came back here to do this job.'

'And what did you tell Andrew?'

'Nothing – I just left. I couldn't face him again, he was so angry.'

'Not as angry as he is now!' Wayne is clearly very upset. 'Surely you went back to reason with him, to explain about this job?'

'I just couldn't face him again.'

Wayne decides to accompany Eddie back to site. He despatches Eddie to the project team, and goes to talk to Andrew alone.

'Andrew, first let me tell you that Eddie is back working with your team right now.'

'I should ****ing well think so! I'm very angry about all this. He should never have left. I told him not to.'

'I know you did. You terrified him. You know he's a very talented individual technically, but interpersonal skills are not his strength. Talking to him like that is counterproductive, especially as this whole situation is not his fault.'

'Well, you should have known better than to tell him to leave. We need him here.'

'This is a fixed price contract, Andrew. If you want to pay for Eddie's non-productive time, that's a very different matter. Now we are very committed to meeting your deadline, and Eddie has agreed to work late tonight, to catch up for any lost time today, so I hope that you'll treat him gently when you next see him.'

Next day Eddie was surprised to get an apology from Andrew. The project finished two weeks ahead of schedule.

Here is an excellent example of the consultant pushing back under pressure from the client. Andrew had no right to shout at Eddie, even though what he said did not appear to be abusive in any way. Eddie did not handle the situation well, but, as Wayne pointed out, he should not have been put in that situation in the first place. Wayne was firm with Andrew, and all ended well for both parties.

Insight

How comfortable are you in pushing back when a client is unreasonable? There is always the worry that you could damage the relationship or even lose the account, but this can sometimes be an easy excuse to do nothing. A good client will respect you and the relationship will be enhanced if you do this well when the situation arises.

It is easier to push back when the client is in the wrong, as Andrew was. When the consultant is at fault, it is harder to handle an angry client.

Case study: The angry client (2)

Rosey had been working on the project for two months. In fact she had joined the Blurange Consultancy Company in February, and started on the project two weeks later. She is very keen to impress, and has worked hard to establish a good relationship with the client, Ben, and her boss, Hassan.

Hassan has been working on site full time, and Rosey has sought a great deal of guidance from him. Now he has moved on to another project for a few weeks, leaving Rosey alone on site. Things are all on schedule, and Hassan has left everything in perfect order.

Ben comes to see Rosey the next day, and asks if she can just fit in a little extra job. Hassan has warned her not to accept any work outside the brief without checking with him, but it is only a small thing, and Rosey is anxious to please, especially as Hassan is not there, so she agrees. It is Tuesday, and Ben has asked for this piece of work to be finished by the following Monday morning.

By Friday Rosey is in a real mess. The 'little job' has turned into a nightmare piece of work, and because of this she is now two days behind schedule. Her solution is to work all weekend and make up the time. By Monday morning the 'little job' is still not finished, and she is still two days behind. She is very tired and tells Ben the full story.

'You mean you haven't done that little job I gave you last week?'

'No – it's not a little job, I've just explained. I've spent five days full time on it and I still …'

Ben is angry. 'That is such a stupid thing to do! Why didn't you tell me? I just can't rely on you now. I could have asked someone who knew what they were doing to deal with it, not a novice, which you have just proved yourself to be. I can't believe you have let the schedule slip like this. You don't have a clue about priorities, do you? I'm going to report you to Hassan.'

Rosey bursts into tears and Ben walks off. By the time Rosey has recovered, Hassan is on the phone to her. She gives her side of the story, and detecting that she is still tearful, Hassan makes no comment, other than to say he has an appointment with Ben at 4 pm that day, and will sit down with Rosey at 2 pm.

By two o'clock Rosey is angry. She has done her best, and been shouted at and abused by the client. She relays all this to Hassan, throwing in comments about the law and harassment along the way. Hassan's relationship with Ben is good on a working basis, but he has not built a strong personal relationship with him. As things have been going so well until now, Hassan has not needed to test even the working relationship. He is now very worried about Rosey's aggressive reaction, and is unclear where she stands legally. It is, of course, very obvious that any accusation from Rosey will damage the client relationship, whether she is justified or not.

Hassan calls his HR department, and gets some very woolly information, which would seem to suggest that Rosey's claims are not strong, but might have some validity.

It is time for his meeting with Ben – what advice would you give him? Again, Hassan faces the dilemma of whether to push back or acquiesce, and he is not on firm ground. The fact that Ben reduced Rosey to tears is Hassan's strongest card to use for pushing back, if he decides to.

Here is how the meeting went.

'I'm very unhappy about all this, Hassan. I don't think this girl is competent to work alone.'

'This is very unfortunate, Ben. I'm very sorry that this problem has arisen, but let me say first of all that we can recover very quickly from this, and have the extra task complete and be back on track by the end of the week, with no extra costs incurred at all.'

'I wouldn't expect any less, Hassan.'

'Good. Now let's deal with the specific issue. Rosey is very competent at what she does, but the scope of her role is limited to execution. She was anxious to please you by taking on the extra work, but she should have followed our change control procedure, and referred that decision to me. If she had, I would have been able to tell you that what looks a simple job is not, and is at least three days' work. You and I would then have had a discussion on that subject, and it would have been dealt with by one of our specialists. You don't know that, and Rosey didn't know that. Rosey was at fault in trying to please you and failing, but I don't think she deserved the response you gave her this morning, after she'd been working all weekend to try to put things right. She tells me that you were abusive, and she is very upset indeed.'

'I deny that! I simply told her a few home truths. I did not insult her, I simply criticized what she had done, and she deserved it! I defy anyone to call that abuse.' Ben is now angry again. 'I'm sure you did exactly that, Ben, but the state Rosey was in probably meant that she heard it differently. What left you wasn't what reached her – she was very tired and very anxious. The fact is that you reduced her to tears, and getting angry was probably not the most effective way of dealing with her. Now she is a very good worker, and I'd like to keep her on this project – it really is the best way to get it finished on time. Do you think that there's any way that you can make things up with Rosey?'

Ben replies, 'Let me think about it. I'll call you first thing tomorrow.'

Hassan returns to Rosey. 'I think Ben will calm down now. If he appears with any sort of olive branch, I'd like you to say that you are sorry that this incident occurred, and now want to forget it and get on with the project. Can you do that?'

'Only if he gives me a full apology. I could take him to court for what he said.'

'You might, Rosey, but in doing that you'd lose us a client, and you'd gain a reputation for being difficult to deal with. That's not something that will work wonders for your career. I've told Ben that his manner was inappropriate, but he swears to me that he did not criticize you, only what you had done, therefore his remarks were not abusive. Of course no client has the right to shout at you or otherwise verbally abuse you, no matter what they're paying, but if there's another way out of this, wouldn't it be better to take it? Bottom line is, if you want to pursue this legally you must speak to HR at once and get advice – it's your decision.'

'Let me sleep on it.'

After Ben and Rosey had had time to calm down, they exchanged awkward conciliatory words, and the project continued to a successful conclusion, with rather more input from Hassan than he had planned. However, he felt that was preferable to having to deal with lawyers! He made an extra effort to build a more personal relationship with Ben after that, and discovered that Rosey was not the only person to suffer from his temper. He had quite a reputation amongst his staff, it turned out, and Hassan regretted not having done more research before. He could at least have alerted Rosey, and she might then have had the sense to call him when that 'little extra job' came up.

Insight

Know your client is easy to say, and sometimes you think you do, and then find they behave differently under pressure. Active but subtle research will pay dividends in avoiding situations like this one.

Hassan had also conceded doing that extra work for nothing, in order to smooth things over. He decided that this was a price worth paying, otherwise it would have prolonged the discussion about Rosey's competence.

KEY MESSAGES

▶ *Do your homework on your clients. It is useful to know if they have marked personal characteristics, such as being uncommunicative, or prone to lose their temper.*

▶ *Be firm with clients who abuse their position – particularly with junior consultants. Push back when you need to, it will restore the balance of respect, as well as protecting the innocent, or nearly innocent.*

▶ *Ensure that clients 'own' the change control procedure, as well as your own team.*

▶ *Avoid confrontation; find ways to pour oil on the situation, but without sweeping it under the carpet.*

▶ *Although clients do not have the right to shout at you, taking the moral high ground is likely to jeopardize the account, so the reality is that you find as civilized a way forward as you can.*

▶ *Keeping the account has to be your priority, even when you are in the right.*

Case study: The obstructive client

Henry is a very experienced consultant, who is in the middle of a twelve-month project, which is based almost entirely on the client site. He has requested some information from Lisa, the management accountant, but to date she has not delivered. He has asked her twice, very nicely. Now he approaches her for the third time.

'Hi Lisa! Busy as ever? I don't suppose ...'

'Sorry, Henry, it's like a madhouse here. I'm desperately trying to get to your stuff, but you know how it is.'

'I do, Lisa, but unfortunately my stuff is now getting urgent. I have a deadline to produce the report for the Project Committee by the 14th. It's the 6th today, so that's not very long, and Joe asked to see it before the meeting. I'm afraid I'm going to need it by Monday, at the very latest. Can I come and collect it at – say – 2 pm?'

'Well, I can't promise anything, but it will be nice to see you!'

'Lisa, shall I speak to Joe about it? He is the person most interested in this report, after all. In which case it helps that he's your boss. Perhaps he could help with your workload in some way, to give you time for this.'

'Talk to him if you like – it won't do any good. He just expects me to deliver on everything, all the time. That's the way it is around here. Let me know what he says, anyway.'

Henry goes to see Joe, the Finance Director: 'Joe, I'm worried about Lisa. She seems to be under so much pressure. I've been asking her for this data we need for the Committee report, but she just hasn't got time to get it for me, and if this continues, the report will be late. I just thought I'd check with you that there's no problem in my having this information, is there? It occurred to me that she might be worried that I shouldn't see it, and this is her way of dealing with the problem.'

'Well, Henry – first of all there's absolutely no confidentiality issue here, and Lisa knows that. Secondly, she's not overworked, she's just a bit behind schedule at the moment. I'm sure she'll deliver on time.'

'I hope you're right, Joe. I'll let you know on Monday.'

Monday afternoon comes and goes, and Lisa makes the usual excuses. Henry calls into Joe's office, but is told he's out until Wednesday morning. The Committee meets on Friday.

Insight

Imagine that you are Henry, and consider his options. It would be easy for him to wait, as he's clearly in the right, but that won't do his image any good in the long run. It can be hard to keep supporting the client, when they are clearly in the wrong!

He could prepare the report without Lisa's data, and just put in estimates. He knows for a fact that estimates won't do at this stage, and he will be the one who is blamed for this in the Committee, not Lisa. He discounts this option.

He could tell Joe he will not be doing anything at all until Lisa delivers. This is not a helpful approach, and smacks of toys being thrown out of his pram! He discounts it.

He could wait until Joe gets back, and ask him to get the data from Lisa. This is a real possibility, but it delays things.

He could stand over Lisa, and refuse to leave without the data. This is the option Henry chooses: he decides to have one last go at Lisa.

'Lisa, would it help if I sit down with you now and we do this together? I've got to the stage where I'm stuck without it, so I may as well give you a hand.'

Henry then discovers that the data he needs is in a complete mess, which is why Lisa was so reluctant to give it to him. He tells her that he will sort it out sufficiently for his needs, and say nothing to Joe. Lisa moves from being an obstacle to an ally. She takes the data home that evening, and delivers something usable to him in the morning. It is far from perfect, but it is enough for the report.

If Henry had decided to leave the problem to Joe, would the resolution have been any different? We can speculate that Lisa would have done the same thing, except she would have been under duress, so probably more hostile to Henry. Also the data would have arrived at least 24 hours later, leaving Henry far less time. Joe would probably not have been happy to be given this task, which he would probably expect Henry to sort out for himself. If there were ill feeling generated between Joe and Lisa, they would probably both blame Henry for it, albeit unjustly. Henry would have done well to make himself scarce whilst all this was happening. If he had witnessed their interchange, there would be some embarrassment, probably on all sides, and they would blame him even more!

All in all, Henry's chosen route proved by far the best. It did not expose either Lisa or Joe, it strengthened his relationship with Lisa, and possibly also with Joe, and it achieved the fastest result.

With hindsight, it would have been best to have specified the required data as part of the project plan, and to request it be provided at the start of the project. That really would fix it, but not every piece of data required is known at the beginning of a project, and so this fix will not work every time. Foreseeing this type of problem is a good way of focusing your thinking when drawing up the project plan, however!

KEY MESSAGES

▶ *Specify your data requirements in advance.*
▶ *Find out why someone is being obstructive, it will normally enable you to solve the problem.*

- Deal with the individual directly to build a positive relationship.
- Use senior level pressure only when you are sure there is no other way. It will usually alienate the individual, and annoy the manager too.

Case study: The antagonistic client

Simon is the project leader for a small team who have been working on the client site for eight months. The project is scheduled to run for a further six months, and everything is running very smoothly. Simon has a reasonable working relationship with the project sponsor, Tony, but sees little of him. Simon tends to deal directly with the client project team, as their team leader, Chris, is very laid back, and in Simon's view, rather ineffectual. Simon ensures that he more than compensates for any of Chris's project management shortcomings, and Chris appears very happy to let him. They have a beer occasionally, and Simon makes a big social effort to build the relationship.

Simon comes in one morning to see a stranger in the team. Chris immediately comes to introduce him. 'Hello Simon, can I introduce you to Brian, who's replacing Dave. Dave's had to go and help on another project – bit of a crisis, actually. Anyway, Brian's very senior and really experienced, so I'm sure he'll soon be steaming ahead.'

Simon shakes Brian's hand and exchanges a few pleasantries. Brian barely responds and is clearly not one for small talk. Simon tries to suppress feelings of instant dislike, but later, at an informal review meeting, Brian makes a few negative comments. Simon lets them go, but remains worried.

A few weeks go by, and the situation has become critical. Brian is clearly telling Chris what to do, and he and Simon have a fundamental disagreement over the next stage of the project. Simon takes Chris out for a beer.

'Chris, I'm concerned about Brian. He has very strong views, and he seems to be imposing them on everyone.'

'He's very experienced, Simon, more so than I am. I'm very happy to take his advice.'

'You're also paying me to give you advice, you know!' Simon tries to make this sound like a slightly humorous remark, and fails.

'Mmmm, well you obviously both feel strongly on this issue, so I have to rely on my own man.' Chris is clearly uncomfortable. 'Another beer?'

'Yes, I'll get them in a minute. Look, you know that Brian and I are both right, both solutions will work, it's just that I know mine is better. Better for you that is, I'm not trying to cut corners here.'

'I didn't think you were, Simon, it's just that Brian thinks ...'

'Shall we escalate it then, Chris? I can bring in my boss, and we'll invite him and Tony to a meeting and present both sides and then let them decide. Will that fix the problem?'

'I'd rather not do that. I'd rather just follow Brian's solution, you said yourself that it will work. If we drag in our bosses, it looks like we can't manage things on our own. I wouldn't want to give that impression.' Chris's normally amiable expression is almost stern. Then he smiles an uncomfortable smile. 'Isn't the customer always supposed to be right? Now how about that beer!'

The next morning, Simon telephones his boss. 'Adrian, I've got this problem.' He then describes the situation to date.

Insight

If you were Adrian, how would you respond to Simon? You rate him as a project manager, and you trust his judgement. You'd prefer not to upset him, but you don't want to upset the client either ...

'And what's your view of Brian?'

'Very arrogant and very competent.'

'So there's nothing wrong with his proposal?'

'It's not the best way, Adrian, it just ...'

'Will it deliver the same result?'

'Yes.'

'On schedule?'

'Yes, but my way would have saved us some time, we would have been ahead of schedule, have some useful contingency and ...'

'Don't you have contingency built in?'

'Yes, but ...'

'It seems to me, Simon, that we don't have a leg to stand on. If the client wants it that way, go ahead with what he wants. We will still be on track, the fact that we might have gained by it is hardly worth discussing. It sounds like you've taken a dislike to this Brian, and want to win this battle for personal reasons. I challenge you to win him over and build a relationship. We don't want an enemy in the camp, and just winning this battle is not going to win him over, it will make him keen to look out for the next one. Let me know how you get on.'

Adrian hangs up, and Simon goes out for some fresh air to help him calm down. Later that day he tries to have a conciliatory chat with Brian, and to tell him, before he tells Chris, that he will be supporting Brian's plan. 'Took you a while to see sense, didn't it?' is all he gets out of Brian. Simon immediately tells Chris, who is clearly very relieved.

Simon and Brian have a number of disagreements over the next few months. Simon manages to avoid the type of confrontation they originally engaged in, but he cannot bring himself to try to build a better relationship with Brian, and they remain in an uneasy truce only because Brian knows he will get his way on most things.

Towards the end of the project, Chris leaves and Brian takes his place. He immediately calls Adrian and requests a meeting, where he gives him his view of Simon's shortcomings, and requests that he be replaced.

Adrian is very firm. 'I'm sorry Brian, I know you and Simon have your disagreements, but he's doing a good job for you and there are only two months to go. By the time I've re-organized my team, and brought in someone else, you'll be behind schedule.'

'Isn't that your problem?'

'No, I rather think it's ours. If I throw more resource at the project, that won't replace Simon's expertise. I know the situation is not ideal, but it's what's best to get the project finished on time.'

Insight

Adrian gave Simon short shrift over his view of Brian. Now Adrian is being just as firm with the client and pushing back hard over what he knows is an unreasonable request. All in the name of completing the project successfully, which is difficult for Brian to argue about.

Brian accepts this, but gives Simon a very hard time for the next two months, until the project reaches a successful and punctual conclusion.

Case study: The abusive client

Sometimes it is necessary to change personnel, if you have that option, when client and consultant really do not get on.

David Mitchell spoke about an experience where one of the Partners returned from an initial client meeting very upset indeed: 'The Finance Director was a working class Scot, who called a spade an f***ing shovel, and the Partner was a very formal Englishman – chalk and cheese just did not describe it. The client also held the belief that all consultants are money grabbing so and sos, and are therefore to be shouted at and abused to keep them in line.

'We agreed that I would take over the account, and I gave the client as good as he got – being a fellow Scot did help, but it was more the way I matched his style. In a meeting one day, the client was out of line. I took a piece of paper from my pocket and said to him, "Jimmy, you know the rules of football?"

"Of course I bloody do!"

"Well this is a red card! You're way out of project scope, so get back into line!" We laughed, and he did as he was told, and I had no trouble with him at all after that.'

This is a nice example of building rapport by careful matching of the other person's style and interest, with good use of humour to round it off.

In larger organizations, changing staff on an account can be the best way to deal with a problem client, as here. However, if you are small, and do not have that option, then sometimes the best option is not to take on the account at all, if you recognize the problem early enough.

Vic Hartley had a good example: 'An experience of the client from hell is the senior management who hire you, and then, not wanting to be seen to get their hands dirty, delegate to a relatively junior manager who resents your presence. I can think of one particular individual who said to me, "We do the telling, and you do the jumping". Of course, you can refer back to senior level, but they just want you to get on with it, and so you have to manage the antagonism and try to win them over. Sometimes it happens that the calibre of the staff lower down the organization is part of the problem. I must say that if I get a whiff that I don't like the way a client operates, then I won't go back. You risk a narrower spread of clients that way, but I'd rather have clients that I can work with.'

> ### Insight
> Turning business away is hard for a consultant to do, but an impossible client can damage your reputation, not to mention the effect they may have on your stress levels!

Mark Brown takes a similar view: 'I must have a degree of respect for what the client is doing – I would not work for a tobacco company unless it was to help them get out of tobacco. Personally I need to like the client and understand their wavelength. Clients usually become friends, and I will not work with a company if the chemistry is not right. When working on innovation, you need the kind of special relationship where you build on each other's ideas, and one and one make three. That's hard to achieve with someone you don't like.'

KEY MESSAGES

▶ *As a consultant, you need to operate at a level above personal likes and dislikes.*
▶ *Your professionalism will not reveal any negative feelings towards an individual.*
▶ *You can therefore be objective about the project.*
▶ *If this does not work for you, then ask to change project, or give up the client.*

Conclusion

Difficult clients are a special challenge, and one of the key areas to think about is loyalty. You owe your own company loyalty, of course, but what about the loyalty to a client project team member – who may take the view that you are betraying them to their own manager. Openness is the ideal, which can be difficult at times between client and supplier, but whenever possible, make it the rule. It will build trust between you.

Maintaining at least a civilized relationship is critical at all times, but that doesn't mean that clients can walk all over you, and sometimes you need to push back. Maintaining a level of mutual respect is a fundamental of any client relationship.

Closing thoughts

Respect yourself and others will respect you.

Confucius

Be careful that victories do not carry the seed of future defeats.

Ralph W. Sockman

STEPS TO SUCCESS

▶ Do your homework on your clients, ideally while they are still prospects.

▶ Take time to consider problems – avoid knee-jerk reactions.

▶ Consult your manager or a colleague if you see a problem arising.

▶ Maintain your professionalism in the face of any emotion.

▶ Make keeping the account your priority over being right.

▶ Avoid confrontation, but deal with the issue – be as open as you can.

▶ Push back when you need to, and maintain a level of mutual respect.

19

Dealing with internal relationships

This chapter covers:
- **working alone on site**
- **working in a team**
- **working with other contractors**

In this chapter we will deal with the challenges you may face in various project situations where the issues are less likely to come from the client, but from your colleagues, your company, or your fellow suppliers or subcontractors.

Working alone on site

If you are working alone on a customer site for several months or more, a number of things may happen to you, quite apart from those related to the project you are working on. The consequences have rather more implications if you are an employee than if you work for yourself, but there are some close parallels.

There are three major issues involved here:

▶ *A sense of becoming cut off from your company.*
▶ *A feeling of divided loyalties.*

▶ *A feeling of belonging to the client, otherwise known as 'going native'.*

You might think that the three are a progression, which they could be, but it is possible to suffer (or enjoy!) any one of them.

Insight

If you work alone and are self-employed, the problems described here are less serious for you, but you can still find yourself slipping into your client's way of thinking, or losing sight of your own business goals.

CASE STUDY: LOYALTIES

Let us look at the case of Harry, who has been working on a software project for eight months. During that time he has got to know Dan, the client project manager, very well. They have much in common, and going to the pub at Friday lunchtimes has become a tradition. Harry's boss was given international responsibility in the last year, and has been travelling a great deal, so Harry doesn't see much of him, but he doesn't really mind, he is pretty self-sufficient and the project is going well.

One Friday lunchtime, Dan becomes very conspiratorial: 'Harry, I'm going to tell you something I probably shouldn't. I'm going to recommend that we buy your product for phase two of the project. I don't think anyone will question it, so it will be pretty much a done deal. You will be able to take quite a lot of credit for the decision, I should think, and of course, we will need you to implement it!'

Far from being delighted, Harry is very alarmed. The phase two proposal was presented to Dan by Harry's boss in April – just two months ago. Harry called into the office last week, and was told that there are serious problems with the new product, which will not be ready for several months. He is now in a quandary. Does he say nothing, let his company get the order, and then let Dan down, or does he tell Dan the truth, and risk losing the order completely, not to mention more work for him in this very congenial environment.

Dan continues: 'There's a Board meeting this afternoon, I'm going to propose it then. I really want to impress them by being ahead of the game.'

Harry cannot see his friend risk losing his reputation. 'Dan, you don't have to do that today, do you?'

'No, but the sooner the better, otherwise it will be another four weeks. Why do you ask?'

'I would just like to check on a few things in the proposal – things we didn't know about two months ago.'

'Like what?'

Harry is now on the spot. He waffles, and Dan is not convinced.

'Are you trying to tell me something, Harry?'

'Not yet I'm not. I just want to be sure that whatever you put in front of the Board is absolutely right, that's all.'

'Are you telling me the price is going up?'

'Not at all. I just want to make sure everything's right.'

Dan responds in a suspicious tone, 'Well you've certainly convinced me not to do anything today, Harry. I'm now concerned about the proposal, and you'd better ask your boss to come in and re-present it to me in the next two weeks, so that it's ready for the next Board meeting – if I decide to put it forward, of course.'

When Harry eventually manages to contact his boss, on his mobile in Germany, he is not pleased. 'So why am I re-presenting this proposal, Harry?'

'Well, I heard about the problems with our new product, and that it just won't meet their timeframe, and I thought …'

'So what exactly did you tell Dan?'

'Nothing. I just said I wanted to check out the details of the proposal, that's all.'

'So now he's really suspicious! Why did you have to say anything? We would have just got the order, and the schedule would have been a bit delayed, at worst. Now we might have lost the whole thing, thanks to you.'

'I didn't want to let the client down – the schedule could be affected by several months. Don't you think …'

'No I don't! Get the order first, and worry about the schedule later. There's usually a way round these problems anyway, once you get going – they're never as bad as R&D make them seem. You should know that by now. I'm in London on the 7th and 8th – see if you can fix the presentation for then.'

Harry duly arranges the appointment, and is cross-questioned again by Dan. 'You don't look very happy about this, Harry. Tell me what the problem is.'

Harry was torn before, but now his boss has made things much worse. He is not happy about his apparently cavalier approach to the client's schedule, but on the other hand he knows that his boss may be right, and that the schedule may not be affected nearly as badly as he first thought. He has now upset both his boss and Dan, and he is seriously worried that Dan won't trust him any more.

Insight

What would you do in Harry's place? Tell Dan everything, say nothing, or do something in between? You are effectively choosing where your loyalties lie – with your company or with the client.

Harry says, 'Look Dan, when I was in our office last week, I heard a few rumours about this new product – nothing major. That's normal with any software, as you know, and normally I wouldn't have said anything, but, well, we know each other pretty well now, and I didn't want you to lose any credibility with the Board.'

'So what were these rumours?'

'Oh, the usual – bugs, delays, what you always get with any new software. It's nothing major, as I said, and Dan, I'd be very grateful if you wouldn't mention this conversation to my boss. You can ask him all these questions without needing to refer to it, can't you?'

'Of course, Harry. Thank you for being straight with me, but I have to say that you may just have lost your company the order. I shall have to investigate alternatives now, and your nearest competitor has an existing product that can do the job, so I won't have to worry about bugs in a new version.'

Harry's loyalty to the client has meant disloyalty to his employer. It is not difficult to predict that Harry's future might lie outside his current company.

You could argue that Harry was just being honest, which is what every good supplier should be with their clients. Business realities are different, and Harry's boss will view this as straight disloyalty. The situation is set up for Harry to leave the company now, so the company needs to be clear on whether it wishes to retain an honest employee, or lose a disloyal one. If the employment market is difficult, it may well wish to take the positive view and keep Harry. In which case, bridges need to be built very quickly.

If you find yourself in Harry's place, do not assume that your company will automatically reject you because they see you as disloyal. If you really want to stay with your present employer, you might suggest a change of client, to alleviate the problem, together with either a shorter project, or a project where a team of people are involved, and you are not left alone on site for months on end.

KEY MESSAGES

▶ *Be clear on where your primary loyalties lie.*
▶ *Take the initiative if you feel you are slipping in a direction you do not want to take.*

CASE STUDY: THE VICTIM

Susan had been working alone on site for four months, and it was driving her mad. She was in an office on her own with no windows and poor light; the client staff were friendly but really busy, and had little time to socialize. It was also the type of work that she had done several times before, and despite her requests for broader experience, she always seemed to end up doing the same thing. She has asked to go on a training course, but nothing has happened.

When she sees her manager, Helen, there is only time to talk about the project and then she's off to her next meeting. Susan sent her an email, requesting the training, but she has not replied.

If you were Susan, what would you do now?

▶ *You could pick up the newspaper and start job hunting.*
▶ *You could complain to HR.*
▶ *You could demand time with your manager to discuss these issues.*
▶ *You could just soldier on and hope for the best.*

It would be easy to go down a negative route at this point – either complaining or leaving. What can be very effective is simply to take the initiative, and see what happens.

Susan goes to see the client, and asks if she can move into a different working area. After a week, this is arranged without difficulty, and she now sits with the client team.

Susan writes an email to her manager, telling her that she will be making a booking for the training course, which will take place in two months' time. She then rings the HR department, makes the booking, and asks them to organize the signoff procedure with her boss, as she is out on site all the time.

She then rings her boss's secretary, and asks her to block out two hours for her next site visit, not one, as she wants a personal discussion. She emails her manager to confirm this. When that meeting does eventually take place, her manager is a little taken aback at the things that Susan has done, but can hardly complain that she was not informed about them, and ends up by applauding the proactive stance that Susan has taken. This is Susan's cue to extract a promise that, after her training, she can work on a different type of project, to which her manager readily agrees. Susan already knows that she will have to identify this project in advance, and perhaps do a little selling to the project manager, and then she can present the decision on a plate to her manager.

Susan has switched from the 'lost consultant on site as victim' mode, to the 'I am in control and I will get what I want' mode, which produces much better results!

Insight

If you work for yourself, you won't need to ask anyone's permission, but sometimes it's easy to be put upon by the client – stuck in a dark corner somewhere, with no time for training – you need to give yourself permission for that!

KEY MESSAGES

▶ *Recognize when you are in danger of going native, and decide where your loyalties lie.*
▶ *If you have been 'disloyal' and still want to work for your employer, take proactive steps to rebuild the relationship.*
▶ *If you feel neglected and in 'victim' mode, take the initiative, and make something happen, whilst keeping your manager informed.*
▶ *Make a formal request for some of your manager's time for a personal discussion, if necessary.*
▶ *Take responsibility for implementing your own training and development plan.*

Working in a team

As a consultant, you will probably find yourself working frequently in a project team. By their very nature, they tend to form quickly for relatively short periods, so there is little time for the 'forming, storming and norming', which is the natural process that many teams go through on their way to stability and effectiveness.

Insight

If you set about your role as a team member in a proactive way, you can make a significant contribution to the process of building a team quickly, and help the team leader, rather than leaving all the responsibility to them, as many team members do.

As a good team player, you will be:

▶ *a good communicator who listens, informs, and asks for information*
▶ *open and honest*
▶ *nice to people, but not afraid to deal with conflict if it arises*
▶ *helpful to other team members, looking out for them, and not purely focused on your own role*
▶ *loyal to the team*
▶ *positive, with a sense of humour.*

COMMUNICATION

In this context it is helpful to hold two presuppositions: the map is not the territory, and the meaning of communication is in the response you get. These two will focus your thinking on the views of other people and their 'map' or view of the world, and on the fact that what people hear is often not what left your lips!

CASE STUDY: DIVIDED LOYALTIES

Sarah and Brian have been working for the company for a long time, often on the same projects. Ian knows how close they are, but the team leader, Robert, is a very recent arrival, and is struggling to get to know everyone. Ian overhears Sarah telling Brian about a problem she is having. 'Brian, this looks really messy, I'll need your help.'

'No joy, Sarah, just stick with it. I've got enough on my plate for now.'

'Seriously, Brian, this looks like a show stopper – I might have to tell Robert.'

'Don't be silly – he doesn't know anything about anything. I'll look at it later.'

Ian is worried by what he hears, and is now in a quandary. He knows that it is Sarah and Brian's style not to tell the rest of the team what they are doing. Should he tell Robert? Should he tell Sarah to tell Robert? Should he say nothing?

If he tells Robert he could be seen to be telling tales, and alienate Sarah and Brian. If he tells Sarah, he will have to confess that he has been eavesdropping. If he says nothing, he could be letting the whole team down, or there might just be nothing to tell.

In the end he contrives a conversation with Sarah when Brian is not there, and asks her how things are going, but she tells him everything is fine, and he cannot push the questions too far. He decides that all he can do is ask questions at the team meeting, which again produces no result.

Insight

Ian does nothing more. Is this the right decision? Should he have told Robert, and put the project needs before his team loyalties?

It later emerges that there was a serious problem, and the project was delayed. Ian feels very unhappy, but cannot see what else he could have done without ruining his relationship with Brian and

Sarah. Robert never learned that Ian had this information, but if he had, he would no doubt have taken the view that Ian should have told him, and left him to 'find out' without implicating Ian. The problem would have been that Ian did not know Robert well enough to trust him with that information.

This case study illustrates classic communication problems in a team – Brian and Sarah happily talk to each other, but do not feel any responsibility to the rest of the team. Ian has tried to be a responsible team member, but Sarah will not co-operate, and Ian has to choose between his team relationships and his duty to the project. Someone more skilled might have managed to get something out of Sarah, and then persuaded her to talk to Robert. That would have been the best outcome.

KEY MESSAGES

▶ *Take active steps to be a responsible team member, but not if it breaches team loyalty.*
▶ *Try to get other members of the team to take responsibility, without upsetting the relationship.*
▶ *As a good team member, aiding the communication process is one of the most important roles you can perform, especially in team meetings, when you can ask questions for clarification, or to encourage someone to speak when you know they have something to say.*
▶ *Teams rarely fail because of over-communication, but things often go wrong for the opposite reason.*

CASE STUDY: COMMUNICATION

An extreme example of communication difficulties is described here by David Mitchell, who was sent out to an eastern bloc country to retrieve a public utilities project, which was slipping by six weeks every month.

'For the project to slip at this rate was quite an achievement, and it proved a real challenge. I was the only English-speaking person there, and I was assigned a full-time interpreter. It was the middle of winter, very cold, with no heating in the main office, and the canteen's very best effort was tripe and beetroot, both of which I hate!

'When I got there, I discovered the problem was that no one could make a decision. In the post-Communist world, where previously the State had decided everything, no one had any idea how to make a decision, or, more importantly, how to take responsibility for it. I analysed the situation from the top to the bottom of the organization, and it was the same throughout. However, the people at the top did say that they were happy for the people at the bottom to make decisions, to which the people lower down immediately asked: "Which ones can we make?"

'To break this mould, I spent time coaching the team and the project managers in making decisions, and more important than that, encouraging them to make mistakes and see that the consequences were not fatal. I decided that working from the bottom up would be most effective, and so it proved. The major challenge was that all this had to be done through an interpreter, but I succeeded and put the project back on track to a successful conclusion. It was very rewarding to help to empower people and to see them respond to this new-found freedom.'

You may think that this is a problem generated by Communist rule, but fear of making decisions can hold a team back in any political culture – even the most democratic. However, the issue is easier to address if you do not need an interpreter!

CASE STUDY: MANAGING CONFLICT

This again tends to be an area that people feel they should leave to the team leader to sort out, which can sometimes be the right decision, and sometimes not.

Julia walked into a meeting room to find Ben and Steve arguing violently.

'Hey guys, what's the problem?'

'Don't ask, Julia, just leave us to it!' Ben is very angry.

Steve stares at the floor.

'Steve, is there ...'

'Julia!' Ben almost shouts at her and holds the door open.

Steve gives her a forlorn glance as she leaves.

Julia bumps into Jonathon, the project manager, as she leaves.

'Hey, Julia, anything the matter? You look a bit upset.'

'Yes. Er, no, not really Jonathon, I have to dash, see you later.'

She escapes to the Ladies, and reflects on the situation. Since she does not want to be flayed alive by Ben, she will not be telling Jonathon anything. However, she could see that Steve was in bad shape, and decides to have a chat to him later.

He tells her nothing, just says that he and Ben have sorted it all out, and to forget it. She is not convinced, but decides to do as he asks. A few days later she overhears a snatch of conversation which tells her that things are far from sorted out. Before she can do anything, Jonathon asks her if she has noticed any problem between Steve and Ben.

'Why do you ask, Jonathon?'

'Things seemed strained between them when I talked to them yesterday. What do you think?'

'I think you should follow up on what you observed, Jonathon. I can't add anything.'

Jonathon talks to the two of them, but gets nowhere, as they assure him that all is well. Only when a project delay arises as a result of their inability to work together can Jonathon address the problem.

KEY MESSAGES

▸ When two people are in conflict, you can only ask them if they want help, or an arbiter – who would normally be the team leader. Sometimes people welcome help, sometimes it is the last thing they want.

▸ The key thing is not to ignore conflict, because it can seriously damage the function of the team, but if those in conflict hide their disagreement, it is no one's business but theirs, until it affects the project in some way.

OPENNESS AND HONESTY

In the last two case studies, we have seen what would appear to be the opposite of open and honest behaviour, with team members hiding information from their team leader. This is because they have put loyalty to the other team members as their highest priority, and strictly speaking, the information they had was not theirs to give. Being open with people is the fastest way to build trust, and trust is the foundation of an effective team. When the information is yours, then share it – be it good news or bad. If there is a problem, then you are giving others the opportunity to help you to solve it. If that makes you feel exposed in front of the rest of the team, then console yourself with the fact that they are valuing your open and honest approach.

BEING POSITIVE AND SUPPORTIVE

Have you ever been in one of those project meetings where someone always takes the negative view? They think that they are pointing out difficulties in a constructive manner, but the message that leaves them is not the one that the rest of the group hears, for example:

'Well, I think we should stop and review the whole thing.'

'Simon, that would put the project back at least a week.'

'But this is a serious problem. If it goes the way I predict, then we're on the road to complete disaster.'

The rest of the team now argue with Simon, and tell him he is being a pessimist, and over-reacting. Simon gets upset. The team leader over-rules his objections, and the meeting ends on a sour note.

If Simon had framed his issue in a positive way, he might have had a different response, like this:

'Now look, folks, I know you're going to hate me for raising this, but I've found what could be a serious problem.'

'Not again, Simon!'

'I'm afraid so. Now I don't want this to cause a project delay, so can we examine this together and see if we can solve it here?'

At this point Simon gets murmurs of assent, and he is off on a positive track, taking the team with him.

In addition to a positive approach, active support for other team members really helps to build a team fast. This can mean any number of things: paying a compliment in public or in private; helping someone with a problem; supporting someone's contribution to a meeting.

KEY MESSAGES

▶ *Take active responsibility for helping the team to work well together.*
▶ *Communicate to clarify and inform, and to help other team members do the same.*
▶ *Be open and honest.*
▶ *Deal openly with conflict if it involves you directly.*
▶ *Oil the team wheels with good humour and positive remarks.*
▶ *Be loyal and supportive to the team.*

Working with other suppliers

When you are working on larger projects, you will often find that you are working with other suppliers in various ways. You may be the prime contractor, or you may be one of a number of small subcontractors. You may have been chosen by the client, or by the prime contractor.

Each of these scenarios can present operating problems, not necessarily because of the nature of the other suppliers, but just the complexity of a three-tier relationship. There is plenty of scope for communication problems to arise, for example. The key is to recognize the situation, and anticipate as much as possible. As prime contractor, you will obviously take responsibility for agreeing objectives and managing the progress and quality of the work of other suppliers, but as a subcontractor, it is in your interest to make sure that this is done well, and not just to take a passive role. Whatever your relationship, spend as much, if not more time on setting up the project parameters with other suppliers as you would with the client – this is the best way to avoid problems.

However, no amount of agreement of objectives and project milestone reviews will solve political problems. Understanding the politics, and finding a way around them or above them is the key, and this is covered in the section on politics in Chapter 16. If you have politics between suppliers and within the client, then you have the most challenging situation to deal with. Political issues aside, let us look at some typical situations that can arise.

CASE STUDY: MOTIVES AND COMMUNICATION

You are the prime contractor, and have set a really tight project plan, and taken pains to agree it in full detail with your subcontractors. In a lunchtime conversation with your client, you discover that extra work has been taken on by Joe, one of your subcontractors, without your knowledge. The client is surprised that you are not aware of it, as he assumes that Joe has told you. You do not want the client to think that there is an issue between you and one of your contractors, so you make light of it, but immediately go to see Joe. He tells you it is just a small thing, hardly worth discussing, which is why he has not mentioned it yet. He was going to, of course, at the next meeting.

You have a choice now: you can get heavy-handed with Joe, and give him a lecture on working to agreed standards. You can have a similar, but more moderated conversation with the client, who should have put the request through you, as it could involve additional expense. Your response will depend on a number of things, not least the size of the work. If it really is trivial, then a few words with Joe and a casual mention to the client are probably all it needs, just to reinforce the principle without making a big issue of it. The big question in all these situations is to know whether the client and Joe deliberately broke the rules, or whether they genuinely believed that what they did was acceptable to you.

CASE STUDY: CLIENT OWNERSHIP

The most delicate situations arise between suppliers where future business is concerned. You are the prime contractor on a project, where you have used one subcontractor. Their team leader is Mike. All has gone well and you are coming to the end of the project, with the next one clearly in your sights. You have a 'gentleman's agreement' with the client that this will be awarded to you, on the strength of your work to date.

However, you have recently noticed that your client, Karl, is spending a lot of time with Mike, and when you joined them for lunch in the canteen the other day, they seemed ill at ease, as if you had interrupted something they did not want you to hear. You will not need to subcontract Mike's company for the next project, as you have identical skills in this area. Seeing Karl and Mike getting together again for lunch yesterday fills you with misgivings – is Mike trying to steal this work from you?

You sit down to consider your options. If you raise the subject, you risk planting an idea where one did not exist before – both with Mike and with Karl, although the risk is much lower with Mike, who will undoubtedly be aware of the business potential. If you just wait, you are potentially giving Mike more time to do a deal with Karl.

You decide to talk to Mike.

'I see you and Karl in deep discussions these days, Mike. Is it anything I should know about?'

'Not really. Mainly about meeting the deadlines for the final stage.'

'Nothing to do with the next project?'

'Meaning?'

'You know what I'm asking.'

'Well, I didn't raise it, but Karl did ask me if I would be part of your project team for the next stage, and I said no, you have the expertise for that. So he asked me if I'd be interested in doing it, and of course I said yes, but that's as far as it's gone, he didn't say any more, and I didn't push it. I was waiting to see what happened, as I know it's your client, and however it works, you'll be involved in some way.'

Insight

What does a genuine and honest subcontractor do when a client asks him 'off the record' if they can work together directly after this contract is over? This situation can create havoc between suppliers – but ultimately the client holds all the cards.

You have no way of knowing if that is what happened, but you decide to take it at face value, and say nothing to Karl, simply continue as before, assuming you have won the work. If Karl wants Mike in the next stage, he will need to ask you, and it can be arranged through you, which is what Mike is acknowledging. He is behaving properly as a subcontractor, although it would have been better if he had volunteered the information that you have just extracted from him.

As the client, Karl has every right to buy whatever services he wishes, whether a 'gentleman's agreement' exists or not. You can have no issue with Karl, simply offer him what he asks for, and price it accordingly.

CASE STUDY: DISAGREEMENT BETWEEN SUPPLIERS

Major problems can arise when suppliers disagree over something major. Helen and Nigel just cannot agree on a project milestone, twenty-four hours before the client review meeting.

'We're there, Nigel! No need for all this extra work you're proposing ...'

'Sorry Helen, I just don't agree, and as it's ultimately my company's responsibility, I'm going to have to tell the client there will be a week's delay.'

'I can't support that. You are wasting time.'

'We must present a united front to the client.'

'Not when it wrongly shows my company in a bad light, I'm not!'

'It won't look too good if we can't agree, though will it?'

'But I really believe I'm right, and we're not running late, and I want the client to know that.'

'They'll end up doing what I recommend, as prime contractor.'

'That's as maybe, but at least I'll have put my case.'

Nigel positions the topic very carefully at the client meeting the next day: 'Helen and I have discussed this point at length, and have agreed to disagree. Helen believes that we have reached the milestone. I do not. I strongly recommend that we take another week to do this. Would you like us to debate this with you, or will you accept my recommendation?'

This is the best form of damage limitation that Nigel can achieve. He has maintained a clear position of control, and has avoided an argument in front of the client. If the client asks for a debate, it will be a measured presentation of views, with no antagonism. Nothing upsets a client more than being faced by squabbling contractors offering conflicting advice.

An extension of this problem is where suppliers not only disagree, but start blaming each other.

As an example, Helen might have blurted out in the meeting:
'I don't agree with Nigel because in not agreeing to the milestone, he is implicitly blaming my team for their work. That is a completely unfounded criticism, and I can prove it to you!'

Now the client is being asked to arbitrate between the two of them, and the client hates being put in this position, so think of their perspective before you leap to the defence of your company.

Ultimately supplier relationships are about mutual benefit, loyalty and trust. If you approach your fellow suppliers in an open and positive manner, whilst holding those values, you will go a long way along the road to achieving that mutual benefit.

KEY MESSAGES

▶ *Understand the nature of your supplier relationships in any project.*
▶ *Take care to clarify all the project parameters with them.*
▶ *Present a united front to the client.*
▶ *Aim for openness, loyalty and trust as your prime values in any supplier relationship. If you start from there, with positive expectations, you are more likely to get positive responses in return.*

Closing thoughts

You get the best out of others when you give the best of yourself.

Harry Firestone

No man is wise enough by himself.

Titus Maccius Plautus

STEPS TO SUCCESS

▶ *Remain alert to the quality of the relationship you have with:*
  ▷ *your employer or colleagues*
  ▷ *your working team*
  ▷ *external organizations.*

▶ *Anticipate any conflict of loyalty, and face the issue squarely.*

▶ *Work proactively to make the team effective.*

▶ *Deal with any conflict so that the client sees a united front.*

20

Marketing your services

This chapter covers:
- *what are you selling?*
- *the lure of the brochure*
- *the value of personal contacts*
- *review of marketing tools*

This is a subject which will vary in importance to you, according to your employment status, but even as the most junior employee on a large project team, you are still a part of the marketing process. As you go up the employment ladder, this responsibility increases, and sales frequently becomes a key part of the job. If you are self-employed, it is critical.

If we start where the need is greatest, it will illustrate the principles most clearly. Although the subsequent execution may vary greatly by size of company, these principles will apply equally to someone employed by the top consulting groups and to the newly fledged one-man band.

What are you selling?

From the very start of this book we have been clear that people buy integrity, reliability and credibility, before they buy technical expertise from a consultant. Integrity and reliability cannot easily be sold. If they are thrust at a client, they are likely to reject them, and this is the intrinsic difficulty in marketing consulting services using any of the traditional methods, such as advertising or mailings. You can promote your technical expertise, and if that is sufficiently rare, people will respond. Unfortunately few of us are offering such a rare commodity, and the client's key to choosing between all the competitive technical offerings is to find ways of testing their need for integrity and reliability.

Insight

Be very clear what it is your clients value in your service, apart from integrity, reliability and credibility. You may be an HR expert, but it could be your ability to set HR in the complete organization context, or to take a hard financial view of HR that people really value.

The most obvious route is to seek recommendations from friends or colleagues – people whose opinion they trust. Failing that, they will look at track record, and ask to speak to previous clients.

What they are almost certainly not buying is a services product. They want to know that you have experience in setting up call centres. They do not want your standard formula for doing so, because their call centre is going to be different. Bear this in mind if you decide you need a brochure: the essence of what you can 'sell' in a brochure is your professionalism (often conveyed by the physical elements of the brochure itself), your technical expertise, your flexibility to meet differing client needs, and your track record of success. If a client senses that they are going to be strait-jacketed into your standard solution, this will be a great turn-off for them.

The lure of the brochure

For consulting services, a brochure will never be a major element in the sales process, but it can detract from it, if not well done. At best it plays a professional but relatively small supporting role.

If you are just starting up as a consultant, do not go down the brochure route, you will be wasting your not-yet-earned money at this stage! Vic Hartley produced some real pearls of wisdom on this subject:

'It is important to be really clear about what you are providing to the marketplace. I created a brochure of my services, and I got the names of managing directors of the companies I was targeting. So I sent out 200 personal letters with my brochure, and I got one reply! It's so obvious to me now that that's what will happen, so my advice is to design a brochure, so that you are clear in your mind what you want to offer, and then throw it away! Having a focus, that's the important thing. I might use a brochure after I have held a first meeting with a prospect, but otherwise, they are not useful. Indeed you could say that, since you are offering a tailored service to meet the client's needs, then it's not congruent to offer them a brochure. You cannot sell a tailored service with a standardized mailing.

'At the same time as designing a brochure, I listed 17 names of people to approach, just contacts on a scrap of paper. I followed them up, and out of 17 names I got work from eleven, whereas my mailing of 200 had produced one lead and no work! Service is about talking to people and selling yourself. You need contacts to get to know people and move outwards from there.'

Insight

You may feel that unless your marketing is translated onto paper or PC screen, it's not real marketing. Wrong! Clever organizations never spend a thing other than on business cards and a minimal website. All their business comes from recommendations and referrals – that's real marketing!

Mary Ahmad had a similar story: 'I went through the stage of writing lots of marketing letters, which I think everybody does, but nothing much comes of them, and then I moved on to networking opportunities – things like the IOD, the American Chamber of Commerce, etc.'

The message of experience is consistent – successful marketing of consulting services is about networking, contacts and referrals.

Someone who has taken another successful route is Peter Honey, who keeps a very high profile through his writing. Not only is he a well-known author, but he appears regularly in professional magazines, which, in addition to profile raising, enhance his credibility and reinforce his technical expertise, which, since it is laid out so openly for public inspection, provides a big step towards establishing integrity.

Review of marketing tools

Here is a checklist of each of the marketing elements, with commentary on their appropriateness for marketing consulting skills.

Advertising
Often expensive. Not an effective medium for the personal message you need to convey. Good if you have a special skill or a unique offering and/or a tightly targeted audience. For example, if you are the only mobile computer expert in your area, it is a good idea to advertise in the local newspaper or parish magazines. Your expertise is not unique, but your location and mobility are, and your audience is tightly targeted, and not expensive to reach.

On the other hand, if you are a management consultant specializing in salary systems, unless you have a narrow focus – for example, you cover the bee-keeping market, where there are specialist magazines – then advertising will do nothing for you.

PR
Writing 'technical' articles for relevant magazines can be a very effective marketing exercise, as evidenced by Peter Honey. Getting any kind of positive press coverage is good, although do not waste your time trying to woo journalists unless you know you have something really interesting for them to write about.

PR also covers things like sponsorship and corporate
entertainment. Sponsorship is normally about raising the
profile of your company, and is a very indirect route, if indeed a
route at all, to increasing sales. Corporate entertainment can be
useful, as it comes under the heading of making contacts, and
direct contact with prospects is the only sure way to create
a sale.

Direct mail
Not appropriate, as described above by Vic Hartley.

Telesales
Could be used to get appointments for a first contact, otherwise
inappropriate as a bought-in service. If you are calling prospective
clients yourself, then it is entirely appropriate.

Exhibitions
Inappropriate unless you are targeting those bee-keepers again!

Internet
Marketing using the Internet can take a number of forms:
through your own website, via emailings, circulating a newsletter,
advertising with Google through a sponsored link. These are the
most obvious methods, and some can be very cost-effective.
The Internet works hardest when you have something concrete
and specialist to offer: so if you design children's play areas,
or build personalized photograph albums, you will be much
easier for potential clients to find than a financial adviser or a
life coach.

Seminars/webinars

Another means of generating contacts, and therefore useful, if you have the funds to set them up. Offer real content, and make it clear that this is not a sales pitch in disguise. Work on an acceptance rate of one in ten, even with warm, rather than cold contacts. Send a written invitation, and then do all the follow-up on the telephone. For small organizations, all this hard work may not pay off, and you may do better to put the same effort into setting up individual meetings. Alternatively you can consider webinars – the online version of a seminar. They are much cheaper to run, but question again whether your effort should go into networking or selling face to face.

Networking

This is a vital marketing activity, and falls into two areas:

First, using all your personal contacts, and then all their contacts. To quote Mary Ahmad again: 'The advice is to contact everyone you know, so I would ask them all, "If you were me, who would you be talking to?" I said this to avoid asking them the question directly. The good thing is that your contacts tend to move around between jobs, and spread the word around.'

The second form of networking is via organized groups, such as the Institute of Directors, or any of the myriad of local meetings set up by the local Chamber of Commerce, or the local group of IT companies, etc. If you are working alone, or as a very small business, these groups can be an invaluable source of contacts and leads, but possibly also of colleagues you may wish to collaborate with, or use as a sounding board.

In addition to these business groups, there are also specific organizations for consultants, such as the IMC, or Magenta Circle, as well as for specialist consulting groups, such as the British Computer Society. (See 'Taking it further', page 304 for details.)

> ### Insight
> Approach networking as a proactive task, not as a by-product of other things you do. Actively cultivate your network, and plan to enlarge it systematically. You are not looking for an immediate return, which is why it needs regular attention.

Nigel Wyatt founded Magenta Circle when he became a consultant, and he revealed an interesting fact. As an individual consultant in the financial training arena, he has had more business from competing consultants than from complementary ones: 'They understand exactly what I do, and when they have too much work, or a client isn't right for them, they come to me!' Collaborating with your competitors is an interesting path to follow, and many consultants do so very successfully.

Intermediaries

Everyone is familiar with the contract agency, which has served the IT industry in particular, for a long time. The recent changes in tax legislation have made this market less attractive, but these agencies remain a useful source of work for many independent consultants.

Now the Internet has produced a new breed of intermediaries, who operate quite differently, and provide a virtual marketplace for consultants. You pay a small annual fee as a consultant to belong to the service, and the employer pays a bigger fee on hiring. You provide your details to the service, and the employers provide details of their opportunities, and then you negotiate directly, with no other fees involved. Examples of organizations that provide this service are Magenta Circle and Skillfair (details in 'Taking it further', page 306). As this is a young and dynamic marketplace, it is likely that new organizations will have appeared by the time you read this book, so do an Internet search for consulting agencies, to find out what is available to you now.

Selling

Many consultants find selling a great challenge, and prefer to use intermediaries, or become associates of other consulting companies, in order to avoid having to generate business themselves. As we have seen, there are many effective alternatives to direct selling, as far as making the first contact is concerned, but at some point you will need to sell yourself and your service. The key is to identify the client's problem, so that you can offer them a solution. Then you are not selling, you are helping them. If you can frame your discussion in this way, it will flow naturally, since offering help is second nature, and a million miles from the 'foot in the door' image of sales that everyone seems to carry in their heads! (For an excellent book on how to sell, see 'Taking it further', page 307.)

Your daily marketing activity

In reality, the best marketing you can do is to market yourself really well to your current client, by doing and being seen to be doing an excellent job. Towards the end of a project you might ask them for leads. Do they know of anyone who might need your services – now or in the future? As you carefully cultivate each client, they will become a source of repeat or referral business, and this is marketing at its very best.

Closing thoughts

We aim above the mark to hit the mark.

Ralph Waldo Emerson

Only those who dare to fail greatly can ever achieve greatly.

Robert Francis Kennedy

STEPS TO SUCCESS

▶ *The marketing of consulting services needs to involve personal contact to be effective.*

▶ *If you are small, focus on contacts, networking and intermediaries.*

▶ *If you are larger, then enhance contacts and networking with seminars and PR activities.*

21

Starting and running
your own business

This chapter covers:
- *three success stories*
- *critical success factors for a consulting business*
- *finance, tax and legal status*
- *choosing an accountant*
- *setting fee levels*
- *minimizing set-up costs*

Three success stories

For those of you who are about to set up your own business, or are planning to do so in the future, this chapter contains advice on the basics, and also the experience of three very different consultants, who have made a success of setting up on their own. If we start with their experiences, then what you need to do in order to follow in their footsteps will become clear.

PETER HONEY, PETER HONEY LEARNING

After graduation, Peter Honey did four jobs for two major companies, Ford and British Airways, and then decided that a couple of years as a consultant would give him breadth of experience. Those two years turned into a working lifetime, during which there has been only one summer when he has had nothing in the pipeline. Asked about his obvious success in building a business,

he replied: 'I was never conscious of doing any marketing.'
However, if you consider that Peter has written over twenty books
and a hundred articles, and has a worldwide reputation for his work
on learning styles, you will understand a key attribute of his success.

'In the early days I depended on word of mouth and referrals. I'm
cynical about respect for the published word – I've written because
I love it.

'There are consultants who are truly learned experts. I believe in
being a learning consultant. I have a low opinion of management
consultants who dish out answers. Diagnosis is so vital – it's more
than half the job. I work with a client, I'm not an expert on a
pedestal, and I don't have ready-made answers. With many clients
it's a learning together relationship. I tell them that there is no need
for me to know everything that they know, otherwise they will
have spoiled the distinctive competence I bring – a fresh approach.

Insight

It's so easy to become professionally arrogant as a consultant –
you are the expert, after all! Peter so clearly lives by his
belief in the learning consultant, and most particularly the
consultant who does not have all the answers ready-made.

'My advice is to do a real job first, to learn the fundamentals of the
world of work and particularly to understand the politics, before
you become a consultant.'

MARY AHMAD, CORPORATE HR PARTNERS

Mary Ahmad started her own business from a very different point
in her career. She explained: 'Once you get to be an HR Director,
you don't do much HR. You spend your time managing managers
and the relationship with the parent company.

'One day I was talking to a multinational about a job they
had, because they had different departments in different locations,

and they wanted an HR person to integrate them. They had several marketing departments for different parts of the company, and I said that I expected that that would create a lot of problems, and they said it did, and suddenly I could see it all, and I realized that I didn't want to do this any more. I didn't want any more of the politics – I can do the politics, but I didn't want to – I just didn't have another corporate in me. I was 48.

'I had always said that I didn't want to be in corporate life after 50, so I took some time and I thought about what I might do. I realized, after some fanciful ideas, that people would pay me for what I know. My brother-in-law is a consultant, and I didn't want to appear to be a one-man band, working from home, so I shared his office. That meant I had someone to speak to, which was important on the days when I didn't feel motivated. My brother-in-law's business was called Corporate Venture Partners Ltd, so I called myself Corporate HR Partners. So I had an office and a name, now I needed to develop a business.

'The advice you get is to contact everyone you know, so I would ask them all, if you were me, who would you be talking to? This to avoid asking them the question directly. The good thing is that your contacts tend to move around between jobs, and spread the word around.

'I also worked with other people who had been consultants for longer than I had, which was very helpful. It was slow to start with, and there were days when I thought, "Am I doing the right thing?" But I'm not someone that quits, and I couldn't think of anything I was better suited to do. I worked on the basis that small companies and start-ups need more HR than an established company in a maintenance phase.

'I went through the stage of writing lots of marketing letters, which I think everybody does, but nothing much comes of them, and then I moved on to networking opportunities – things like the IOD, the American Chamber of Commerce, etc.

> **Insight**
>
> Mary's story clearly shows how hard it can be to start up
> from scratch. It requires gritty determination, and someone
> to talk to when your motivation is low. She used what
> she thought were the 'right' marketing tools, and then she
> dedicated her efforts to contacts and networking.

'I was two years on my own, and it was OK. Those were the hardest years, especially if you are used to the corporate life, and enjoy team working and discussion. What's very different is that everything you normally decide on is discussed first. When you're on your own, that no longer happens, unless you seek someone out as a sounding board.

'I started in 1995. At the beginning of 1998 my fellow Director, Andrew, joined and that made a significant difference. We now have clients on retained services, and a more complete HR offering. It took off more. We have never been there to carve out a major consulting organization, because we want do the work/home balance thing, that's really hard to do when working for a large corporate.

'I'm lucky now that Andrew is the worrier about the business. Do we have too much work? Or we don't have enough work! We are very comfortable about what we are doing. Each year we have different key clients, as their work goes in cycles. We work with them to answer the key corporate question, "How can we be the employer of choice?" Then things change, so we bring out the skills we have in cutting back, and in motivating people.

'We run the West Thames HR Exchange Club, and another group called HR4DOTCOMS – both meet quarterly. We find people are thinking more about the work/home balance. The demographics of the future are going to force companies to make this a reality for people. Younger people are asking now "Is it worth it?"

> **Insight**
>
> Note that Mary manages a network of existing and potential
> clients, where they share HR information. This is an excellent
> technique, if you can pull it off! What could be better than to

organize meetings of your customer and prospect base, where they talk about their problems and requirements.

'My advice to people setting up on their own:

▶ *Find people to talk to – people in similar situations. You need a support network, as it can be lonely.*

▶ *You set off with a business goal, and you may well need to modify that, as what you think people want and what you discover they want may not be the same thing.*

▶ *Be careful about your choice of partner in a business. I have a partner who I'd previously worked with for 20 years, who has complementary skills to me, and who I respect and trust. I would never question his integrity, and we have a very successful partnership. We did have a third partner, but it did not work as well, not because of lack of trust and respect, far from it, but because our goals and values were different. They were at a different stage in their life, and wanted different things. It was amicable, but it did not work because of that and so we parted company.*

▶ *As a consultant you need confidence and belief in yourself. You have to have broad experience if you are going to set out on your own. You need to become your own IT expert, to buy the stamps and un-jam the photocopiers; in other words, to operate at lots of different levels.'*

VIC HARTLEY, VERTEX CONSULTANTS

Vic Hartley has a varied consulting background, in that he has worked for a large consulting group, has set up his own business, and also runs courses on advanced consulting skills. He used to work for Deloittes as Head of Organization Development and Training for the Group. Vic then went on to head up Corporate HR and Management Development for Mercury Communications, which was very much an operational position, before setting up his own business over eight years ago. He talked about the transition from a corporate environment to self-employment.

'There was a lot of liberation, but a lot of things I'd taken for granted were not there. In the early stages it was difficult to get to grips with things like computer problems, or finance. Not only did this create problems, it also diverted attention from selling and building up your business.

'Another transition difficulty people have is working on their own. They often feel the need to coalesce, and maintain some of the structure of corporate life – being together and working together. I dabbled with one or two of these associations, but then I realized that the infrastructure they created was again taking me away from clients. There was also the problem of how to divide up and value any business that was won. It was very difficult to reward all the parties effectively. This can become very difficult, and many people have fallen out over it. Every time I see a partnership, I think it must be recent, because generally they don't last.

Insight

Vic clearly identifies a tension in working alone as a consultant – you need colleagues, but they can become competitors, and the relationship can go sour. He has set some simple ground rules to avoid this problem.

'I've found that the best way to operate is with a network of peers, which means that I keep my friends. If I sell work and pass it on, I keep a small percentage and they get the rest, and they know that. They do the same with me. Everything is open and up front – everyone recognizes that the sales process has a value, and that's fine.

'What this means is that my network overlaps to a small degree with theirs, and then they have their own network and so it goes on. If you trust them, then you can trust anyone they recommend in their network, and so clients also know that they will get people they can trust. The difficulty is in selling the concept that a small company can do as good a job, if not better, than the big names. I know a company in a permanent dilemma because they are very concerned about costs, but always go for the big names. It's a good measure of the confidence and maturity of a client that they are able to employ a small company rather than having to rely on the reputation of a big name. Going for big names often shows that they lack confidence.

Insight

This could be a very neat 'emperor's clothes' pitch to use if you are a small consulting company, selling to a large one, but it needs to be done very carefully!

'The key skills of a consultant are to listen, keep an open mind, and not to go in with a ready made diagnosis. Recognize that people are different, and different does not mean inferior. See things through the client's eyes, and help the client to solve the problem, rather than telling the client what to do. If the client loses ownership of a project, then the consultant has to take the blame, because that feeling of shared ownership is critical to success. It's also important to acknowledge that the consultant is not always right, just as the customer is not always right, even though you help them to think that they are for much of the time!

'The difference that makes the difference for me is remaining hungry. By hungry I mean that you have the drive and energy to keep the relationships going, or to make that phone call, or to do the report on time, even though you know they won't look at it for several days. That's what works for me. If I'm just like their own people, then why should they hire me? I've got to be more rigorous, when I hate the detail, more quality aware, more delivery focused.'

Insight

Vic's question gives a very useful focus: why should a client hire me, instead of using their own people? Or, what do I have to offer that the client cannot get from other consultants?

Vic's business is about consulting in organization development. 'I help organizations to achieve things that are significant to them, which means I have a very wide portfolio, from designing an appraisal system through to downsizing. I was asked by a client to create a programme for consultants covering advanced consulting skills, and that has become a product that I regularly deliver. I did not set out to offer it as part of my portfolio, but it emerged from client needs.'

Critical success factors

So here we have three very different people going into consulting from very different points in their career. The messages that we derive from their experience and advice are:

▶ *Setting up on your own will almost certainly be lonely. Get yourself a support network, or at least one person who can be your sounding board.*
▶ *You need to be a jack-of-all-trades when you start your own business. It will be strategy one minute and sticking on stamps the next.*
▶ *Do not waste money on expensive brochures. Write the copy, to get clarity of focus on what you are about, but do not print it!*
▶ *Use contacts, contacts and more contacts, and build your network, both as a source of leads, and working associates.*
▶ *Do not go into partnership unless your working relationship is tried and tested. If it is, then check that your skill sets are truly complementary, and finally check that your life values match. For example, long-term versus short-term gain, work/home balance. If you get positives to all these, take some more time, and possibly seek some advice, before you decide to take the plunge!*
▶ *Start with a clear idea of what your service is, and then be very prepared to modify it to meet the needs of your clients.*

Finance

The final part of this chapter deals with a subject which often worries would-be start-ups, or in some cases, does not worry them enough!

We can offer you some general advice here, but no specific detail, because personal and business circumstances can differ greatly, and also legislation changes regularly, and what is good advice today might not be so good after the next budget.

LEGAL STATUS

A vital question to ask is what your business status should be. At the moment, looking at the subject very simply, in the UK you have the choice of being a sole trader, a partnership, or a limited company.

With current tax legislation, you may have more scope to minimize your tax and National Insurance contributions if you are not a limited company. People often assume that limited company status confers some kind of authority on a small company. In fact, all it often means is that you pay more in National Insurance and accountant's fees. If you use contract agencies, they will normally force you into limited status, but if you do not, then consider all the options carefully before you commit to this route. If you are thinking of the benefit of limiting your liability, look at the current laws on director's liability, and you will find that there is very little protection in a limited company, so little, in fact, that it is unlikely to count as a factor in your decision.

Insight

Do not sleep-walk your way into limited company status because your accountant thinks it's a good idea, and you don't know about this legal stuff! There is not much to know, and you can find out very quickly what will suit you best.

As a sole trader or a partnership, you can pick any name you like, such as ABC Consulting, and you do not need to register it. You will almost certainly pay less to your accountant for the annual accounts, since they do not have to be formally audited. As the law currently stands, you will pay less in National Insurance contributions, and may have scope to pay less tax than if you were the sole employee of a limited company, where effectively you continue on PAYE. Investigate all the options, as tax rules change all the time, and they obviously vary by income level.

Consider getting some one-off, independent tax advice from a specialist, and then find an accountant to deal with the financial routine. Sometimes you find the two skill sets combined, but often they are not, and by consulting an accountant about tax, you may be doing the equivalent of asking your GP to do a little brain surgery while you wait. Also bear in mind that accounting fees are usually higher for a limited company, so an accountant might be inclined to send you in that direction for reasons that are more to do with their fees than your business success. There is a Teach Yourself book on tax for small businesses which you may find useful (details in 'Taking it further', page 307).

GETTING ADVICE

The best and cheapest place to start in the UK is with the government-sponsored agency which is designed to help people to set up small businesses. This is called Business Link, and consists of about 45 regional operations, which are set up to offer you advice. What they do for you in each region varies, but as a minimum they will offer a 'sign-posting' service free of charge. If you ring them up and say 'I'm thinking of setting up on my own, and I need advice,' then they will help you to decide who you need help from, and then recommend people to you who are likely to be affordable. Details are to be found on page 307, and they have an excellent website, full of useful information.

Choosing an accountant

Choosing an accountant is a challenging exercise, if you don't know one, and it enables you to experience all the difficulties your clients face when they are choosing you! There is a formal qualification, so that is a useful start, but how to choose after that? This is where you immediately seek recommendations – ring up your friends, anyone you know who has a small business. If you cannot get a personal recommendation, then try Business Link, who will certainly have some names to give you. How well researched those names are will vary, but usually they will be current service providers to other Business Link users.

Would you look on the Internet? Unlikely. *Yellow Pages*? Possibly, but then how do you know how good they are? If you received a brochure in the mail, would you keep it for just this moment? If you had kept it, would you try someone who, unusually for this profession, wasted their money on brochures – that must mean their fees are expensive. Unless it is a cheap looking brochure, then maybe they are a cheap outfit – a bit dangerous for an accountant. Either way, brochures are not a medium you are likely to respond to in this context.

Insight

It is very interesting to think through this process yourself as a buyer, and then apply it to the marketing of your own business. It does clearly illustrate how difficult it is for a buyer to assess quality of service, and how few marketing mechanisms, except personal recommendations, really help with that assessment.

'Should I do it myself?' is a question you may ask. As a small business, it is possible to do your own accounts, and dispense with an accountant. In the same way it is possible to build your own computer, or knock up a simple desk to work at. If you have skills in a particular field, by all means use them, and doing your own book keeping may be sensible. However, as Vic Hartley said, if this is not your strength, then doing these things is a distraction from your business, not a benefit. However, if you do decide to have a go, there is a Teach Yourself book on small business accounting (see 'Taking it further', page 307 for details).

IR 35 – TAX RULE FOR CONSULTANTS

The effect of this legislation has been to force a consultant who only works for one client to be treated as an employee of that client, rather than as an independent entity. The rules may change, but at the moment the message is to demonstrate a spread of different clients, to prove your independence. How many is a spread? That is down to negotiation with your tax office, but if one client is more than 75 per cent of your turnover, you may wish to take advice. There is currently a website for those concerned with this issue. Details in the references section.

Fees

Setting your fee level can be a challenge. The rule is to do lots of research, and find out what the rates are for your marketplace. Be clear, first of all, exactly what is your marketplace. Rates can be dramatically different for the same service in different sectors. The most obvious of these are the public versus the private sector, and the large corporate versus the small business marketplace. Small businesses in particular, are renowned for demanding the most for the lowest possible fees.

In arriving at a fee rate, it may be helpful to consider the pay for your kind of work as an employee, but it is far more important to find out what fees your consulting competitors charge. Do not take an annual salary figure as a basis for your daily rate: you need to take account of pension, car, holidays, offices, rates, lighting etc., – all those invisible costs that sit on top of straight salary. You also need to allow for the fact that you will not be earning fees full time as a consultant: you will be very lucky indeed to work for 5 days a week for 48 weeks of the year. You will need time for tax returns, and finding new clients, always assuming that your pipeline flows wonderfully smoothly from one project to the next. 'Feast or famine' is a well-used expression in the world of the independent consultant, who is either overwhelmed with work, or waits for weeks or months for a fee-earning project to materialize.

When you know what the market rates are for your kind of consulting, you need to determine where to position yourself – too cheap, and people may wonder about the quality of your service; too expensive, and they may go elsewhere.

If you decide to vary your rates, be sure to apply a consistent structure. Some consultants charge different rates according to the type of work they do, and some charge different rates for different customers – their fees are less to local government, for example. Imagine all your customers in one room, with all the fees they have paid in public view, and now explain your pricing structure to them. If you can do this with integrity, then your structure is sound.

It can be easier to quote a rate for a complete project, but only if you are very confident of how long it will take. When in doubt, quote fees per day to your client, as people have made serious losses on fixed price contracts.

Set-up costs

There is a temptation, when you start on your own, to emulate the major corporations with nice literature, a good business address: all the things that will impress your clients. The joy of setting up as a consultant is that most of the investment is already made – in your head! It also means that clients generally expect you to go to them, and not to be invited to your prestigious city-centre address.

You will need business cards, of course, and possibly letter-headed paper, although you can create your own on your PC, and so much correspondence is by email these days, that printing stationery may not be worth it. So apart from the business cards, avoid going into print. See the section on marketing, which will probably eliminate your brochure needs.

You may want to invest in a little design effort to make your cards look stylish, but you do not need a logo! If you are in love with the idea, save it until later, as it will not bring you more business!

Insight

Don't get carried away when you set up a new business – keep your costs low, and promise yourself that new computer or business logo from the fat profits of your first project.

Something that will have a little more impact is your email address – the shorter, the better, and you obviously want to avoid being associated with any of the commercial addresses – such as a supermarket! However, you are unlikely to lose a deal because your email address is inelegant!

Like a business card, a website is now a basic requirement. Do the minimum if it is only to establish your presence as a proper business. If you occupy a specialist niche, then a website is definitely worth more of an investment. Business Link will be able to give you contacts who operate at the start-up level of charges. Having got the site, which is, let us say, for guided potholing holidays for the over-60s in Turkey, then the important part is to ensure that you are registered with all the relevant search engines for potholing, over-60s holidays, Turkish potholing, etc. With a tightly targeted market like this you can really get the web working for you. If, on the other hand, you offer general programming skills, a basic website is all you need, so that people can look you up, make sure your business is real, and email or phone you.

OFFICE

The question of an office is often down to economics. Unless you offer a service where clients need to visit you – to use specialized equipment, for example, then why waste your money? This presupposes, of course, that you have a study or spare room at home where you can close the door and be undisturbed. If this is not the case, then perhaps sharing space, as Mary did, is the next best option. If you are tempted into that prestigious address, think how much extra business it will bring you, and the answer will always be – not enough to cover the expense. People buy you and your skills; where you keep your computer and your paperwork is not an issue, as long as they know you can reach their own offices easily.

EQUIPMENT

It goes without saying that you need to be equipped with the tools of your trade, whatever they may be, but if you are a landscape gardener, you do not necessarily need a new PC to write to all your clients. The old one will do. Certainly, if you have to buy some new tools, and perhaps a different vehicle, then a new PC can certainly wait. Ask yourself if you really need all those new garden tools too.

Insight

Sometimes people go into 'new broom' mode with a new business, kitting themselves out with everything new for this fresh start. The result is that you have made a loss before you have even started, and that puts a burden on you that you can do without.

Keep your set-up costs to a minimum, ideally just business cards, a website and some advice. By all means make a shopping list, with the headings: essential, desirable and nice to have. You can then purchase only the essentials at the outset, and when you have recovered that cost and made some profit, you can consider the desirables. However, keep asking yourself the same question: will this item bring in more business – and you will be surprised how few things pass this test!

Closing thoughts

The whole world steps aside for the man who knows where he is going.

Anon

Luck is good learning meeting opportunity.

Ian Cunningham

STEPS TO SUCCESS

▶ Get your company status right – do not be pressured into becoming 'limited' without checking all the options.

▶ Get some one-off tax advice from a specialist at the outset, to be clear on your company status.

▶ Find a business accountant (who is probably not a tax specialist).

▶ Be aware of the implications of IR 35 if most of your business comes from one client.

▶ Keep set-up costs to an absolute minimum – pay for good advice, a website and business cards only.

▶ If you need to spend more on set-up, ask the test question 'Will it bring in more business?' before you make the decision. Mostly it will not!

22

Balancing your work with the rest of your life

This chapter covers:
- *how to recognize the pressures of your role*
- *the importance of pushing back on clients*
- *creating personal balance*
- *how to manage your time*

Frank Milton gave a good list of reasons not to be a consultant: They are:

▶ *travel*
▶ *irregular hours*
▶ *less chance of financial windfalls*
▶ *need for structure (the consulting culture won't provide it)*
▶ *need to like people (do something else if you don't like working with people!).*

As far as home/work balance goes, the structure of the consultant's role is going to work against it. As soon as you move from Manchester to Reading, you can be sure your next project will be nine months in Warrington! The hours you work will be closely monitored by the client, if you are working on site, so slipping away early on Friday afternoons will not be an option.

All this is guaranteed to play havoc with your home life, as you have no doubt discovered! The fundamental structure of a consultant's role is not going to change, but there are a number of things you can do to ensure that you still have a life, and social trends are working with you in this regard. It is no longer considered the 'right' thing to be a complete workaholic, and with increasing publicity given to work-related stress problems, employers have a strong motive to ensure that their staff are not pushed too hard. If you are your own boss, then it is in your own interests to 'keep the machine running at peak performance'. This means proper rest, taking breaks, and not working long hours, which are proven to be counterproductive after a while.

Insight

Noel Coward once said, 'Work is more fun than fun!' If you are in that happy position, you can work for longer and enjoy it. However, you can still get tired and jaded after too much fun, so the rules of balance still apply.

The first thing to check on is your organization's stance on this, if you are employed, and your boss's in particular. If you are self-employed, your boss will be your client. It may be lots of corporate lip service, together with a boss who tells you he believes in lots of R&R (rest and recuperation), but only after the project is complete! Whatever the answer, at least you know where you stand, and it may be that the organization expects less of you than you think.

Pushing back on clients

The next step is to ensure that you are not being tyrannized by the client into overwork. Penny Stocks had strong views on this: 'I sometimes have to rescue consultants who haven't learned how to push back with clients. I educate clients in how to treat consultants – that they are not available to them 24 hours a day, seven days a week. Also, an inexperienced consultant may find themselves over-committing, because they haven't properly understood the requirement, have thought they can just wing it, or haven't thought to ask for help.'

These are both ways in which the inexperienced consultant can find themselves overworked unnecessarily by the client.

Creating personal balance

The final step you can take is to create sufficient personal counterweight to balance a heavy work project. If work is very demanding, and not much is happening at home, the scales will weigh in work's favour, and it will creep further into your personal life. If, on the other hand, you have just taken up golf, and cannot wait to get onto the course, or have just booked a weekend away with your partner, then that will ensure that a better balance is maintained, and that you are in better shape to cope with work when you return to it refreshed. Put as much effort into planning your personal life as you would into a project, and the balance will follow. Do not expect it just to happen. Of course there will be times when you are up against a deadline and that dinner date has to be cancelled, but if that is the exception, then whoever is on the receiving end of that cancellation will be far more forgiving.

Insight

If you are about to become a consultant, talk to your partner about what it means. Discuss ways of coping with nights away from home, or long days on the client site. This is definitely a good time to share the problem, before it actually happens.

Steven Hunt has suffered a great deal of personal upheaval in his consulting life, and copes with the following philosophy: 'I believe that work should not be the be all and end all of life. I'm a very keen mountaineer, and I think it's really important to have interests outside of work, otherwise it can consume you, and you may come to resent that.'

If you have that feeling of resentment, or perhaps of discomfort, outside of normal working hours: that nagging feeling that you should be doing something else, then it is time to evaluate how you are spending your time, and how you would like to spend your time.

'I know I'm putting my family second, and I'm not happy about that,' is not an unusual remark. Often this is true, but sometimes it may not be. Sometimes the reality is that work is exciting, and the kids are tiring, and you do not want to admit it, but you actually prefer being in the office. It is a well-known fact that people find the time to do the things that are really important to them, so when someone tells you that 'I just haven't had a moment to do ...', what they mean is that it has not appeared high enough on their priority list.

ANALYSING YOUR TIME

If you are unhappy about how you spend your time, analyse how you spend it, and how it fits with what is important to you in life. It may be that you are unhappy working late, not because you are missing an evening in front of the TV, but because your partner complains about it. So your problem is keeping your partner happy, and that does not necessarily mean you have to arrive home on time every evening.

If, on the other hand, you really do look forward to going home, and work is stopping you getting there, then you have a completely different problem, that you solve by attacking the work end of things, and perhaps discussing the problem with your manager or a buddy.

Insight

Keep asking yourself: 'Is it worth it?', 'Is this how I want to spend my life?' Then you will know what to change – how you work, when or where you work, or what work you do.

When you do the time analysis, beware of telling yourself that you'll put up with this 'until I've got myself established' or until some other milestone event happens in your life. What tends to happen is that one follows another, and you always have some reason to defer good use of your time, and of your life. You may look back on your 50th birthday and realize how much you have missed. Few people have on their tombstone, ' I wish I'd spent more time at the office.' This can be a difficult perspective to hold in your 20s and 30s, when you are building your career, but more immediate questions are 'Am I really enjoying life?' and 'Will I regret missing this special event one day? Will I get this opportunity again?' The most obvious of these, and most frequently regretted, is the parent who misses seeing their children grow up.

WASTING TIME

If you have been truly honest in your analysis, you may discover that you waste time. You procrastinate, and find all sorts of reasons not to write that report, or make that phone call. You half look at things, and put them to one side to deal with later, doubling the time you spend on them.

If you are working alone, self-discipline can be a challenge to maintain, and it is important to recognize patterns that you run, and find ways to deal with them. If you are an 'always put it off until the last minute' person, then do just that, and design yourself a sensible last-minute schedule! Do not waste time starting too early, if you know you need the pressure to make it happen. If you put things off because you do not like doing them, then look at ways of changing that dislike, as described in Chapter 12 on report writing.

The technique described there is effectively the ten-minute plan. If there is a task you dislike and keep putting off, tell yourself you will look at it for just ten minutes today – preferably now. When the ten minutes is up, the task can go back on the 'too difficult' pile, but with another ten minutes booked for tomorrow. What you will usually find is that by breaking the task up into small chunks, it becomes less daunting, and you are soon able to get to grips with it.

Insight

This technique for dealing with your 'too difficult' pile is really effective, so if you find that your analysis of how you use (and waste) your time is slipping onto that pile, use the ten minute technique now!

Take every time wasting habit that you have, face it square on, and find creative ways to make it work for you, not against you.

TIME FOR LEARNING

All this is about the job itself, but there is also the small question of your learning to fit into all this. When are you going to find time to do all those rehearsals for the big client presentation in between work and all these personal commitments?

If you have someone at home, with a vested interest in your working hours, then it is a great idea to involve them in your learning. Even if they are not well equipped to help you, you will get support through their involvement, and they may have more to contribute than you expect. As a minimum, they will understand when you tell them that you will be staying late at the office to do a rehearsal for the big day.

Many of the skills we have reviewed in this book are applicable to life, not just to consulting. For example, you can apply managing conflict to your home life just as well as to the office, and so your partner may be very interested in the content, and in helping you to apply it. Your learning therefore ceases just to occupy the work side of the scales, and comes into balance. The natural consequence is that what you are undertaking here is personal development in the broadest sense: in becoming a better consultant, you are acquiring life skills.

Closing thoughts

Time is the coin of your life. It is the only coin you have, and only you can determine how it will be spent. Be careful lest you let other people spend it for you.

Carl Sandburg

Imagine life as a game in which you are juggling five balls in the air. You name them – work, family, health, friends, and spirit – and you're keeping all of these in the air. You will soon understand that work is a rubber ball. If you drop it, it will bounce back. But the other four balls – family, health, friends, and spirit are made of glass. If you drop one of these, they will be irrevocably scuffed, marked, nicked, damaged, or even shattered. They will never be the same. You must understand that and strive for balance in your life.

Brian Dyson,
CEO of Coca-Cola Enterprises, 1959–1994

STEPS TO SUCCESS

▶ Recognize that travel and irregular hours are going to be an additional obstacle to achieving the work/home balance.

▶ Check on your employer and client expectations (if self-employed, set yourself some working standards which ensure you are able to contribute at peak performance).

▶ Push back on clients who demand 24-hour service.

▶ Create an equal and opposing force to your work demands in your personal life. If you do not have an interest that completely absorbs you, then find one!

▶ Analyse how you actually spend your time, and how you would like to.

▶ Be honest with yourself, and recognize what actions to take in order to bring your life into balance.

23

Going forward

This chapter covers:
- *key messages to take with you*

Key messages

One of the critical points in the chapter on presentations was that an audience can only remember three things afterwards, and you therefore need to ensure that you deliver three key messages. The same may well be true of a book, which would be a bit depressing for an author, were it not for the fact that a book has a physical presence, and readers can refer to it as often as they like.

This summary will therefore be a bit longer than three points, but not a great deal longer, because they are the key things to take away with you, as opposed to the things you can always look up in the text.

From all the interviews and discussions, the following messages were repeated frequently and emphatically:

▶ Act with integrity
▶ Listen to your clients
▶ Keep learning

Those are the three messages that occurred most often, and although they all sound like pleas to 'be a good consultant' in the ethical sense, do not be fooled. They are the most frequent pieces of advice because they work – they deliver business, repeat business and referrals – the lifeblood of your future as a consultant.

To reinforce these messages, here they are in context, together with further key points, all in groups of three. This way, you can choose the three which mean the most to you.

As a client, I buy:

- ▶ Integrity
- ▶ Reliability
- ▶ Credibility

before I buy your expertise.

As your prospect, I need you to:

- ▶ Listen to me with your whole body
- ▶ Step into my shoes
- ▶ Offer a solution designed just for me

As your client, during a project I need you to:

- ▶ Agree with me precisely what you are going to deliver
- ▶ Set my expectations
- ▶ Involve me

As a learning consultant, I need:

- ▶ Self-belief
- ▶ To be ready to fall down one ski run in ten
- ▶ To be petrified at least twice a week!

And to help you on your twice-weekly ski slope, you will find some useful references in the next section ('Taking it further'), which is the end of this book, but the start of a new journey. Begin it now.

Closing thoughts

> Success is not a destination that you ever reach.
> Success is the quality of your journey.
>
> Jennifer James

> Whatever you can do, or dream you can, begin it now.
> Boldness has genius, magic and power in it. Begin
> it now.
>
> Goethe

Taking it further

This is a list of all the references in the book which could be useful to you as a consultant.

General

E-LEARNING

The e-learning program which accompanies this book, is called 'The Consultant's Guide to Consulting'. It covers all the key areas of consulting skills, and is designed to be very interactive, with many more case studies, all different from those in the book, so that the two do make ideal companions.

Details of the program can be found at www.avenuemanagement.com.

LEARNING

Peter Honey's website is the place to go if you want to find out about your learning style. To complete the Learning Styles Questionnaire online, go to www.peterhoney.com and click on Learning Styles.

TRAINING/CONSULTING

Vic Hartley is a partner in Vertex, which focuses on advanced skills for corporate consultants, and also offers consulting on client management to professional firms.
Telephone: 00 44 (0)1444 456473.

Q Learning offers many courses and coaching for corporate consultants. In particular they specialize in areas like outcome thinking and strategies for success, as well as the specifics like project management: www.qlearning.com.

Mind maps were originated by Tony Buzan, and he has produced a great deal of related material which you can find at: www.mind-map.com.

Irene Nathan is the Managing Director of the Interpersonal Relations Group, and founder President of the Federation of Image Consultants: 'Consultants can volunteer to be a model on a training course for image consultants. They are often looking for people, and of course there would be no charge.' The Federation website has details of recognized training providers: www.tfic.org.uk.

Professional bodies

Whatever your technical field, there will probably be a professional body of some kind offering qualifications. Often these extend to non-technical skills too. A good example is the British Computer Society (BCS). If you are a consultant in the IT field, you may wish to consider the BCS Certificate in Consultancy Practice as a qualification. It covers the broadest spectrum of non-IT subjects, from change management to project risk assessment, and details can be found on the BCS website: www.bcs.org.uk.

Apart from specific professional bodies, there are also broader churches, so to speak, like the Institute of Business Consulting (IBC). They also offer a qualification as a Management Consultant, as well as maintaining a register of consultants, and various other services: www.ibconsulting.org.uk.

For small business consultants

ADVICE

An obvious starting place for free advice on setting up and running your own business is Business Link: 'The national network of advice centres for businesses great and small.' They will always 'know a man who can', and their excellent website will tell you about any small business issue you can think of, from accounting to websites: www.businesslink.gov.uk.

All the following organizations charge an annual subscription, in return for advice, information and networking opportunities, and they all have a local presence.

British Chambers of Commerce

www.britishchambers.org.uk

Institute of Directors

www.iod.com

Federation of small businesses

http://www.fsb.org.uk/

If you decide to pay for some advice, then you will get good value from Initiatives in Business Development Ltd – a national network of advisers to small businesses. As they are specialists, they know your problems, and know what you can afford: www.ibd-uk.com.

NETWORKING

The organizations below provide networking opportunities:

Magenta Circle is dedicated to self-employed consultants, and does not have the strict attendance rules that can apply to some networks. There are monthly meetings in different locations, and the aim is to facilitate networking, both for business opportunities, and for mutual support. Details of Magenta Circle can be found on their website: www.magentacircle.ning.com.

The best-known and established networking groups are BRX and BNI. They have a long track record in this field, and generally work on the basis that you must attend meetings very regularly, and they do not normally allow competitors in the same group. However, there are lots of local groups, so this should not be an issue. BRX is the Business Referral Exchange: www.brxnet.co.uk. BNI is Business Network Inc.: www.bni-europe.com.

Remember too that you can network online with groups such as Linkedin: www.linkedin.com, and Ecademy: www.ecademy.com, which is primarily, but not exclusively, for online networking, and also via small business websites such as Millipod, www.millipod.com.

There are a number of specialist network groups for women running small businesses, such as Women in Business Network (www.wibn.co.uk), Women in rural enterprise (www.wireuk.org) or Women on Top (www.womenontop.com). These examples demonstrate how specifically networking groups are now targeted, and it is a very dynamic area, so it is worth searching for the one that matches your needs.

ONLINE MARKETPLACE

This area of the Internet is one that is moving fast, and well worth exploring if you are an independent consultant.

Here is just one example of the type, called Skillfair, which is run by Gill Hunt. Skillfair is an online project exchange for independent consultants in the UK. Clients search for quality checked consultants in Business and IT disciplines or ask Skillfair to find the right person for the project: www.skillfair.co.uk.

TAX

To find out the latest on IR 35, go to: http://www.hmrc.gov.uk/ir35/.

To find out if you need to register for VAT, go to the Business Link website (www.businesslink.gov.uk) where a simple questionnaire will tell you all you need to know.

Further reading

For comprehensive advice on how to set up a small business, refer to the sister volume in this *Teach Yourself* series, *Set Up A Successful Small Business*, which covers the range of topics you might need, from cash flow to premises. Also, in the *Teach Yourself* series, financial matters are covered by *Small Business Accounting* and *Understand Tax for Small Businesses*.

Tom Lambert is known as the consultant's consultant. He has written a number of books on the subject, the most well known being *High Income Consulting*.

For a complete introduction to project management, see *Improve your Project Management* in this series, covering all aspects from risk assessment to closure.

Sharon Drew Morgen has written an excellent book on selling, which matches the consultant's style really well: *Selling with Integrity*.

Index